THE
ILLUSTRATED
GUIDE TO

BIBLE
CUSTOMS
& CURIOSITIES

GEORGE W. KNIGHT

BARBOUR
PUBLISHING

ACKNOWLEDGMENTS

About 150 years ago James M. Freeman wrote a book titled *Manners and Customs of the Bible*. This book explained the meaning of some of the strange and puzzling customs mentioned in the Bible in order to make God's Word more understandable and timely for the Bible students of his time.

This book, *The Illustrated Guide to Bible Customs and Curiosities*, builds on the groundbreaking work of Freeman's book. Many of the customs mentioned by him have been included here, but the material has been totally rewritten for a modern audience. New information, such as that brought to light by biblical archaeology since Freeman's day, has been included to bring the book up to date.

Full-color illustrations—landscape photographs, artifact images, and details from paintings—have been included to make this book a valuable source on the customs and curiosities of Bible times.

My thanks to Paul Muckley of Barbour Publishing for sensing the potential for this book and encouraging me in its development. I am also grateful to my wife, Dorothy, for her assistance with word processing, proofreading, and indexing parts of this publishing project.

INTRODUCTION

In Bible times people expressed their grief and distress much more openly and emotionally than most of us do today. For example, they tore their clothes, threw ashes or dust on their heads, and wore clothes made of a rough material known as sackcloth. This was an unmistakable way of showing others that their grief and despair were overwhelming and inconsolable.

The Bible, particularly the Old Testament, is filled with accounts of strange practices like these. The Israelite people understood the meaning of these expressions, but they have lost their meaning for modern readers. That's what this book is all about. It explains the customs and curiosities of the ancient world that are mentioned in the Bible in order to make God's Word more relevant and meaningful for modern readers.

The Illustrated Guide to Bible Customs and Curiosities takes an orderly approach to this subject, beginning with verses in Genesis that reflect ancient customs and continuing through Revelation. You will find explanations of customs from every book of the Bible. But some books—Genesis, for example—contain a larger number of entries because of their greater length and antiquity. Read the verses on the outside edges of the pages for the biblical context of each custom or curiosity. Then read the accompanying entry on the inner portion of the page for insight into its real meaning.

Sidebars, illustrations, and photographs also appear throughout the book to enrich and expand your understanding of the various biblical customs under discussion. At the back of the book, you will find a topical index to aid in your search for specific customs and where they are mentioned in the Bible.

My hope is that this book will enrich your Bible study and make God's Word a bright and guiding light for your daily walk with the Lord.

GEORGE W. KNIGHT
NASHVILLE, TENNESSEE

GENESIS

The Term *Father*

In the ancient Middle East, the originator of a custom was frequently referred to as the "father" of that custom. Thus, Jubal was called "the father of all such as handle the harp and organ" because he invented those instruments.

Jubal. . .was the father of all such as handle the harp and organ [flute, NIV].
GENESIS 4:21

The Messiah is called "the everlasting Father" (Isaiah 9:6), meaning He is the giver of eternal life. God is called "the Father of mercies" (2 Corinthians 1:3), "the Father of glory" (Ephesians 1:17), and "the Father of lights" (James 1:17).

The word *children* is also used in a similar way in the Bible (see note on Mark 2:19).

OTHER FATHERS

1. Lot's son Moab was the father of the Moabites (Genesis 19:37).
2. Lot's son Benammi was the father of the Ammonites (Genesis 19:38).
3. Isaac's son Esau was the father of the Edomites (Genesis 36:9).
4. Joseph called himself a "father to Pharaoh" because he saved the Egyptian people from a famine through wise planning (Genesis 45:8).
5. The Jewish people referred to Abraham as their father because of the covenant promise God made to him and his descendants (Genesis 12:1–3; Luke 1:73).

A Sign of Peace

This dove with an olive leaf was God's assurance to Noah that the floodwaters were going down. It also showed that God's creation was once again in a peaceful relationship with Him. Even today, a dove with an olive branch is considered a symbol of peace.

And the dove came in to him [Noah] in the evening; and, lo, in her mouth was an olive leaf.
GENESIS 8:11

Bricks in Babylonia

Many of the bricks used in Babylonia, where the Tower of Babel was built, were sun-dried. But others were cured by being baked in a kiln, just like those used in this tower. Fire-cured bricks were stronger, so they were sometimes laid next to a wall of sun-dried brick to give it strength and stability.

The slime or tar spoken of in this passage is bitumen, which still bubbles from the ground in parts of the Middle East. It was used as a mortar to hold bricks and stones together.

Bitumen was also used to waterproof the basket in which

They [builders of the tower of Babel] said. . . Let us make brick, and burn [bake, NIV] them throughly. And they had brick for stone, and slime [tar, NIV] had they for morter.
GENESIS 11:3

7

the baby Moses was hidden (Exodus 2:3), and it served as caulk for Noah's ark (Genesis 6:14). Large deposits of bitumen existed near the cities of Sodom and Gomorrah around the Dead Sea (Genesis 14:10).

A FAMINE IN CANAAN

Famines occurred in the ancient world when the crops failed because of a scarcity of rain. The land of Canaan to which Abraham migrated was especially subject to this problem because of its dry climate and upland location.

Abraham sought refuge in the land of Egypt, where the rich, moist bottomlands along the Nile River always seemed to produce an abundance of food.

This camel is finding little to eat in a field that has been ravaged by famine.

And there was a famine in the land [Canaan]: and Abram went down into Egypt to sojourn [live, NIV] there.

GENESIS 12:10

BIBLICAL FAMINES

1. Joseph predicted—correctly—that a seven-year famine would strike Egypt and surrounding nations (Genesis 41:27-30, 50).
2. Naomi and her family were forced to move to Moab because of a severe famine that devastated their homeland (Ruth 1:1).
3. God punished King Saul for his sin and rebellion by sending a three-year famine against the entire nation (2 Samuel 21:1).
4. The prophet Elijah announced God's judgment in the form of a famine against King Ahab of Israel (the Northern Kingdom) (1 Kings 17:1; 18:1-2).

THE EGYPTIAN PHARAOH

The princes also of Pharaoh saw her [Sarah].

GENESIS 12:15

Pharaoh is the title of the Egyptian kings mentioned in the Bible (see also Genesis 47:13–20; Exodus 5:1–12:33; 1 Kings 7:8). The word does not mean "king," as most people think, but is a reference to the sun.

This title was given to the ruler of Egypt because he was considered the representative on earth of the sun god Ra, the supreme god of the Egyptian religious system. Sun worship was a common practice among the pagan peoples of the ancient world (see note on Deuteronomy 4:19).

The Term *Brother*

In Genesis 11:31 Lot is clearly identified as Abraham's nephew, not his brother (Lot was the son of Haran, Abraham's brother). This discrepancy is explained by the ancient Middle Eastern custom of referring to any male relative as a "brother."

Thus, Jacob told Rachel that he was her father, Laban's, brother (Genesis 29:12). But he was actually Laban's nephew (Genesis 28:5).

He [Abraham]. . .also brought again his brother [relative, NIV] Lot.
GENESIS 14:16

A Solemn Oath

This was Abraham's way of taking a solemn oath. He swore before the Lord to the king of Sodom that he would not keep any of the spoils of war that belonged to the king.

Swearing with a raised hand is similar to the oath required of witnesses in a modern courtroom. This practice is also mentioned in Daniel 12:7 and Revelation 10:5–6.

Abram said to the king of Sodom, I have lift up mine hand unto the LORD, the most high God.
GENESIS 14:22

A Startling Sign

A few hours before this event, the Lord had made a covenant with Abraham. He promised to bless Abraham with many descendants and make them into a nation devoted to Him.

To seal the covenant, Abraham cut several animals into two-piece sections and walked between them. This was a solemn declaration of his intention to keep the covenant. Just as the two separate pieces belonged to one animal, so the two people making this agreement were of one mind about the terms of the covenant.

When darkness fell, God caused a burning lamp or torch, signifying His divine presence, to pass between the two sections of the slaughtered animals. This was a bold and startling sign to Abraham that God would keep His promise.

It came to pass, that, when the sun went down, and it was dark, behold a smoking furnace [firepot, NIV], and a burning lamp [torch, NIV] that passed between those pieces.
GENESIS 15:17

A Child by Hagar

In the ancient world, not to be able to have children was considered a curse. A desperate childless couple would sometimes try to bear children by using a substitute mother—in this case, Sarah's maidservant, Hagar. From the union of Abraham and Hagar, a son named Ishmael was born.

He [Abram] went in unto Hagar, and she conceived.
GENESIS 16:4

Midday is the time to escape the heat of the day by resting inside one's tent.

A RELIGION OF NAMES

The Egyptians worshiped many pagan gods. They assigned to each of these gods a name that represented its specific characteristics. Since Hagar was an Egyptian (Genesis 16:3), it was natural for her to give the supreme God a name that acknowledged that He appeared to her and encouraged her in the wilderness.

Some interpreters believe the Israelites were influenced by this "religion of names" during their long period of enslavement in Egypt. Perhaps this is why Moses asked God at the burning bush, "When I come unto the children of Israel, and shall say unto them, The God of your fathers hath sent me unto you; and they shall say to me, What is his name? what shall I say unto them?" (Exodus 3:13).

A SIGN OF THE COVENANT

These instructions were delivered by the Lord to Abraham, but they applied to the entire nation of Israel. Circumcision—the cutting away of the loose flesh from the male sex organ—was a symbol, as well as a visible reminder, of the covenant between God and His chosen people.

Circumcision expressed the idea of moral purity (Isaiah 52:1). God was holy, and He expected His people to be persons of integrity who were devoted to Him. In a figurative sense, people could have uncircumcised hearts (Leviticus 26:41) or uncircumcised lips (Exodus 6:12). This meant they failed to fulfill God's purpose in their lives.

RESTING IN THE TENT DOOR

Abraham and his family were wandering herdsmen who lived in tents. They moved their tents from place to place to stake out grazing lands for their livestock. The tent door was a flap that could be closed at night for protection, then opened during the day to let in light and air.

Abraham was sitting in his tent door at midday—"in the heat of the day." This was the time when people of the ancient Middle East rested in the shade of their tents or trees to escape the oppressive heat (see note on Micah 4:4).

Total Body Bowing

There were several different ways of bowing in Bible times. These ranged from lowering the head to bending the knees to kneeling down before another person.

The Hebrew word for "bowed" in this passage indicates that Abraham exercised the most extreme form of bowing before these strangers. He knelt down, then leaned forward and placed his head on the ground. This indicated his attitude of respect, reverence, and humility toward these men.

Abraham's kindness toward these three strangers shows ancient Middle Eastern hospitality at its best. He placed all of the resources of his household at their disposal and insisted that they would be doing him a great favor if they stayed awhile.

For other examples of such hospitality toward travelers or strangers, see Genesis 19:2–3; Judges 6:14–19.

When he [Abraham] saw them [three strangers], he ran to meet them from the tent door, and bowed himself [bowed low, NIV] toward the ground, and said, My Lord, if now I have found favour in thy sight, pass not away, I pray thee, from thy servant.
GENESIS 18:2–3

BOWING DOWN IN RESPECT

1. Jacob bowed seven times before his brother, Esau, to appease his anger and hostility (Genesis 33:3).
2. Joseph's brothers bowed to him when they came to Egypt to buy grain because he was a high official of the Egyptian government (Genesis 42:6).
3. Ruth bowed to Boaz to show her thanks when he treated her kindly and allowed her to glean left-behind grain from his fields (Ruth 2:10).
4. David bowed to Saul to show his respect for the kingly office, even though he knew the king was trying to kill him (1 Samuel 24:8).
5. The sons of the prophets bowed to Elisha in acceptance of his role after he succeeded Elijah as the prophetic leader in Israel (the Northern Kingdom) (2 Kings 2:15).

Foot Washing

Walking in sandals along the primitive roads of the ancient Middle East led to dirty feet. It was just as important for a host to provide for the washing of his guests' feet as it was to feed them and put them up for the night. Abraham made sure this service was provided for his guests.

The most famous example of this practice occurs in the New Testament. The washing of feet was usually done by a household servant (1 Samuel 25:41). Jesus set an example in humble service by washing the feet of His disciples (John 13:4–15). The Master of all became the servant of all.

The Bible mentions the washing of feet several times (Genesis 24:32; 43:24; 2 Samuel 11:8; Song of Solomon 5:3; Luke 7:44; 1 Timothy 5:10).

Let a little water, I [Abraham] pray you, be fetched [brought, NIV], and wash your feet, and rest yourselves under the tree.
GENESIS 18:4

BREAD BAKING

Abraham hastened
[hurried, NIV] into the
tent unto Sarah, and said,
Make ready quickly three
measures of fine meal
[flour, NIV], knead it, and
make cakes [bread, NIV]
upon the hearth.
GENESIS 18:6

The "fine meal" from which Sarah baked bread for her guests was probably wheat flour that had been finely sifted. This was considered choice flour. Only the best was good enough for Abraham's guests.

The "hearth" on which Sarah baked the bread was probably a primitive oven, consisting of stones. The stones were heated by a fire, then the coals were raked away and the bread cakes were placed on the stones for baking. Bread baking is also mentioned in 1 Kings 17:11–13.

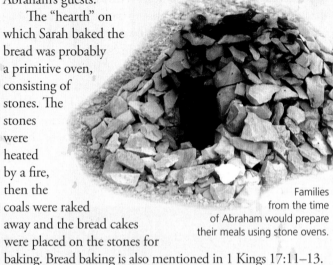

Families from the time of Abraham would prepare their meals using stone ovens.

AN ANCIENT MEAL

Abraham ran unto the
herd, and fetch a calf
[selected a choice, tender
calf, NIV]. . .and gave it
unto a young man; and he
hasted to dress it. And he
took butter [curds, NIV],
and milk, and the calf
which he had dressed,
and set it before them.
GENESIS 18:7–8

This is a good description of an ancient Middle Eastern meal in Old Testament times. The meal consisted of bread baked from wheat flour (Genesis 18:6), milk, butter or curds, and meat from a freshly slaughtered calf (see note on Genesis 43:16). A typical meal of this period consisted of a vegetable stew with no meat, so Abraham probably provided the meat as a special delicacy for his guests. The milk was probably goat milk.

Utensils and plates were not used in Bible times. People ate by scooping vegetables and meat from a common cooking pot with pieces of bread. Jesus referred to this method of eating when He predicted that Judas would betray Him. "It is the one to whom I will give this piece of bread when I have dipped it in the dish" (John 13:26 NIV).

The cooking pot in the foreground was used both to cook and to serve a meal.

SITTING AT THE CITY GATE

Cities of the ancient world were surrounded by massive defensive walls made of stone (see note on 2 Chronicles 8:5). People gathered at the gateway through the city wall to conduct business, pass the time with friends, catch up on the latest news, or just watch the passing crowds.

Lot happened to be sitting in the gateway of the city of Sodom, just as evening was falling, when these two angels entered the city.

There came two angels to Sodom at even [in the evening, NIV]; and Lot sat in the gate of Sodom.
GENESIS 19:1

HAPPENINGS AT CITY GATES

1. Boaz met the elders of the city at the city gate to make arrangements to take Ruth as his wife (Ruth 4:1–10).
2. Eli the priest suffered a fatal fall beside the city gate of Shiloh when he learned that his two sons had been killed and the ark of the covenant had been captured by the Philistines (1 Samuel 4:17–18).
3. Joab, commander of David's army, assassinated Abner in the gateway of the city of Hebron because Abner had supported David's rival to the throne (see note on 2 Samuel 3:27).
4. Jesus raised the son of a widow from the dead near the gate of the city of Nain (Luke 7:11–15).

TENTS AND PERMANENT HOUSES

Some time before this event in Sodom, Abraham and his nephew Lot had gone their separate ways (Genesis 13:7–12). Abraham continued to live in a tent (see note on Genesis 18:1), while Lot moved to the city of Sodom, where he settled into a permanent house.

Most of the Israelites were tent dwellers for many centuries beyond Abraham's time. They probably had permanent houses during their enslavement in Egypt (Exodus 12:7). During the wilderness wandering years, they became tent dwellers again (Deuteronomy 1:33). Not until the Israelites conquered the land of Canaan under Joshua did they settle for good into permanent houses.

The people from "every quarter" in this verse reminds us of modern cities that have many smaller communities within the larger metropolitan area. People of similar ethnic background, social status, or occupation often live in the same section of the city. Did this same practice exist in Bible times?

Possibly, since people from "every quarter" of Sodom gathered at Lot's house. We know that Jerusalem had a "bakers' street" during the prophet Jeremiah's time (Jeremiah 37:21).

Before they [two angels who were lodging with Lot] lay down, the men of the city, even the men of Sodom, compassed the house round. . .all the people from every quarter.
GENESIS 19:4

DEAD SEA CAVES

He [Lot] dwelt [lived, NIV] in a cave, he and his two daughters.

GENESIS 19:30

The region around the Dead Sea where the cities of Sodom and Gomorrah were located has many caves. When Sodom was destroyed by the Lord because of its wickedness, Lot and his family moved into one of these caves.

This is the same area where the Dead Sea Scrolls were discovered by a shepherd boy in 1947. Hundreds of ancient manuscripts, some dating back to as early as 250 BC, had been placed in clay pots and hidden away in several caves around the Dead Sea. These documents have been an important source of information for biblical scholars and researchers.

A manuscript fragment from the Book of Noah. Dead Sea Scroll manuscripts like this reveal how people living between the Old and New Testament times interpreted the Old Testament.

WEANING FEAST

In Bible times a child was kept on his mother's milk until well into the toddler stage—or about two to three years of age. His weaning marked an important stage in his development. It was celebrated with a special feast.

Abraham made a great feast the same day that Isaac was weaned.

GENESIS 21:8

GETTING UP EARLY

Abraham rose up early in the morning, and saddled his ass [donkey, NIV], and took. . .Isaac his son.

GENESIS 22:3

Most people in Bible times got up early in order to schedule their work around the oppressive heat of the midday (see note on Genesis 18:1). Abraham followed this custom to get an early start on his trip to Mount Moriah with his son.

When Abraham "saddled" his donkey, he was not putting anything like a modern saddle on his animal. It was probably nothing more than a blanket, a piece of cloth, or an animal hide. Saddles were not developed until many centuries after his time.

OTHERS WHO GOT UP EARLY

1. Abraham got up early and sent his concubine, Hagar, and her son off into the desert (Genesis 21:14).
2. Jacob awoke early after his dream about ascending and descending angels; then he dedicated the rock on which he had rested his head as a memorial to the Lord (Genesis 28:12, 18).
3. Moses got up early to climb Mount Sinai and receive the Ten Commandments from the Lord (Exodus 34:4).
4. Job got up early to present a burnt offering to God on behalf of himself and his children (Job 1:5).
5. David the psalmist vowed to commune with the Lord in prayer early in the day (Psalm 63:1).

GOING AND COMING

Notice that Abraham did not say, "I am going," but "I will go and come again." In his culture this was probably a polite way of saying good-bye, similar to our saying, "I'll see you later," or "We'll talk again."

CEREMONIAL MOURNING

This seems to be a formal, ceremonial type of mourning, not that Abraham didn't feel the loss of Sarah in a personal way. But here his mourning was expressed in a public way, in accordance with the standards of his community. Every culture has accepted standards for the formal demonstration of sorrow in honor of the dead.

MONEY BY WEIGHT

Abraham paid Ephron the Hittite four hundred shekels of silver for a plot of ground as a burial site for his family (Genesis 23:1–20).

Coins and paper money did not exist in Old Testament times, so Abraham paid Ephron in silver bullion. This bullion weighed four hundred shekels—the agreed-upon price. Money had to be weighed rather than counted by bills and coins, as we do today.

The exact weight of a shekel is not known. The word *shekel* (from the Hebrew *shukal*, "to weigh") indicates this method of figuring money by weight rather than by number of coins or bills. The weighing of money is also referred to in Jeremiah 32:9–10 and Zechariah 11:12.

STRIKING A BARGAIN

These two verses conclude a lengthy bargaining session between Abraham and Ephron the Hittite that began with verse 3 of Genesis 23. This passage is a good example of an ancient business deal.

Abraham wanted to buy a plot of land from Ephron as a burial site (Genesis 23:3–9). So he first contacted Ephron's clan to get them to talk with Ephron on his behalf. Even after Abraham began talking with Ephron face-to-face, the clan members were present during these negotiations (Genesis 23:10). Perhaps they had to agree on the transfer of any land from within the clan to a foreigner such as Abraham.

After a deal was reached and Abraham paid Ephron for the land, the transaction was "made sure" (Genesis 23:17), or witnessed, by members of Ephron's clan, as well as others who passed through the city gate. In Bible times business was transacted in the gateway of the city (see note on Genesis 19:1).

Abraham said unto his young men. . .I and the lad [Isaac] will go yonder [over there, NIV] and worship, and come again.
GENESIS 22:5

Sarah died in Kirjath-arba. . .and Abraham came to mourn for Sarah, and to weep for her.
GENESIS 23:2

Abraham weighed to Ephron the silver. . .four hundred shekels of silver, current money with the merchant [according to the weight current among the merchants, NIV].
GENESIS 23:16

The field of Ephron. . . and the cave which was therein. . .were made sure unto Abraham for a possession [deeded to Abraham as his property, NIV] in the presence of the children of Heth, before all that went in at the gate of his city.
GENESIS 23:17–18

BURIAL IN CAVES

Abraham buried Sarah his wife in the cave of the field of Machpelah.

GENESIS 23:19

This is the first burial recorded in the Bible. Sarah was probably buried soon after she died. In the hot climate of Palestine, a body would quickly begin to decompose.

Burial caves were common in the biblical world. In Sarah's case, a natural cave was used. But tombs were sometimes hewed out of solid rock (Isaiah 22:16). This is the type of cave in which Jesus was buried (Matthew 27:60).

The Machpelah, built by King Herod, marks the traditional location of the cave in which Sarah was buried.

SWEARING BY ABRAHAM'S CHIEF SERVANT

Abraham said unto his eldest [chief, NIV] servant of his house, that ruled over all that he had, Put, I pray thee, thy hand under my thigh: and I will make thee swear by the LORD.

GENESIS 24:2–3

The word *eldest* in this passage expresses authority rather than age. The most competent and faithful servant in a household was appointed supervisor of the other servants. This trusted servant probably kept the account books on Abraham's extensive livestock holdings and made sure the household ran smoothly. Although Abraham's chief servant is not named in this passage, we learn from Genesis 15:2 that his name was Eliezer.

Earlier, Abraham had made a solemn promise by raising his hand (see note on Genesis 14:22). Here, he required Eliezer to swear by placing his hand under Abraham's thigh. The word *thigh* is actually a euphemism for the male sex organs. Abraham's servant was swearing to find a wife for Isaac among Abraham's kinsmen in Mesopotamia rather than among the pagan Canaanites.

Perhaps the placement of the servant's hand emphasized the rite of circumcision that God had commanded for the

Israelites (see note on Genesis 17:11). It could have been a reminder of the covenant between God and His people and the seriousness of the oath the servant was taking.

Another possible explanation is that the placement of the servant's hand symbolized the influence his mission to find a wife for Isaac would have on Abraham's future descendants. This strange way of swearing an oath occurs only one other time in the Bible (Genesis 47:29).

A Bride for Isaac

In Bible times marriages were arranged by the parents, and their children were expected to abide by their choice. Thus, Abraham sent his chief servant back to Mesopotamia—a distance of more than five hundred miles—to select a wife for his son Isaac from among Abraham's kinsmen.

A proposal of marriage was usually initiated by the father of the groom (Genesis 38:6). After his offer was accepted by the father of the bride, the groom's father paid a dowry, or bride-price, to the bride's parents. This was to compensate them for the loss of the household services of their daughter.

Occasionally a young man would ask to be allowed to marry a girl of his choice (Judges 14:1–3). But his parents still had to give their approval and make the necessary arrangements for the marriage.

Community Wells

When Abraham's chief servant arrived at Nahor in Mesopotamia, he stopped just outside the village to rest and water his camels at the community well. Villages were usually built near wells or springs for convenience. But these water sources were just far enough away so the settlement was not disturbed by the noise and traffic.

The task of collecting and carrying water was generally done by women. In the New Testament, Jesus talked with a Samaritan woman who had come to the well outside the town of Sychar to draw water (John 4:3–26).

Collecting Water from a Well

This well at Nahor had steps around the wall that provided access to the water supply. Rebekah had to go down into the pit, fill her pitcher, then trudge back to the top with

Thou [Abraham's servant] shalt go unto my country, and to my kindred [my own relatives, NIV], and take a wife unto my son Isaac.

Genesis 24:4

HAPPENINGS AT WELLS

1. Jacob helped Rachel water her sheep from a well near Haran (Genesis 29:10).
2. Isaac clashed with the Philistines over wells that his father, Abraham, had dug in southern Canaan (see note on Genesis 26:15).
3. Three of David's soldiers risked their lives to bring him water from a well near Bethlehem (2 Samuel 23:15–17).
4. Jesus talked with a sinful Samaritan woman at the well outside the village of Sychar (John 4:5–14).

He [Abraham's servant] made his camels to kneel down without [outside, NIV] the city by a well of water at the time of the evening. . .that women go out to draw water.

Genesis 24:11

her heavy load. Archaeologists have discovered a well of this type at ancient Gibeon near Jerusalem. It extended more than fifty feet deep through solid rock.

The water from other wells of Bible times was collected in containers that had to be let down and drawn up by hand. The well where Jesus met the Samaritan woman must have been this type of public water supply. When He told her that He could give her living water, she replied, "Sir, thou hast nothing to draw with, and the well is deep: from whence then hast thou that living water?" (John 4:11).

JEWELRY FOR THE NOSE AND ARM

Because of Rebekah's kindness to him, Abraham's servant presented her with gifts of jewelry. The "earring" was actually a nose ring. The servant said later that he had put this piece of jewelry "upon her face" (Genesis 24:47).

It was common for women of Bible times to wear nose rings. They were generally about one to two inches in diameter. Made of silver or gold, they were often inlaid with precious stones. The term *shekel* indicates the weight of the gold or silver in the nose ring (see note on Genesis 23:16). Isaiah 3:21 and Ezekiel 16:12 also refer to nose rings (see NIV translation).

Abraham's servant also gave Rebekah two bracelets. Made of gold, silver, or bronze, these were worn by both men and women in Bible times. Sometimes the lower section of each arm was almost covered with bracelets. Bracelets are also referred to in Numbers 31:50 and Ezekiel 16:11; 23:42.

A bracelet discovered at Succoth. Women of the biblical world frequently wore bracelets similar to this one.

OTHER BRIDAL PRESENTS AND PAYMENTS

After Abraham's servant had secured an agreement for Rebekah to marry Isaac (see note on Genesis 24:4), he gave her additional bridal presents (Genesis 24:22). These included expensive "raiment," or items of clothing.

Clothes were often presented as gifts in Bible times. Naaman, a Syrian military commander, took ten changes of clothing to present as gifts to the prophet Elisha if he would heal him of his leprosy (2 Kings 5:1–5).

The gifts that Abraham's servant presented to Rebekah's relatives were probably a dowry, or bride-price. In Bible times the father of the groom—in this case, Abraham—compensated the bride's father for the loss of her household services as a daughter. Rebekah's father must have been deceased, since this payment was made to her mother and brother.

REBEKAH'S NURSE

When Rebekah left Mesopotamia to marry Isaac in Canaan, she was accompanied by several servants (Genesis 24:61), as well as her "nurse." This was the servant who had breast-fed her as an infant and had become as close to her as her own mother.

Even after Rebekah had become an adult, this servant had remained with her family as her special helper and friend. Since Rebekah was marrying into a family whom she had never met, her nurse would provide continuing comfort and companionship.

We learn later that the name of Rebekah's nurse was Deborah. She stayed with Rebekah in Canaan until she died (Genesis 35:8).

COVERING THE FACE WITH A VEIL

We know from other passages that Israelite women in Bible times did not wear veils in public. For example, when Abraham's servant first met Rebekah, he could see that she "was very fair to look upon" (Genesis 24:16). This would not have been obvious if she had been wearing a veil.

Rebekah's covering of her face with a veil when she met her future husband, Isaac, was a sign of modesty and respect. In many modern weddings, the bride wears a veil in the presence of the groom. The veil is lifted at the conclusion of the wedding ceremony.

A WIFE JOINS THE CLAN

There is no evidence of any special religious ceremony in Isaac's marriage to Rebekah. His father, Abraham, had already arranged the marriage and paid a dowry, or bride-price, to Rebekah's relatives (see notes on Genesis 24:4 and Genesis 24:53). The marriage was sealed when Isaac took his bride from her father's house and escorted her to the tent of his father and mother.

In Old Testament times, parents and their children and grandchildren of succeeding generations lived as a clan in a compound housing arrangement.

They [Rebekah's relatives] sent away Rebekah their sister, and her nurse.
GENESIS 24:59

The servant had said, It is my master [Isaac, NIV]: therefore she [Rebekah] took a vail, and covered herself.
GENESIS 24:65

Isaac brought her into his mother Sarah's tent, and took Rebekah, and she became his wife.
GENESIS 24:67

When Israelite women veiled their faces, it was a sign of modesty and respect.

Transfer of a Birthright

Isaac had twin sons, Esau and Jacob. As the older of the two (Genesis 25:22–25), Esau had certain "birthright" privileges. A firstborn son would become head of the clan when his father died. This responsibility meant he would inherit twice as much of his father's estate as each of his other brothers born into the family (Deuteronomy 21:17).

This right of the firstborn son could be transferred by the father to another son if the elder son proved unworthy (1 Chronicles 5:1–2). Or the elder son could sell or trade his birthright to one of his brothers.

This is what happened with Esau. In a moment of weakness brought on by hunger, he traded his birthright to his brother, Jacob, for a bowl of stew.

Vegetable Stew

The pottage or stew that Jacob cooked for his brother, Esau, in exchange for his birthright was made from a vegetable (lentils) similar to our modern peas. These lentils were cooked with herbs and spices to form a thick reddish-brown stew. Lentil stew was a common dish in Old Testament times. This vegetable was also crushed and used as an ingredient in bread (Ezekiel 4:9).

Jacob gave Esau bread and pottage of lentiles [lentil stew, NIV]; and he did eat and drink, and rose up, and went his way: thus Esau despised his birthright.

GENESIS 25:34

Controversy over Wells

Springs and streams were scarce in the hot, dry climate of the ancient Middle East. Shepherds had to dig wells to provide water for their flocks and herds.

The wells that Abraham had dug for his animals years before in the unoccupied territory of southern Canaan had given him and his heirs the right to graze their flocks in this region. But after Abraham died, the Philistines had filled these wells with dirt, denying Isaac the right as Abraham's heir to continue using these pasturelands.

All the wells which his [Isaac's] father's servants had digged in the days of Abraham his father, the Philistines had stopped them, and filled them with earth.

GENESIS 26:15

Isaac and the Philistines eventually reached a compromise that allowed him access to the grazing lands around a productive well that he named Sheba ("productive well"). The ancient city of Beersheba ("well of Sheba") took its name from this well (Genesis 26:17–23).

A Covenant Feast

Isaac and the Philistines ate a special meal together to celebrate their agreement over access to pasturelands in southern Canaan (see note on Genesis 26:15).

This was a common practice when covenants were sealed in Bible times. When Isaac's son Jacob reached an agreement with his father-in-law, Laban, in later years, he marked the occasion with a meal of celebration (Genesis 31:25–54).

He [Isaac] made them [the Philistines] a feast, and they did eat and drink. And they rose up. . .in the morning, and sware one to another.
Genesis 26:30–31

Seasoned Meat

The term *savoury meat* means "seasoned meat." Thus, the aging Isaac asked his son Esau to prepare him a dish flavored with herbs and spices such as garlic, saffron, and mint.

The Israelites were fond of highly seasoned food. While in the wilderness, they especially missed the garlic they had enjoyed in Egypt (Numbers 11:5).

Go out to the field, and take me [Isaac] some venison [wild game, NIV]; and make me savoury meat [tasty food, NIV], such as I love, and bring it to me, that I may eat.
Genesis 27:3–4

A Deathbed Blessing

Esau had already traded his birthright as Isaac's firstborn son to his brother, Jacob (see notes on Genesis 25:31, 33 and Genesis 25:34). But it was still up to Isaac to decide which son would receive his final blessing—or his formal declaration of God's favor and goodness.

Isaac intended to bless Esau, but Jacob tricked his father into pronouncing his blessing on him instead. It was through Jacob and his descendants that God's covenant with Abraham would be carried on. This blessing, once given by Isaac, could not be revoked (Genesis 27:34–40).

It came to pass, as soon as Isaac had made an end of blessing Jacob, and Jacob was yet scarce gone out from the presence of Isaac his father, that Esau his brother came in from his hunting.
Genesis 27:30

Days of Mourning

Esau was referring to the period of formal or ceremonial mourning for the dead (see note on Genesis 23:2), which usually lasted for seven days (Genesis 50:10; 1 Samuel 31:13).

When Job's friends came to comfort him because of the losses he had suffered, they mourned with him for seven days and seven nights (Job 2:13).

Esau said in his heart, The days of mourning for my father [Isaac] are at hand.
Genesis 27:41

He [Jacob] lighted upon [reached, NIV] a certain place, and tarried there all night. . .and he took of the stones of that place, and put them for his pillows, and lay down in that place to sleep.

GENESIS 28:11

He [Jacob] dreamed, and behold a ladder [stairway, NIV] set up on the earth, and the top of it reached to heaven: and behold the angels of God ascending and descending on it.

GENESIS 28:12

Jacob rose up early in the morning, and took the stone that he had put for his pillows, and set it up for a pillar, and poured oil upon the top of it.

GENESIS 28:18

SLEEPING UNDER THE STARS

Jacob was accustomed to the life of a shepherd. And shepherds usually slept out in the open to keep watch over their sheep at night (Luke 2:8). He probably used his outer cloak as a blanket and took off his head covering and placed it on the stones to form a makeshift pillow.

A STAIRWAY TO HEAVEN

This ladder or stairway in Jacob's dream symbolized access to God. The travel of angels up and down this stairway between heaven and earth symbolized God's revelation of Himself to Jacob and His assurance that Jacob was heir to the covenant promises that God had made to Abraham (Genesis 12:2–3).

A MEMORIAL STONE

To commemorate God's revelation to him through a dream (see note on Genesis 28:12), Jacob dedicated the stone that had served as his pillow as a memorial to the Lord. This stone would be a permanent reminder of God's glory and of His covenant promise to His people.

OTHER STONE MEMORIALS

1. The waters of the Jordan River were miraculously divided by the Lord so the Israelites under Joshua's leadership could cross safely into Canaan. The people set up twelve stones in Canaan as a perpetual reminder of the Lord's mighty acts on their behalf. The twelve stones represented the twelve tribes of Israel (Joshua 4:2-9).
2. Joshua set up a stone under an oak tree in the land of Canaan after challenging the people to remain faithful to the Lord. Because this rock had heard "all the words of the LORD" that Joshua had delivered, it was a constant reminder of God's commands (Joshua 24:26-27).
3. Samuel set up a stone and named it Ebenezer, meaning "hitherto hath the LORD helped us," because God had given the Israelites victory over their Philistine enemies (1 Samuel 7:8-12).

They [Jacob, along with Laban's servants] rolled the stone from the well's mouth, and watered the sheep, and put the stone again upon the well's mouth.

GENESIS 29:3

A WELL COVER

Livestock in Bible times were often watered from a well that had been dug near where they grazed (see note on Genesis 24:15–16). The top of a well was covered with a huge stone to keep out trash and blowing sand. It took several men to roll away the stone to gain access to the water.

A well cover may be referred to in Job 38:30: "The waters are hid as with a stone."

RACHEL THE SHEPHERDESS

Sheep tending was normally done by men. Perhaps Laban's younger daughter, Rachel, had been given this responsibility because he had no sons when Jacob arrived on the scene (Genesis 29:16).

A KISS OF GREETING

Male relatives and friends of Bible times often greeted one another with a kiss, although the exact nature of this kiss is unknown. It may have been a hug in which they touched their cheeks together, first on one side of the face and then on the other.

LEAH'S WEAK EYES

The phrase *tender eyed* actually means "weak" or "dull." In comparison to her sister Rachel, Leah had eyes that were not lively or sparkling. Bright eyes were considered a mark of beauty for women in Bible times.

MARRIAGE AMONG RELATIVES

Laban was the brother of Jacob's mother, Rebekah (Genesis 29:10). This relationship would have made Laban's daughter Rachel—the woman whom Jacob wanted to marry—Jacob's first cousin.

Sometimes the term *brother* was used loosely in Bible times to refer to any male relative such as a nephew or an uncle (see note on Genesis 14:16). So Rachel may have been a distant relative of Jacob.

Marriage among distant relatives from the same tribe or bloodline was common in Old Testament times. Abraham sought a wife for his son Isaac from among his kinsmen in Mesopotamia (see note on Genesis 24:4).

While he [Jacob] yet spake [was still talking, NIV] with them [Laban's servants], Rachel came with her father's sheep: for she kept them.
GENESIS 29:9

When Laban heard the tidings [news, NIV] of Jacob his sister's son. . . he ran to meet him, and embraced him, and kissed him.
GENESIS 29:13

Leah was tender eyed [had weak eyes, NIV]; but Rachel was beautiful and well favoured [lovely in form, NIV].
GENESIS 29:17

It is better that I [Laban] give her [Rachel] to thee [Jacob], than that I should give her to another man.
GENESIS 29:19

23

In Bible times a dowry, or bride-price, was paid by the family of the groom to the family of the bride (see notes on Genesis 24:4 and Genesis 24:53).

If the groom or his family could not afford to pay a dowry in money or livestock, the bride's father could require the groom to pay off the debt in labor expended in his service. This is what Laban required of Jacob for the privilege of marrying his daughter Rachel.

A MARRIAGE FEAST

After Jacob had worked seven years for Laban, he requested that he be allowed to marry his daughter Rachel. To celebrate the marriage, Laban invited his friends and neighbors to a marriage feast in the couple's honor. This customary feast lasted for seven days (Genesis 29:27).

According to the Gospel of John, the first miracle performed by Jesus took place at a similar marriage feast in the city of Cana in Galilee. This feast had gone on for several days, and the host had run out of wine. Jesus turned water into wine, and the guests continued the celebration (John 2:1–10).

OLDER DAUGHTER FIRST

Jacob worked seven years for the privilege of marrying Rachel, only to discover that Laban had tricked him into marrying Leah instead. Laban defended his trickery by explaining that it was customary in a family for the older daughter to marry before the younger daughter.

This ancient custom is still observed today in many countries—especially in those cultures where marriages are arranged by the parents (see note on Genesis 24:4).

A CHILD OF HOPE

Jacob loved Rachel, but he only tolerated Leah—perhaps because he had been tricked into marrying her (Genesis 29:25). When Leah gave birth to a son by Jacob, she probably thought this would change his attitude toward her.

So Leah named her son Reuben, meaning "See! A son!" The birth of a son—especially a firstborn son—was considered a special blessing (see note on Genesis 25:31, 33). Parents of Bible times often gave their children names that represented their character, the circumstances of their birth, or the hope they represented.

Jacob served seven years for Rachel; and they seemed unto him but a few days, for the love he had to her.
GENESIS 29:20

Jacob said unto Laban, Give me my wife. . . . And Laban gathered together all the men of the place, and made a feast.
GENESIS 29:21–22

Laban said, It must not be so done in our country [It is not our custom here, NIV], to give the younger [Rachel] [in marriage] before the firstborn [Leah].
GENESIS 29:26

Leah conceived, and bare a son, and she called his name Reuben: for she said, Surely the LORD hath looked upon my affliction [misery, NIV]; now therefore my husband will love me.
GENESIS 29:32

FRUIT OF THE MANDRAKE

The mandrake plant grew wild throughout the Mediterranean region. It produced an orange-colored fruit similar to the modern carrot. Also referred to as the "love apple," it was believed to promote fertility.

Rachel had not been able to have children. This is why she asked Leah to give her the mandrake fruit that Leah's son Reuben had found in the field.

STOLEN HOUSEHOLD IDOLS

These "images" that Rachel had stolen from her father were household idols known as teraphim. Small statuettes in human form, they may have represented deceased ancestors of the family. They were consulted in a superstitious way for guidance and direction in everyday life.

Why did Rachel steal these images when she and her sister, Leah, fled Laban's household with Jacob? Perhaps she thought Laban would consult them to determine the route they had taken. Or she could have thought these images would provide protection for her and her sister on their journey with Jacob to a strange land.

Many Israelites apparently saw no conflict between keeping these superstitious teraphim in their homes and following the Lord. Not until the days of King Josiah centuries after Jacob's time was an effort made to abolish the practice of consulting household images (2 Kings 23:24).

TABRET AND HARP

The Hebrew word for "tabret" is also translated in other places in the Bible as "timbrel" and "tambourine." It was a hollow, hand-held percussion instrument with small bells or pieces of brass attached. Often used to accompany

Mandrakes depicted in a Byzantine floor mosaic. This common plant was thought to promote fertility.

Reuben. . .found mandrakes in the field, and brought them unto his mother Leah. Then Rachel said to Leah, Give me. . . of thy son's mandrakes.
GENESIS 30:14

Laban went to shear his sheep: and Rachel had stolen the images [household gods, NIV] that were her father's.
GENESIS 31:19

I [Laban] might have sent thee [Jacob] away with mirth [joy, NIV], and with songs, with tabret [tambourines, NIV], and with harp.
GENESIS 31:27

The harp or lyre is the stringed, musical instrument mentioned more times than any other in the Bible.

dancing, the tabret made a distinctive rustling sound when shaken.

The harp is mentioned more than any other musical instrument in the Bible (see 1 Samuel 16:16, 23; Psalm 147:7). The Hebrew word for "harp" is also rendered as "lyre" in some modern translations. It was an ancient stringed instrument (Genesis 4:21), probably dating back to as early as 2700 B.C. Similar to the modern harp, it varied throughout biblical history in size, design, and number of strings.

PEACE-TREATY STONES

Laban said, This heap [of stones] is a witness between me and thee [Jacob] this day.
GENESIS 31:48

Laban pursued Jacob and his daughters and overtook them as they traveled toward Canaan (see note on Genesis 31:19). After Laban and Jacob agreed to treat each other as friends and go their separate ways, they stacked up a pile of stones.

This was more than a memorial or visible reminder of the agreement they had made (see note on Genesis 28:18). Each pledged that he would not pass this pile of rocks to attack the other!

The relationship between Jacob and his father-in-law, Laban, had been stormy during the entire twenty years Jacob had lived among Laban's family in Mesopotamia (Genesis 31:41).

GIFTS FOR A BROTHER

Jacob said, Nay, I pray thee [Esau], if now I have found grace [favor, NIV] in thy sight, then receive my present at my hand.
GENESIS 33:10

In Bible times people presented gifts to others for many reasons: to secure a bride through a dowry, or bride-price (see note on Genesis 24:53); to seal a friendship; or to show love.

In this instance Jacob presented gifts to his estranged brother, Esau, because he had wronged him in the past (see notes on Genesis 25:31, 33 and Genesis 27:30). He hoped his gifts would appease Esau's anger.

BIBLICAL GIFTS

1. Naaman the Syrian commander brought gold, silver, and fancy clothes to the prophet Elisha in hopes of being healed of his leprosy (2 Kings 5:1-9).
2. The Queen of Sheba brought gifts of gold, spices, and precious stones when she came to interview King Solomon (1 Kings 10:1-10).
3. The Magi from the east brought gold, frankincense, and myrrh to the infant Jesus in Bethlehem (Matthew 2:11).

An Offering from Jacob

The Lord appeared to Jacob and renewed the covenant He had made with his grandfather Abraham (Genesis 12:2–3). As a token of his thanksgiving for God's faithfulness, Jacob set up an altar. On this altar of stones he poured a drink offering—probably wine—as well as olive oil, as offerings to the Lord.

Wine and olive oil were valuable commodities in Bible times. God required offerings from His people that represented a sacrifice on their part. The Lord did not need Jacob's wine and oil, since He owns everything. But Jacob needed to offer these valuable items to show his commitment to the covenant-keeping God of Israel.

Jacob set up a pillar in the place where he [God] talked with him, even a pillar of stone: and he poured a drink offering thereon, and he poured oil thereon.
GENESIS 35:14

Joseph's Unusual Coat

Joseph's "coat of many colours" has been translated in various ways by modern translations ("richly ornamented robe," NIV; "long robe with sleeves," RSV). The precise meaning of the Hebrew word behind this phrase is uncertain.

This "coat" may have been the long tunic or outer robe that was worn by both men and women in Bible times. It was different from the robes worn by Joseph's brothers, thus setting him apart as his father's favorite son.

Israel [Jacob] loved Joseph more than all his children, because he was the son of his old age: and he made him a coat of many colours.
GENESIS 37:3

A Cistern Prison

The Hebrew word for "pit" may also be translated as "cistern." Since the pit into which Joseph was thrown was designed to hold water, it must have been an abandoned, dry cistern.

Runoff water from rainfall was channeled into cisterns. They served as an important backup water supply during the dry summer months. Cisterns differed from wells (see notes on Genesis 24:11 and Genesis 24:15–16) in that wells were filled constantly with fresh water from the underground water table.

Abandoned cisterns were sometimes used as prisons, as in the case of Joseph. His brothers probably intended to leave him there to die, but they changed their minds and drew him up and sold him into slavery in Egypt.

The prophet Jeremiah was also imprisoned in a cistern. But his "cell" was more uncomfortable than Joseph's: "There was no water, but mire [mud, NIV]: so Jeremiah sunk in the mire" (Jeremiah 38:6).

They [Joseph's brothers] took him, and cast him into a pit [cistern, NIV]: and the pit was empty, there was no water in it.
GENESIS 37:24

MERCHANTS IN CARAVANS

This was a group of Arabian merchants traveling in a caravan. They were carrying their wares to sell in Egypt, following a familiar trade route across the desert.

Merchants of Bible times often traveled in groups like this to minimize the dangers of these hazardous trips. Robbers were always a threat. They were less likely to attack a large caravan. Caravans are also referred to in Isaiah 21:13 and Luke 2:44.

EXPRESSIONS OF GRIEF

Joseph's brothers led his father, Jacob, to believe that Joseph had been killed by a wild animal (Genesis 37:31–33). Jacob expressed his grief by tearing his clothes. This custom symbolized the deep, emotional anguish Jacob felt over his son's death.

Jacob also expressed his emotional distress over Joseph's death by wearing clothes made of sackcloth. This material was woven from goat or camel hair or some other rough fiber such as hemp. The discomfort associated with wearing clothes made of such rough cloth symbolized the anguish and turmoil of those who had lost loved ones.

CAPTAIN OF THE GUARD

The literal meaning of the Hebrew word for "captain of the guard" is "captain of the executioners." Joseph became a slave in the household of Potiphar, a royal official who was responsible for the keeping of prisoners. His title suggests that he also executed the sentences that had been pronounced against these prisoners.

The king of Babylon had an official with similar duties in his service (Jeremiah 39:13).

DRESSED IN SACKCLOTH

1. King Ahab of Israel (the Northern Kingdom) expressed his remorse by wearing sackcloth when the prophet Elijah declared he would be punished by the Lord for his sin and idolatry (1 Kings 21:17–27).
2. King Hezekiah of Judah (the Southern Kingdom) wore sackcloth when the Assyrians were threatening to overrun the nation (2 Kings 19:1).
3. Mordecai wore sackcloth when he heard about Haman's plot to wipe out the Jewish people throughout Persia (Esther 4:1).
4. Job's suffering was so severe that he pictured himself as having sackcloth sewed permanently to his skin (Job 16:15).
5. The citizens of Nineveh repented in sackcloth after the prophet Jonah proclaimed God's judgment against them (Jonah 3:5).

JOSEPH'S PRISON IN EGYPT

This is the first mention of an official state prison in the Bible. The place where Joseph was confined was apparently a room or special section of the house that belonged to Potiphar, captain of the guard in Pharaoh's administration (see note on Genesis 37:36). Two of Pharaoh's household servants were also in this prison.

Official state prisons were sometimes located in the king's palace complex (Jeremiah 32:2) or in the house of an important royal official (Jeremiah 37:15).

CARRYING THINGS ON THE HEAD

In Bible times it was common practice for people to carry things by balancing them on their heads. Over time a person's neck muscles would become so strong that he could carry extra-heavy loads—such as the three baskets of Pharaoh's servant—in this way. This custom is still observed today in many parts of the world.

During Bible times, people often would carry items by balancing them on their head.

ROYAL BIRTHDAY FEASTS

Kings of Bible times celebrated their birthday by sponsoring feasts for members of their court and setting selected prisoners free. In this case Pharaoh pardoned his chief butler, or cupbearer, but refused to pardon his chief baker.

In the New Testament, a birthday celebration for King Herod was the occasion for his issuance of an execution order against John the Baptist (Matthew 14:6–10).

THE NILE RIVER

When the Egyptians referred to "the river," they had the Nile in mind. One of the longest and most important streams in the world, it was literally a life-giver to the Egyptian people (see note on Exodus 7:20–21). The Nile's annual flooding produced the rich soil that provided crops for their sustenance. Its waters were also used to irrigate the land.

He [Pharaoh] put them [his servants] in ward [in custody, NIV] in the house of the captain of the guard, into the prison, the place [same prison, NIV] where Joseph was bound [confined, NIV].
GENESIS 40:3

I [Pharaoh's chief baker] also was in my dream, and, behold, I had three white baskets on my head.
GENESIS 40:16

It came to pass the third day, which was Pharaoh's birthday, that he [Pharaoh] made a feast unto all his servants. . . . He restored the chief butler [cupbearer, NIV]. . .but he hanged the chief baker.
GENESIS 40:20–22

At the end of two full years. . .Pharaoh dreamed: and, behold, he stood by the river.
GENESIS 41:1

EGYPTIAN MAGICIANS

Pharaoh dreamed that seven skinny cows gobbled up seven fat cows along the Nile River. Many people in Bible times believed that dreams carried hidden messages, so he called on the magicians of the land to tell him the meaning of his dream.

These magicians belonged to an order of priests who were held in high esteem in a land that had a magical, superstitious approach to religion. But their "black magic" formulas and incantations failed them in this case.

Ironically, a foreigner, Joseph the Israelite—who worshiped a God unknown to the Egyptians—was brought out of prison to interpret Pharaoh's dream.

Centuries later, other magicians of Egypt clashed with Moses and Aaron when they appeared before Pharaoh to demand the release of the Israelites from slavery (Exodus 7:11–12).

EGYPTIANS AND FACIAL HAIR

Egyptian men did not grow beards, but the Hebrews did. Apparently it was considered inappropriate for a bearded man to appear before Pharaoh, so Joseph was required to shave.

JOSEPH'S PROMOTION

Pharaoh was so pleased with Joseph's interpretation of his dream and his proposal for how to avoid a famine that he promoted him to a high position in his administration. This dramatic reversal of fortune—from a lowly prisoner to an Egyptian potentate—showed God at work in the life of His servant Joseph.

PHARAOH'S SIGNET RING

The ring that Pharaoh placed on Joseph's finger was probably his official signet ring. Used to authenticate documents much like a signature is used today, it may have contained an engraving of the state seal of Egypt. Thus, Pharaoh was giving Joseph the authority to act on his behalf in setting up a system of storing and dispensing grain throughout Egypt.

Other symbols of Joseph's authority and prestige among the Egyptians were his linen robe and the gold chain that Pharaoh placed around his neck.

BIBLICAL SIGNET RINGS

1. King Ahasuerus of Persia gave Haman his signet ring to use in issuing a death decree against the Jews (Esther 3:10–12).
2. King Ahasuerus of Persia gave Mordecai the Jew, Haman's successor, his signet ring to use in issuing an authorization for the Jews to defend themselves against Haman's death order (Esther 8:2, 8, 10–11).
3. God declared that He would designate Zerubbabel, governor of Judah after the Babylonian exile, as His signet ring—or authorized representative—to rebuild the temple in Jerusalem (Haggai 2:23).

Storage for Grain

Joseph made arrangements to store the surplus wheat and other grain produced during the years of plenty in Egypt. During the coming years of famine, the storage facilities would be opened to feed the people.

The storage of grain and other commodities was done routinely by most people in Bible times. What made this situation in Egypt unique is that grain was stored for seven years for a famine that was expected to last for seven years (Genesis 41:29–36).

Some granaries of the ancient world were nothing more than pits dug in the ground and lined with plaster to keep the grain dry. Archaeologists have discovered such an underground storage facility at Megiddo, an ancient city mentioned in connection with King Solomon's administration (1 Kings 9:15–19).

He [Joseph] gathered up all the food of the seven years, which were in the land of Egypt, and laid up [stored, NIV] the food in the cities.
Genesis 41:48

The round depression is the granary at Megiddo. Underground silos like this were lined with stone and sealed with plaster to keep the grain dry.

Grain Containers and Feed Sacks

The "corn" that Joseph's brothers carried back to Canaan from Egypt was actually wheat or some other grain. They had two types of "sacks" with them—containers for the grain they had bought and sacks of feed ("provender" or fodder, Genesis 42:27) for their animals.

When the brothers opened their feed sacks to feed their animals during the return trip to Canaan, they discovered their grain money had been mysteriously returned (Genesis 42:27–28).

Joseph commanded to fill their [his brothers'] sacks with corn [grain, NIV], and to restore every man's money into his sack.
Genesis 42:25

Joseph served his brothers fresh meat when they came to Egypt. The cattle and pyramid, seen here, are located in Faiyum, one of the storage cities built by Joseph.

SUPERFRESH MEAT

In Old Testament times, there was no way to preserve meat. An animal was slaughtered immediately before the meal at which meat was to be served (Genesis 18:7–8; 1 Samuel 28:24).

JOSEPH GREETS BENJAMIN

Joseph was particularly eager to see Benjamin because he was Joseph's full brother. Both of them had been born to Rachel (Genesis 30:22–24; 35:16–18). Joseph's other brothers were half brothers—offspring of other wives of his father, Jacob.

Joseph's esteem for his younger brother, Benjamin, comes through in his elaborate greeting.

Joseph. . .said to the ruler [steward, NIV] of his house, Bring these men [Joseph's brothers] home, and slay [slaughter an animal, NIV], and make ready; for these men shall dine with me at noon.
GENESIS 43:16

He [Joseph]. . .said, Is this your younger brother [Benjamin], of whom ye spake unto me? And he said, God be gracious unto thee, my son.
GENESIS 43:29

He [Joseph] washed his face, and went out. . . .and said, Set on bread [Serve the food, NIV].
GENESIS 43:31

EATING BREAD

Bread was such a staple of the daily diet in Bible times that any meal—even though it might include meat and vegetables—was often referred to as "eating bread" (Genesis 37:25; Exodus 2:20; 1 Samuel 28:22–25).

In the Model Prayer, Jesus taught His disciples to pray, "Give us this day our daily bread" (Matthew 6:11)—or food to meet our daily physical needs.

THREE GROUPS AT ONE MEAL

This interesting passage shows the social distinctions that existed in Egypt. Although Joseph, along with a group of Egyptians, ate with Joseph's brothers in the same room, they were seated in three separate groups.

Joseph was the highest in rank, so he ate by himself. The Egyptians who had been invited to the meal ate in a group by themselves, since they considered all foreigners unclean. Joseph's brothers were Israelites, so they were placed in a third group because of this Egyptian pecking order.

Later, when Joseph brought his family to Egypt, he used this Egyptian distaste for foreigners to settle the Israelites in a region known as Goshen.

This section of southern Egypt had rich soil that had been deposited by the annual flooding of the Nile River. It grew lush pastures to support the flocks and herds of the Israelites. Here Joseph's people could live to themselves without being contaminated by the pagan religious practices of Egypt.

This segregation suited the Egyptians just fine, since they had a special contempt for foreigners who tended livestock for a living (Genesis 46:31–34; 47:1–6).

SEATED BY AGE

Joseph had apparently arranged with his servants in advance to have his brothers seated at the meal (see note on Genesis 43:32) according to their birth order—from oldest to youngest. This would have placed Reuben first (see note on Genesis 29:32) and his favorite brother, Benjamin, last (see note on Genesis 43:29).

While the brothers noticed this arrangement and wondered about it, they still didn't realize they were in the presence of their long-lost brother. But Joseph was dropping strong hints that he knew who they were.

FIVE TIMES MORE FOR BENJAMIN

At mealtimes a host would often pay special respect to an important guest by sending him a choice morsel of food or serving him a larger portion than the other guests. A royal official, for example, would generally receive a double portion.

Benjamin and his brothers must have been shocked when he was served five times more than they had received. This was Joseph's way of expressing his special esteem for his younger brother (see note on Genesis 43:29).

JOSEPH'S SPECIAL CUP

Joseph had his silver cup—probably his personal drinking cup—planted in the grain sack of his favorite brother, Benjamin. He planned to have all of them searched during their return trip to Canaan. Then he would claim that Benjamin had stolen the cup.

When Joseph's servant found the cup, he asked, "Is not this it in which my lord drinketh, and whereby indeed he divineth?" (Genesis 44:5). Divining cups were used by the Egyptians in a magical way to foretell the future. Did Joseph use his cup in this way? Or did his servant call it a "divining cup" to emphasize the seriousness of the crime that Benjamin was being accused of?

We don't know. But it is clear that Joseph was using this trumped-up charge as a test for his brothers. Would they come to Benjamin's defense? Or would they abandon him as they had betrayed Joseph so many years before?

They set on for [served, NIV] him [Joseph] by himself, and for them [Joseph's brothers] by themselves, and for the Egyptians, which did eat with him, by themselves: because the Egyptians might not eat bread with the Hebrews; for that is an abomination unto the Egyptians.
GENESIS 43:32

They [Joseph's brothers] sat before him, the firstborn according to his birthright, and the youngest according to his youth: and the men marvelled one at another.
GENESIS 43:33

He [Joseph] took and sent messes [portions, NIV] unto them [his brothers] from before him: but Benjamin's mess [portion, NIV] was five times so much as any of theirs.
GENESIS 43:34

Put my [Joseph's] cup, the silver cup, in the sack's mouth of the youngest [Benjamin].
GENESIS 44:2

An Emotional Joseph

When Joseph's brothers came to the defense of their brother Benjamin, Joseph was overcome with emotion. Finally revealing himself to his brothers, he wept with such an outpouring of feeling that the other officials in Pharaoh's court heard him.

The Israelites were very expressive people. They tended to voice their joy as well as their sorrow with loud cries. The writers of the Psalms often described their deep anguish (Psalm 38:6), as well as their overwhelming joy (Psalm 104:33–34).

Egyptian Wagons

These wagons provided by Pharaoh to bring Joseph's family to Egypt probably had wooden wheels and were drawn by oxen.

They must have seemed strange to Jacob and his family, since they had no need for such carts in Canaan. As nomadic shepherds, they probably moved their goods from pasture to pasture on the backs of camels or oxen.

Gifts of Clothing

Joseph continued his preferential treatment of his brother Benjamin (see note on Genesis 43:34) by giving him five changes of clothes—more than he gave his other brothers. Clothes were often given as gifts in Bible times (2 Kings 5:5; see also note on Genesis 24:53).

Clothing styles did not change from year to year in Joseph's time as they do today. Thus, five changes of clothes would have kept Benjamin outfitted for a long time.

These clothes were probably not normal, everyday clothes but expensive and elaborately decorated outfits to be worn on special occasions.

Eyes Closed at Death

Before Jacob left Canaan, God appeared to him and assured him that his move to Egypt with his family was a part of the divine plan. He also promised Jacob that his son Joseph would be with him in Egypt to close his eyes when he died.

It was customary in Bible times for the next of kin to close the eyes of a person who had died and to give him a farewell kiss (Genesis 50:1).

A Hand of Victory

Before he died, Jacob called his twelve sons together and predicted their futures. He foretold the importance of Judah and his descendants—the tribe of Judah—by using the image of Judah's hand on the necks of his enemies. Placing one's hand on the neck of another was a symbol of superiority and victory in battle (2 Samuel 22:41; Lamentations 5:5).

Judah did become the central tribe in Israel's history. King David was born into this tribe, and it was through David's lineage that the Messiah emerged (Matthew 1:1–17; Judah is spelled "Judas" in the King James Version; see Matthew 1:2).

Judah, thou art he whom thy brethren shall praise: thy hand shall be in [on, NIV] the neck of thine enemies.

GENESIS 49:8

Egyptian Embalming

This is the first of only two references to embalming in the Bible. Like his father, Jacob, Joseph was also embalmed after his death (Genesis 50:26).

The word *embalming* apparently refers to the unique method of preparing a body for burial used by the ancient Egyptians. Different methods of embalming were used, depending on the person's status.

The bodies of kings and people of great distinction were put through a sophisticated process that involved removing the internal organs and soaking the body for many days in a special chemical. Finally, the body was wrapped tightly in strips of linen cloth and placed in a wooden coffin.

Bodies like this (known as mummies) have been discov-

Joseph commanded his servants the physicians to embalm his father: and the physicians embalmed Israel [Jacob]. And forty days were fulfilled for him; for so are fulfilled the days of those which are embalmed.

GENESIS 50:2–3

ered in the ancient royal tombs of Egypt. Many have been in a remarkable state of preservation, even after more than three thousand years in their tombs.

After he was embalmed, Jacob was returned to Canaan for burial by Joseph and his brothers (Genesis 50:4–13).

An Egyptian illustration depicting the embalming of Ramses III. The bodies of Jacob and Joseph were both prepared for burial in this manner.

EXODUS

She [Moses' mother] took for him [Moses] an ark of bulrushes [a papyrus basket, NIV], and daubed [coated, NIV] it with slime [tar, NIV] and with pitch, and put the child therein.
EXODUS 2:3

The daughter of Pharaoh came down to wash [bathe, NIV] herself at the river. . .and when she saw the ark [basket, NIV] among the flags [reeds, NIV], she sent her maid to fetch it.
EXODUS 2:5

Moses was content to dwell with the man [Jethro or Reuel]: and he gave Moses Zipporah his daughter.
EXODUS 2:21

Moses kept the flock of Jethro his father in law, the priest of Midian: and he led the flock to the backside [far side, NIV] of the desert.
EXODUS 3:1

MOSES' PAPER ARK

Moses was hidden by his mother to protect him from the death order issued by Pharaoh against all male children of the Israelites (Exodus 1:15–16).

The "ark" in which he was hidden was probably a basket woven from stalks of the papyrus plant. This reedlike plant grew in abundance along the banks of the Nile River. The Egyptians used papyrus for making paper, as well as shoes and clothes. This basket was waterproofed with bitumen or tar (see note on Genesis 11:3).

BATHING IN THE NILE RIVER

Moses was discovered in his basket by Pharaoh's daughter. Had he been deliberately hidden in this spot so he would be discovered by a member of the royal family? It's possible, since his sister "stood afar off" to see "what would be done to him" (Exodus 2:4).

The Egyptians viewed the Nile River as sacred because it contributed to the fertility of the land (see note on Exodus 7:20–21). This Egyptian princess may have been bathing in the river as part of a pagan worship ritual.

MOSES AND JETHRO (REUEL)

Moses fled to Midian when he became a hunted man for killing an Egyptian slave superior (Exodus 2:13–15). In Midian he joined the family of Jethro. Moses probably worked for Jethro as a shepherd to earn the right to marry his daughter, just as Jacob had worked for the right to marry Rachel (see note on Genesis 29:20).

DISTANT PASTURELANDS

Nomadic shepherds of Bible times often moved great distances to find sufficient grazing lands for their flocks and herds. It may have been during the dry season that Moses moved Jethro's livestock to the "backside" or distant side of the Arabian desert.

Sometimes shepherds would be camped out with their flocks for several weeks at one of these distant locations. It was during one of these times of isolation and solitude that God appeared to Moses in a burning bush (Exodus 3:2).

Taking Off the Shoes

God's appearance to Moses had made the entire area sacred. So he was commanded to remove his sandals as a token of respect and reverence for the Lord. This same action was demanded of Joshua when God appeared to him after the Israelites had entered the land of Canaan (Joshua 5:15).

Jewelry for Israelite Women

God promised Moses that when the Israelites were released from slavery, their women would carry from the land jewelry of silver and gold given to them by the Egyptians.

Some interpreters believe these precious items were payment for the labor the Egyptians had taken from the Israelite slaves. But they had little use for jewelry while living in the desert.

After several years in the wilderness of Sinai, the Israelites donated their items of gold and silver for the building of the tabernacle (Exodus 35:22). Perhaps this was the purpose God had in mind for this jewelry all along.

Egyptian Bricks with Straw

The bricks used in the building projects of ancient Egypt were molded from mud, then placed in the sun to dry. Over time sun-dried bricks would crumble from exposure to the wind and rain.

To give these bricks greater strength and stability, chopped straw from wheat or barley stalks was sometimes added. Pharaoh added to the hard labor of the Israelite slaves by forcing them to forage for straw to be used in the manufacturing process.

Apparently the Israelites were under a quota system. They were expected to produce so many bricks per day—no excuses accepted (Exodus 5:13–14).

He [God] said [to Moses], Draw not nigh hither [Do not come any closer, NIV]: put off thy shoes [sandals, NIV] from off thy feet, for the place whereon thou standest is holy ground.
EXODUS 3:5

When ye [Israelites] go, ye shall not go empty [empty-handed, NIV]: but every woman shall borrow of her neighbour. . .jewels of silver, and jewels of gold, and raiment [clothing, NIV]. . . .and ye shall spoil [plunder, NIV] the Egyptians.
EXODUS 3:21–22

Ye [Egyptian slave supervisors] shall no more give the people [Israelite slaves] straw to make brick, as heretofore: let them go and gather straw for themselves.
EXODUS 5:7

The Israelites made bricks from mud and straw while in Egypt. This painting from the tomb of a nobleman illustrates the steps in that process. (Egypt, New Kingdom)

37

ALL THE POOLS OF EGYPT

This plague against Egypt—the turning of water into
blood—covered all of the water sources of the land. Included
were the Nile River, other flowing streams, irrigation canals,
and ponds that held water for the watering of animals and
for irrigation purposes.

In the dry climate of Egypt, irrigation of crops was
essential. Large holding ponds were constructed to catch
water from the Nile during its annual flooding stage. This
water was released through irrigation canals during the dry
months.

This plague on the Egyptian water supply was a strike
against the livelihood of the land and its people.

A SUPERIOR GOD

The Egyptians viewed the Nile River as sacred because it was
essential to their survival as a nation. They worshiped it as
a god, referring to it as "the father of life" and "the father of
the gods" (see note on Genesis 41:1).

God's turning the water of this great river into blood was
actually a strike at the heart of their pagan religious system.
He was showing that He was more powerful than all of their
gods and that He was the supreme ruler of the universe.

FROM ASHES TO DUST TO SORES

Sores broke out on the Egyptians and their animals when
Moses threw ashes into the air at God's command. God first
turned the ashes into dust and blew it throughout the land.
The Egyptians touched by the dust broke out in sores.

This shows that even something as common as ashes or
soot has great power when wielded by the hand of the Lord.

DEEP DARKNESS

This plague consisted of a thick, heavy darkness that fell
across the land of Egypt for three days (Exodus 10:22).
This must have been an eerie blackness with no sliver of
light, similar to the total darkness a person experiences deep
within a cave when all of the lights are turned out. It was so
frightening that the Egyptians did not venture outside their
houses (Exodus 10:23).

Once again, the Lord proved His superiority over the
Egyptian gods. The Egyptians worshiped the sun through
the sun god Ra (see note on Genesis 12:15). But God was
master over the sun and all other forces of nature.

ALL THE GODS OF EGYPT

To be superior to "all the gods of Egypt" was quite a claim, since the Egyptians are known to have worshiped more than thirty pagan deities. These included the bull god Apis, who ensured fertility; Hathor, the goddess of love; and Thoth, the god of wisdom and books.

But God proved, through the death of all the Egyptian firstborn (Exodus 12:29), that He held the power of life and death over the Egyptians and their religious system. Months later, after Moses had led the Israelites out of slavery in Egypt, God declared to him, "I am the LORD thy God, which have brought thee. . .out of the house of bondage. Thou shalt have no other gods before me" (Exodus 20:2–3).

Egyptian relief of Hathor. The Egyptians are known to have worshipped more than thirty such pagan deities.

UNLEAVENED BREAD

This verse shows the haste with which the Israelites left Egypt after the death of the Egyptian firstborn. The people who were in the process of baking bread didn't even have time to add yeast to the dough to get it to rise before they were commanded by Pharaoh to leave.

A kneading trough was a wooden bowl in which dough was worked by hand before being placed on the fire for baking. Families who were baking bread at the time of the Exodus may have carried their dough with them in these bowls when they left.

The Jewish feast known as the Passover commemorated the release of the Israelites from Egyptian slavery. The meal eaten during this special celebration was known as the Feast of Unleavened Bread (see note on Exodus 23:15). The people ate bread baked without yeast to emphasize the sudden departure of the Israelites from Egypt.

Against all the gods of Egypt I will execute judgment: I am the LORD.
EXODUS 12:12

The people [Israelites] took their dough before it was leavened, their kneading-troughs being bound up in their clothes upon their shoulders.
EXODUS 12:34

The pharaoh of Egypt who released the Israelites from captivity may have pursued them in a chariot like this.

Pharaoh's Chariots

He [Pharaoh] made ready his chariot. . .and he took six hundred chosen chariots. . .and captains over every one of them.

Exodus 14:6–7

After allowing the Israelites to leave Egypt, Pharaoh changed his mind and went after them with his army to return them to captivity. He apparently led the charge from his own royal chariot.

Egyptian chariots were generally drawn by two horses. Staffed with trained soldiers, they were a formidable weapon of war. Each chariot had at least two soldiers—one to drive the horses and the other to engage the enemy.

In addition to these two soldiers, each of Pharaoh's chariots had a "captain." The literal meaning of this Hebrew word is "third man." He probably directed the actions of the other two to make sure the chariot force was effective in battle.

CHARIOTS OF ISRAEL

1. Samuel warned the people of Israel who were asking for a king to rule over them that this king would conscript their sons to serve in his chariot corps (1 Samuel 8:11–12).
2. Absalom gathered chariots and horses to use in his rebellion against his father, King David (2 Samuel 15:1).
3. King Ahab of Israel (the Northern Kingdom) was killed in his chariot during a battle with the Syrians (1 Kings 22:35–37).
4. Jehu, assassin and successor of Joram/Jehoram as king of Israel (the Northern Kingdom), was known as a furious chariot driver (2 Kings 9:20–24).

Old Testament Night Watches

It came to pass, that in the morning watch [last watch of the night, NIV] the LORD looked unto the host of the Egyptians.

Exodus 14:24

During this period in biblical history, the Israelites divided the night into three "watches" or units of time. From sunset until 10:00 p.m. was the "beginning of the watches" (Lamentations 2:19). The "middle watch" lasted from 10:00 p.m. until 2:00 a.m. The time from 2:00 a.m. until sunrise was called the "morning watch" (1 Samuel 11:11).

Thus, God took note of Pharaoh and his army during

the early morning hours before sunrise. God never sleeps; He is always alert and watching over His people.

This method of dividing the night is also referred to in Psalms 63:6 and 119:148. The psalmist meditated on God and His word in the "night watches."

For the method of dividing the night during New Testament times, see note on Mark 13:35.

Dancing with Joy

Miriam and other women celebrated God's deliverance of the Israelites from the Egyptian army by singing, playing timbrels or tambourines (see note on Genesis 31:27), and dancing.

Dancing was a distinctive form of worship and religious expression among the Israelites during Old Testament times. It demonstrated joy and thanksgiving to the Lord. King David danced "with all his might" (2 Samuel 6:14) when the ark was brought home to Jerusalem.

The psalmist called on God's people to praise the Lord through dancing (Psalms 149:3; 150:4).

Miriam. . .took a timbrel [tambourine, NIV] in her hand; and all the women went out after her with timbrels and with dances.
Exodus 15:20

Egypt and the Good Old Days

Soon after leaving Egypt, the Israelites began to whine for the "good old days." They began to think their existence as slaves was preferable to the harsh life of the wilderness.

Flesh pots or meat pots were three-legged metal containers in which the Egyptians cooked meat over an open fire. But it is likely that meat was a delicacy enjoyed only by the elite of Egyptian society. The Israelites exaggerated when they claimed they had eaten meat regularly from these cooking pots.

That's the problem with nostalgia: Looking back, things always seem better than they actually were.

Would to God we [Israelites] had died. . .in the land of Egypt, when we sat by the flesh pots [pots of meat, NIV], and when we did eat bread to the full [ate all the food we wanted, NIV].
Exodus 16:3

A Bread Substitute

In response to the complaints of the Israelites about what they had to eat (see note on Exodus 16:3), God promised to "rain bread from heaven" (Exodus 16:4).

Every morning a mysterious substance appeared on the ground. Each family was to gather enough of this bread substitute to feed their household for that day (Exodus 16:16–19).

The people called this substance manna—a Hebrew word that means "What is it?" To them, it tasted like the seed of the coriander plant, a herb used to season food.

The house of Israel called the name thereof Manna: and it was like coriander seed, white; and the taste of it was like wafers made with honey.
Exodus 16:31

An Omer of Manna

Moses and Aaron were commanded by the Lord to preserve some of this manna as a reminder to future generations of how God had provided for His people in the wilderness. An omer was a unit of dry measure equal to about three and one-half quarts.

This memorial sample of manna was apparently placed in the ark of the covenant after the tabernacle was built (Hebrews 9:4).

The Ephah

A unit of dry measure, an ephah was equal to about one bushel. Ruth gleaned about one ephah of barley in the fields of Boaz (Ruth 2:17). The ephah in dry measure was equivalent to the bath in liquid measure (see note on Ezekiel 45:10).

Clean before the Lord

About three months after leaving Egypt, Moses led the Israelites to the base of Mount Sinai in the wilderness (Exodus 19:1–2). Here they would have a dramatic encounter with the living Lord, who had led them out of slavery.

In order to prepare the people for this special revelation of Himself, God commanded that the people be both spiritually ("sanctify them") and physically ("wash their clothes") clean. Such cleanliness was essential for those who would stand in the presence of the holy God.

The Principle of Restitution

This verse shows the principle of restitution that characterized the Old Testament law. No one was insured against liability in the ancient world. So if a person accidentally caused the loss of another person's property, he was expected to compensate the owner personally for the loss.

Crimes against property, such as by stealing, carried a heavier penalty. The guilty party had to make double restitution for the property he had taken (Exodus 22:7).

The word *stacks* should be rendered as "shocks" or "piles." When wheat or barley was cut in Bible times, the stalks of grain were heaped up loosely into piles, ready for the threshing floor.

Donkeys were commonly used to carry products in the ancient world. Exodus 23:5 required a bystander to assist a donkey if it collapsed under its load.

HUMANE TREATMENT OF ANIMALS

This interesting law required a bystander to help a donkey that had collapsed under its load, even if the animal belonged to an enemy. Thus, humane treatment of animals is not a modern development but a principle established by biblical law.

THREE GREAT FESTIVALS

God through Moses directed the Israelites to celebrate three great annual festivals, or religious holidays, to commemorate God's leadership in the life of their nation. These three festivals were Passover, or the Feast of Unleavened Bread (Exodus 23:15); the Feast of Harvest, or Weeks (Exodus 23:16); and the Feast of Ingathering, or Tabernacles (Exodus 23:16).

These festivals served the same purpose for the Israelites that our holidays serve for us. They gave them rest from their labors, reminded them of important events in their history, and emphasized the values that set them apart as a distinct people.

PASSOVER, OR THE FEAST OF UNLEAVENED BREAD

The first and most important of the Jewish religious feasts was Passover, which commemorated the deliverance of the Israelites from slavery in Egypt.

This celebration was often referred to as the Feast of Unleavened Bread because the people left Egypt in such a hurry that they didn't have time to add yeast to the bread they were baking (see note on Exodus 12:34). They ate

If thou see the ass [donkey, NIV] of him that hateth thee lying under his burden [fallen down under its load, NIV], and wouldest forbear to help him, thou shalt surely help with him.
EXODUS 23:5

Three times thou shalt keep a feast unto me [God] in the year.
EXODUS 23:14

Thou shalt keep the feast of unleavened bread. . .in the time appointed of the month Abib; for in it thou camest out from Egypt.
EXODUS 23:15

43

unleavened bread during this festival to mark this historic event.

Passover was so named because the death angel sent by the Lord to secure the release of His people "passed over" the homes of the Israelites while visiting the homes of the Egyptians (Exodus 12:12–13). The blood of a sacrificial lamb was smeared on the doorposts of Israelite homes as a sign to this messenger from the Lord.

The apostle Paul compared Christ to the Passover lamb that was sacrificed to provide deliverance for Israel: "For even Christ our passover is sacrificed for us" (1 Corinthians 5:7).

The month of Abib during which the Passover was to be observed was the first month of the year for the Israelites. It corresponded to March/April in our calendar. Abib was known as Nisan during the years after the Babylonian exile (Nehemiah 2:1; Esther 3:7).

THE FEAST OF HARVEST AND THE FEAST OF INGATHERING

The purpose of the Feast of Harvest was to express thanks to God for the crops He had provided. This festival was sometimes called the Feast of Weeks because of the "seven weeks" after Passover by which its time was determined (Deuteronomy 16:9–10). It was also called "the day of the firstfruits" (Numbers 28:26), because the first loaves of bread made from the wheat harvest were offered to the Lord on that day.

During New Testament times, the Feast of Harvest was known as Pentecost (from the Greek word *pentekoste*, meaning "fiftieth day") because it fell on the fiftieth day after the Passover celebration. Gathered in Jerusalem to celebrate this feast, early believers experienced a miraculous outpouring of God's Spirit (Acts 2:1–4).

The third annual feast that God commanded the Israelites to observe (see note on Exodus 23:14) was the Feast of Ingathering, generally referred to in the Bible as the Feast of Tabernacles (Leviticus 23:34; see note on John 7:37).

This festival lasted for eight days, during which the people lived in huts made from the branches of trees. These crude dwellings reminded them that this was how their ancestors had lived in the wilderness after their deliverance from Egypt (Leviticus 23:39–43) and that God had been with them during these years.

Thou shalt keep. . .the feast of harvest, the firstfruits of thy labours, which thou hast sown in the field: and the feast of ingathering, which is in the end of the year, when thou hast gathered in thy labours out of the field.
EXODUS 23:15–16

REQUIRED ATTENDANCE

The Lord directed that all adult males must attend the three great religious festivals (see note on Exodus 23:14).

In the early years of Israel's history, at least certain parts of these festivals must have been held at a central gathering place, perhaps around the tabernacle. After Jerusalem was established as Israel's capital city, adult males were required to make a pilgrimage to this holy city, where the temple was located, to observe these holidays.

Jesus was crucified outside Jerusalem while the city was crowded with pilgrims who had come to observe the annual Passover.

Three times in the year all thy males shall appear before the LORD God.
EXODUS 23:17

A FORBIDDEN PRACTICE

This injunction, repeated in Exodus 34:26 and Deuteronomy 14:21, is one of the most puzzling passages in the Bible. Why did God forbid this practice?

Perhaps the best explanation is that this was a fertility rite practiced by pagan peoples of Bible times, maybe the Canaanites. God expected His people to avoid all forms of idolatry and false worship.

Thou [Israelites] shalt not seethe [cook, NIV] a kid [young goat, NIV] in his mother's milk.
EXODUS 23:19

THE CUBIT

God gave the Israelites the exact dimensions for the ark of the covenant, a sacred box that represented God's presence among His people.

The cubit was a unit of linear measure. The word comes from the Latin term *cubitus*, which refers to the lower arm. Thus, a cubit was the length of an adult's lower arm from the elbow to the tip of the middle finger—or about eighteen inches.

This means the ark was about forty-five inches long by twenty-seven inches wide by twenty-seven inches high.

They [the Israelites] shall make an ark [chest, NIV] of shittim [acacia, NIV] wood: two cubits and a half shall be the length thereof, and a cubit and a half the breadth thereof, and a cubit and a half the height thereof.
EXODUS 25:10

BREAD ON THE TABLE

A special bread called shewbread or bread of the Presence was to be set on a table in the holiest place in the tabernacle.

We know from other Bible passages that this bread consisted of twelve loaves, representing the twelve tribes of Israel (Leviticus 24:5–7). The constant presence of these loaves acknowledged that the tribes were guided at all times by the watchful eye of the Lord.

And thou [Israelites] shalt set upon the table shewbread [bread of the Presence, NIV] before me [God] alway.
EXODUS 25:30

QUALITY OLIVE OIL

And thou [Moses] shalt command the children of Israel, that they bring thee pure oil olive beaten for the light.

EXODUS 27:20

The Israelites burned olive oil in their lamps to illuminate their tents and houses (see note on Mark 4:21). God commanded them to produce olive oil of high quality for the lamps that would burn continually in the tabernacle.

Common, everyday oil was made by crushing olives in a press. The "beaten" olive oil specified by the Lord was produced by pressing olives in a mortar. The higher-quality oil burned cleaner and produced less smoke. Only the best was good enough for the sacred place where the people worshiped God.

THE SPAN

Make the breastplate [breastpiece, NIV] of judgment with cunning [skilled, NIV] work. . . . A span shall be the length thereof, and a span shall be the breadth thereof.

EXODUS 28:15–16

This "breastplate of judgment" fit on the front of the ephod, or apron, worn by the high priest. A span was a unit of linear measure, equal to the distance from the tip of the thumb to the tip of the little finger on the fully extended hand of an adult—or about eight to nine inches.

A GOLD-PLATED CALF

All the people [Israelites] brake off the golden earrings which were in their ears. . . . And he [Aaron] received them at their hand, and fashioned it with a graving tool, after he had made it a molten calf.

EXODUS 32:3–4

The word *molten* implies that the calf idol that Aaron created in the wilderness was cast from gold. But thousands of melted-down earrings would have been required to produce such an idol.

It is more likely that the calf image was carved from wood and then plated with a thin layer of gold to produce the final idol worshiped by the people. This method of producing pagan images was described by the prophet Isaiah (Isaiah 40:19–20).

CALF WORSHIP

They [Israelites] have made them a molten calf, and have worshipped it.

EXODUS 32:8

This lapse into idolatry by the Israelites may show how they had been influenced by the pagan worship system of Egypt. The Egyptians worshiped more than thirty pagan gods, including the bull god Apis, who was thought to ensure human fertility (see note on Exodus 12:12).

MIRRORS OF METAL

Mirrors of the ancient world were made from metals such as gold, silver, and bronze. These metals were so highly shined and polished that a person could see his reflection in their surfaces. Glass was not used to make mirrors until several centuries after Bible times.

While in Egypt, some of the Israelites began to worship the Apis bull, which was thought to provide fertility.

These metal mirrors donated for tabernacle construction were probably taken from Egyptian women when the Israelites were delivered from slavery (see note on Exodus 3:21–22).

THE TABERNACLE

More than one-third of the forty chapters of Exodus deal with the tabernacle (see Exodus 25–40)—a sacred tent that served as a place of worship for God's people.

The tabernacle moved with the Israelites from place to place during their years of wandering in the wilderness. Thus, it served as a constant witness of His guidance.

God gave Moses and Aaron detailed instructions on how to build and equip the tabernacle (Exodus 25–27). The actual building of the structure is recorded in Exodus 35–40. Finally, the book of Exodus comes to a close with a description of how the building was organized and furnished for the purpose of worship (Exodus 40:1–38).

The tabernacle was divided into two rooms—the Holy of Holies or "the Holiest of all" (Hebrews 9:3) and the Holy Place (Exodus 28:29)—by a lavishly embroidered linen curtain (see note on Mark 15:38).

It was what the tabernacle represented— the presence of God with His people—that made this structure special.

> *He [Bezaleel the craftsman] made the laver [basin, NIV] of brass [bronze, NIV], and the foot [stand, NIV] of it of brass, of the looking-glasses [mirrors, NIV] of the women. . .which assembled at the door of the tabernacle.*
>
> EXODUS 38:8

> *On the first day of the first month shalt thou set up the tabernacle of the tent of the congregation.*
>
> EXODUS 40:2

> *Thou [Moses] shalt put therein [in the tabernacle] the ark of the testimony, and cover the ark with the vail [curtain, NIV].*
>
> EXODUS 40:3

Reproduction of the Ark of the Covenant.

THE ARK OF THE COVENANT

This ark of the testimony is better known by its alternate name, "ark of the covenant" (Deuteronomy 31:26). It is also called "the ark of God" (1 Samuel 3:3). It was a sacred portable chest that symbolized God's grace and guidance in the lives of the Israelites.

God had already given instructions for the building of the ark (Exodus 25:10–22). In this passage, He directed Moses and Aaron to place it inside the completed tabernacle. It belonged in the most sacred room of the building—the Holy of Holies or Most Holy Place (Exodus 26:34; see note on Exodus 40:2).

Inside the ark was a copy of the law, or

ARK-RELATED EVENTS

1. Priests carried the ark ahead of the people when they crossed the Jordan River into Canaan. The river was miraculously divided when their feet touched the water (Joshua 3:6–16).
2. The Philistines captured the ark (1 Samuel 4:10–11), then returned it to the Israelites when they were afflicted with a strange disease (1 Samuel 5:8–10; 6:1–15).
3. King David danced with joy before the ark when it was lodged in a special place he had prepared for it in Jerusalem (1 Chronicles 15:1, 29).

testimony, that God had revealed to Moses to direct the lives of the Israelites as His covenant people (Exodus 25:21).

According to Hebrews 9:4, the ark also contained Aaron's rod and a memorial sample of the manna that God provided for the Israelites in the wilderness (see note on Exodus 16:32).

THE INCENSE ALTAR

Incense was a sweet-smelling substance burned in the tabernacle as an offering to God. It was offered by a priest on this special altar made of gold. The pleasant aroma symbolized the prayers of the Israelites before the Lord.

Only incense made by using a formula specified by God (Exodus 30:34–38) was to be burned on the incense altar. Two sons of Aaron were destroyed for burning incense by "strange fire" (Leviticus 10:1–3). They may have been offering incense not produced by this divine formula.

THE ALTAR OF BURNT OFFERING

The altar upon which sacrificial animals were burned as offerings to God was located outside the tabernacle in the surrounding courtyard.

This large boxlike altar was filled with dirt (Exodus 20:24), perhaps to catch the blood of animals when they were slaughtered by the priests. It was surrounded by a platform on which the priests stood while officiating at the altar.

The Israelites believed animal sacrifices provided atonement for sin. The death of Jesus Christ—the perfect and once-for-all sacrifice (Hebrews 7:26–28)—ended the need for this ancient custom.

DISTINCTIVE PRIESTLY CLOTHES

The priests of Israel wore distinctive clothes to show that they were set apart by the Lord for ministry to His people. These included linen drawers or breeches (Exodus 28:42; "undergarments," NIV); a linen tunic or shirt (Exodus 28:39–40); a girdle (Exodus 28:39; "sash," NIV) that was worn over the tunic on the upper part of the body; and a linen mitre (Exodus 39:28; "turban," NIV) on the head.

In addition to these pieces of clothing, the high priest wore an outer robe (Exodus 39:22–26) and an ornately embroidered ephod, or apron (Exodus 39:2). His clothes contained twelve precious stones, symbolizing the twelve tribes of Israel (Exodus 28:15–21). His turban also contained the words "holiness to the LORD" (Exodus 28:36–37), showing that the nation of Israel was to be a holy people who were set apart for God's service.

Thou [Moses] shalt set the altar of gold for the incense before the ark of the testimony.
EXODUS 40:5

Thou [Moses] shalt set the altar of the burnt offering before the door of the tabernacle of the tent of the congregation.
EXODUS 40:6

Thou [Moses] shalt put upon Aaron the holy [sacred, NIV] garments.
EXODUS 40:13

LEVITICUS

No Yeast or Honey

Leaven, or yeast, was mixed with dough to cause bread to rise. Any bread brought to the Lord as an offering was to be baked without leaven. Neither was honey, used as a sweetening agent, to be used in any food items presented to the Lord.

The reason for these prohibitions is that both yeast and honey were associated with offerings presented to pagan gods.

Salt in Meat Offerings

Salt was a symbol of permanence and purity, since it was used as a seasoning agent and as a preservative for meat. The use of salt in the meat offerings presented to God by the Israelites represented the covenant that bound them together. They were pledged to Him for eternity, and He had promised them His everlasting presence.

The covenant between God and His people was sometimes referred to as a "covenant of salt" (Numbers 18:19; 2 Chronicles 13:5).

The Burnt Offering

The burnt offering is the first of several sacrificial offerings described in the book of Leviticus: meat offering (Leviticus 6:14), sin offering (6:25), trespass offering (7:1), and peace offering (7:11).

Behind all of these offerings was the principle of atonement. Through making these sacrifices to God, the people hoped to receive forgiveness for their sins and to restore fellowship with God. These offerings were made by the priests on behalf of individual members of the community of Israel.

The burnt offering—as well as the sin, trespass, and peace offerings—involved the burning of a sacrificial animal on the altar in the tabernacle (see note on Exodus 40:6). But these offerings were made for different offenses, and they

Ye [Israelites] shall burn no leaven [yeast, NIV], nor any honey, in any offering of the LORD made by fire.
Leviticus 2:11

Every oblation of thy meat offering shalt thou season with salt; neither shalt thou suffer the salt of the covenant of thy God to be lacking from thy meat offering: with all thine offerings thou shalt offer salt.
Leviticus 2:13

This is the law of [regulations for, NIV] the burnt offering: It is the burnt offering, because of the burning upon the altar all night unto the morning.
Leviticus 6:9

49

were presented in different ways.

For the burnt offering, the animal was left on the fire until it was totally comsumed. Thus, it is sometimes referred to as the "whole" burnt offering (Deuteronomy 33:10; Psalm 51:19). In some of the other offerings involving a sacrificial animal, the meat was removed from the fire before it was consumed and was eaten by the priests and their families.

The purpose of the burnt offering is not stated in the Bible. Many interpreters believe it symbolized the dedication of the Israelites to the Lord after His forgiveness and restoration.

Reconstruction of the Israelite Tabernacle and the Great Altar. The burnt offering was presented to the Lord using this altar.

THE GRAIN OFFERING

This was not an offering of meat but of bread (see note on Leviticus 2:11). Only a portion of the bread brought by a worshiper was burned on the altar; the rest was reserved for support of the priests and their families (Leviticus 2:8–10).

The grain offering may have been presented in association with the sin offering or the burnt offering (Numbers 15:4–6, 9).

This is the law of [regulations for, NIV] the meat offering [grain offering, NIV].
LEVITICUS 6:14

THE SIN OFFERING

This sacrificial offering was intended to atone for sins committed by the entire nation, as well as by individuals.

When the nation had sinned, the elders of the people presented an animal to a priest, who slaughtered it in the outer court of the tabernacle. He then took some of the animal's blood into the Holy Place inside the tabernacle and sprinkled it on the altar of incense (Leviticus 4:13–19).

In cases of individual sin, the priest did not enter the Holy Place but sacrificed the animal on the altar of burnt offering in the outer court (Leviticus 4:22–26).

This is the law of [regulations for, NIV] the sin offering.
LEVITICUS 6:25

THE TRESPASS OFFERING

The trespass offering was required for people who had committed sins of a lesser degree than those for which a sin offering was required. The guilty party had to bring an animal for sacrifice by the priest, and he was expected to make restitution for the wrongs he had committed against others (Leviticus 5:15–19).

This is the law of [regulations for, NIV] the trespass offering.
LEVITICUS 7:1

THREE WAYS OF BAKING BREAD

This verse describes three different ways of baking bread in Bible times.

The "oven" probably refers to a large stone pitcher with space in the bottom for heating small rocks over a fire. These rocks would radiate heat into the upper part of the pitcher, where bread was placed for baking.

The "fryingpan" was a large metal pot placed over an open fire and used mostly for boiling meat. But it could also be used for baking bread.

The "pan" was a flat metal plate that could be heated quickly to bake bread over an open fire. This is probably the utensil referred to by the prophet Ezekiel (Ezekiel 4:3).

All the meat offering [grain offering, NIV] that is baken in the oven, and all that is dressed in the fryingpan, and in the pan [griddle, NIV], shall be the priest's that offereth it.
LEVITICUS 7:9

THE PEACE OFFERING

This sacrificial offering was also referred to as the heave offering (Numbers 31:41) and the wave offering (Leviticus 23:20). The different sections of a sacrificial animal presented by the worshiper were lifted up before the Lord to celebrate His forgiveness and the restoration of fellowship between God and His people.

This is the law of [regulations for, NIV] the sacrifice of peace offerings.
LEVITICUS 7:11

UNCLEAN POTS

These animals were considered unclean and could not be eaten by the Israelites. Their impurity extended even to the things they touched. Thus, if these animals got into a clay jar where water or food was kept, these items had to be thrown away. Even the jar was considered irreversibly contaminated and had to be destroyed.

The weasel, the mouse, the tortoise, the ferret, the chameleon, the lizard, the snail, the mole. . .every earthen vessel, whereinto any of them falleth, whatsoever is in it shall be unclean.
LEVITICUS 11:29–30, 33

REPLASTERING WITH MORTAR

These instructions were intended for the Israelites after they had settled in permanent houses in the land of Canaan. If a plague of mildew or fungus broke out in a house, the owner was to replace the infected stones and replaster the entire dwelling with "morter," or clay.

The mortar of Bible times was made by mixing clay with finely chopped straw. Sometimes sand, ashes, or lime

They [Israelites] shall take other stones, and put them in the place of those stones; and he shall take other morter [clay, NIV], and shall plaister the house.
LEVITICUS 14:42

were added to give this substance more body and to make it last longer.

If this renovation of the house with new stones and new mortar did not eliminate the plague, the dwelling was to be torn down. The debris was to be carried outside the city to "an unclean place" (Leviticus 14:45)—perhaps a garbage dump designated for this purpose.

THE SCAPEGOAT

Once a year, on the Day of Atonement, the high priest of Israel made atonement for the sins of the entire nation. This ceremony included the offering of two goats as sacrifices to atone for the Israelites' sins.

One goat was selected by the casting of lots to serve as the blood sacrifice (Leviticus 16:8–9). The other goat, known as the scapegoat, was kept alive so it could be carried away into the wilderness. This action symbolized the forgiveness and removal of the sins of the nation.

The original meaning of the term *scapegoat* was "far removed" or "going far away." Today it refers to a person who takes the blame for wrongdoing committed by others.

TRANSFER OF SIN

This action by Aaron symbolized the transfer of the sins of the nation to the scapegoat (see note on Leviticus 16:10). Perhaps this passage is what the prophet Isaiah had in mind when he declared of the coming Messiah, "The LORD hath laid on him the iniquity of us all" (Isaiah 53:6).

The goat, on which the lot fell to be the scapegoat, shall be presented alive before the LORD, to make an atonement with him, and to let him go for a scapegoat into the wilderness [desert, NIV].
LEVITICUS 16:10

On the Day of Atonement, the scapegoat was driven away from God's people into the wilderness.

THE DAY OF ATONEMENT

The Day of Atonement was an annual ceremony in which sacrifices were offered to atone for the sins of Israel. Marked by humiliation and fasting, it recognized the people's inability to make atonement for their sins. This required God's intervention and that of His representative—the high priest of the nation.

The high priest first made atonement for his own sins by offering an animal sacrifice (Numbers 29:8). Then he entered the Most Holy Place in the tabernacle and sprinkled the blood of this animal on the ark of the covenant. He left and reentered this sacred room several times with other

Aaron shall lay both his hands upon the head of the live goat, and confess over him all the iniquities [wickedness and rebellion, NIV] of the children of Israel. . .putting them upon the head of the goat.
LEVITICUS 16:21

sacrifices to emphasize the people's need for forgiveness and reconciliation.

Another part of this ceremony was the release of a scapegoat, symbolically bearing the sins of the people, into the wilderness (see notes on Leviticus 16:10 and Leviticus 16:21).

The Day of Atonement was observed on the tenth day of the seventh month.

Goat Worship
The Hebrew word for "devils" in this passage literally means "shaggy" or "hairy" and is more accurately translated by the New International Version. The Egyptians worshiped the goat, as they did many animals. To them, the goat personified the rejuvenating power of nature. The implication of this verse is that some Israelites had offered sacrifices to this goat idol. Perhaps they had been influenced in this practice by the Egyptians.

Sacrifices to Molech
Molech, also referred to as Malcham (Zephaniah 1:5) and Moloch (Acts 7:43), was a pagan god of the Ammonites, whose worship involved child sacrifice. Images of this god portray him with a human body and the head of an ox.

Some interpreters believe Molech was a hollowed-out metal idol. A fire was kindled within the hollow space, and children were placed by their parents in his outstretched arms, where they were consumed by the flames and heat. It is believed that firstborn children were demanded of parents who worshiped this pagan god as proof of their devotion.

In spite of the Lord's prohibition against child sacrifice, it was practiced on occasion among the Israelites. Both King Ahaz (2 Kings 16:3) and King Manasseh (2 Kings 21:6) of Judah made their sons "pass through the fire." This probably refers to this pagan custom.

Forbidden Fruit
These instructions from the Lord probably had a practical bent. Not picking fruit off their new trees in Canaan for the first three years would allow the fruit to be eaten by animals and to have their seed spread. This would lead to more new trees, contributing to the Israelites' prosperity in the land.

This shall be an everlasting statute [lasting ordinance, NIV] unto you [Israelites], to make an atonement for the children of Israel for all their sins once a year.
LEVITICUS 16:34

They [the Israelites] shall no more offer their sacrifices unto devils [goat idols, NIV].
LEVITICUS 17:7

Thou [Israelites] shalt not let any of thy seed [children, NIV] pass through the fire to Molech.
LEVITICUS 18:21

When ye [Israelites] shall come into the land, and shall have planted all manner of trees for food, then ye shall count the fruit thereof as uncircumcised [forbidden, NIV]: three years shall it be as uncircumcised unto you: it shall not be eaten of.
LEVITICUS 19:23

Forbidden Hair Trimming

God instructed the Israelites not to crop their hair close around the ears and not to clip off the edges of their beards because these practices were associated with pagan worship. Full beards and thick hair all the way around their heads were signs that the Israelites worshiped the one true God.

Forbidden Cutting and Tattooing

Many pagan peoples of Bible times made cuts on their arms, hands, and faces as signs of mourning for the dead. God directed the Israelites not to practice this custom. Other references to this ancient practice are found in Leviticus 21:5; Deuteronomy 14:1; and Jeremiah 16:6; 48:37.

Imprinting permanent tattoos under the skin with sharp needles has been practiced since ancient times. But it was a pagan form of body manipulation during Bible times, and thus was forbidden for God's people.

Forbidden Food

This restriction was given for health reasons (see also Exodus 22:31; Leviticus 17:15; Ezekiel 44:31). The meat of an animal that had died of natural causes or had been killed by wild animals was not to be eaten by the Israelites. It might have some disease that could be passed on to humans.

The Drink Offering

A drink offering to God was usually given along with other offerings, such as the burnt offering (see note on Leviticus 6:9), the sin offering (see note on Leviticus 6:25), and the trespass offering (see note on Leviticus 7:1). The drink offering was a quantity of wine. It was presented by the worshiper to a priest, who poured it out at the base of the altar of burnt offering (see note on Exodus 40:6).

Celebration with Trumpets

This one-day celebration occurred on the first day of the seventh month and is sometimes called the Feast of Trumpets or the seventh-month festival. No work was done on this day. The people were summoned to gather for its celebration by the blowing of the two silver trumpets that Moses had been commanded to make for this purpose (Numbers 10:1–10).

The exact reason for this celebration is not known. It may have served notice to the Israelites that they should

God directed the Israelite men to cut their hair in a distinctive way.

Ye [Israelites] shall not round the corners of your heads [not cut the hair at the sides of your head, NIV], neither shalt thou mar [clip off, NIV] the corners of thy beard.
Leviticus 19:27

Ye [Israelites] shall not make any cuttings in your flesh for the dead, nor print any marks [tattoo marks, NIV] upon you.
Leviticus 19:28

That which dieth of itself, or is torn with beasts, he [Aaron and his descendants] shall not eat to defile himself therewith.
Leviticus 22:8

They [sacrificial animals] shall be for a burnt offering unto the LORD, with their meat offering, and their drink offerings.
Leviticus 23:18

begin preparation for the Day of Atonement, which was held ten days later (see note on Leviticus 16:34).

A Year of Rest for the Land

Just as the seventh day of the week, the Sabbath, was a day of rest and worship for God's people, they were to give their land a rest every seventh year. This was known as the sabbatical year.

During this year no crops were to be planted. Food for the Israelites would come from meat and from the grain that grew "of its own accord" (Leviticus 25:5). These spontaneous crops that grew without cultivation were also intended as provision for the poor (Exodus 23:11; Leviticus 25:6).

The Year of Liberty

Every fiftieth year among the Israelites was known as the year of liberty, or the year of jubilee. The Hebrew word for "jubilee" means "to be jubilant" or "to exult or praise." This year was launched on the Day of Atonement (see note on Leviticus 16:34) with a blast from a trumpet or ram's horn, signifying a call to joy and liberty throughout the land.

During this year any Israelite who had sold himself into slavery to a fellow Israelite to pay off a debt was released from his indebtedness and set free. Land that had been lost from a family since the last jubilee to pay a debt had to be returned to the original owners.

The jubilee year was a great leveler in Israelite society. It gave the poor and unfortunate a second chance. It also demonstrated God's concern for justice and fairness among His people.

No Idols or Images

This verse is similar to the first of the Ten Commandments: "Thou shalt have no other gods before me. Thou shalt not make unto thee any graven image" (Exodus 20:3–4). But in addition to graven images—idols cast from metal—this verse mentions two other types of idols: "standing image" and "image of stone."

A "standing image" may have been a statue representing a pagan god, similar to the statue that King Nebuchadnezzar of Babylon made of himself

In the seventh month, in the first day of the month, shall ye [Israelites] have a sabbath [day of rest, NIV], a memorial of blowing of trumpets, an holy convocation [a sacred assembly, NIV].
LEVITICUS 23:24

Six years thou shalt sow thy field. . .and gather in the fruit thereof; but in the seventh year shall be a sabbath of rest unto the land, a sabbath for the LORD: thou shalt neither sow thy field, nor prune thy vineyard.
LEVITICUS 25:3–4

Ye [Israelites] shall hallow the fiftieth year, and proclaim liberty throughout all the land unto all the inhabitants thereof: it shall be a jubile unto you.
LEVITICUS 25:10

Ye [Israelites] shall make you no idols nor graven image, neither rear you up a standing image, neither shall ye set up any image of stone in your land, to bow down unto it.
LEVITICUS 26:1

Household idols like this example from Babylon were common among many ancient peoples. The first of the Ten Commandments specifically forbids the use of such graven images.

and commanded his subjects to worship (Daniel 3:1–5). An "image of stone" was probably a likeness of a pagan god carved out of a rock, perhaps to symbolize permanence.

Pagan High Places

A "high place" was generally a mountaintop or a hilltop on which pagan worshipers bowed down before images of their false gods. They believed these elevated sites would put them closer to their gods and increase their chances of being heard.

God made it clear in this verse that He would judge the Israelites if they adopted the worship practices of their pagan neighbors.

The Shekel and the Gerah

Coins or bills did not exist in Old Testament times, so money was reckoned by weight, with the shekel serving as the standard unit of measure (see note on Genesis 23:16).

The gerah was an even smaller unit of weight. The phrase "a shekel is twenty gerahs" appears several other times in the Old Testament (Exodus 30:13; Numbers 3:47; 18:16; Ezekiel 45:12).

The Tithing Rod

The Lord established the principle of tithing among the Israelites by referring to the method by which shepherds counted their sheep.

When sheep were herded into a sheepfold at night, the shepherd stood by with a rod saturated with dye. He marked every tenth sheep with this dye as they entered the pen. This enabled him to do a quick count to determine if any were missing.

I [God] will destroy your [pagan worshipers'] high places.
Leviticus 26:30

All thy [Israelites'] estimations shall be according to the shekel of the sanctuary: twenty gerahs shall be the shekel.
Leviticus 27:25

Concerning the tithe of the herd. . .even of whatsoever passeth under the rod [shepherd's rod, NIV], the tenth shall be holy unto the LORD.
Leviticus 27:32

NUMBERS

STANDARDS AND BANNERS

God directed the twelve tribes of Israel to camp in three-tribe units on the northern, southern, eastern, and western sides of the tabernacle (Numbers 2:3–31). Each of these three-tribe units had a distinct sign on a pole, known as a standard, around which they gathered to make sure they followed the camping arrangement specified by the Lord.

These standards may have been similar to those used by the Egyptians as military symbols for different units of their army. Many of these Egyptian standards featured images of their pagan gods. The Bible does not say what symbols were used on the Israelite standards.

The phrase "ensign of their father's house" probably refers to a small flag or banner that was carried by each tribe or even the separate clans that made up each tribe.

Every man of the children of Israel shall pitch by his own standard, with the ensign [banners, NIV] of their father's house.
NUMBERS 2:2

DUTIES OF THE LEVITES

Since Levi was a son of Jacob (Genesis 29:34), Levi's descendants evolved into one of the twelve tribes of Israel. It was designated as the tribe that would minister on behalf of all the other Israelites.

Aaron was a member of the tribe of Levi. Aaron's direct descendants became the priests who officiated at the altar (Numbers 3:2–3), offering sacrifices for the people. All the other members of the tribe of Levi were designated as Levites. Their duty was to assist the priests in these sacrificial functions.

The three separate divisions of the Levites were named for Levi's three sons: Gershon, Kohath, and Merari (Numbers 3:17). During the days when the Israelites wandered in the wilderness, these three units had specific responsibilities for setting up and taking down the tabernacle, transporting it, and caring for its sacred objects and furnishings (Numbers 3:23–27).

The Levites assisted the priests by slaughtering sacrificial animals, baking the showbread for the Most Holy Place in the tabernacle (see note on Exodus 25:30), and serving as doorkeepers and musicians in the tabernacle and temple.

Bring the tribe of Levi near, and present them before Aaron the priest, that they may minister unto him.
NUMBERS 3:6

AARON'S PRIESTHOOD CONFIRMED

Some Israelites questioned Aaron's right to serve as priest and his descendants' right to continue his priestly work among the nation (Numbers 16:1–3). So Moses conducted a test to determine who should serve in this leadership position.

Moses placed twelve staffs or sticks, representing the twelve tribes of Israel, in the tabernacle overnight. The next morning Aaron's staff had budded and produced almonds. This miracle served as undeniable proof that Aaron of the tribe of Levi and his descendants had been selected by the Lord for this ministry.

SACRIFICE OF THE RED HEIFER

The Israelites believed that contact with a corpse made a person ceremonially unclean (Numbers 19:11). He could be made clean again by being sprinkled with the remains of a red heifer (female cow) that had been sacrificed and burned to ashes for this purpose. The animal's ashes were mixed with water for this purification ceremony (Numbers 19:17–18).

The death of a person in a tent or house also made the dwelling unclean. It could be made clean again by being sprinkled with the ashes from this sacrificial animal. This mixture of water with ashes was known as the "water of separation" (Numbers 19:21).

ELEAZAR SUCCEEDS AARON

At Aaron's death the special clothes that he wore as high priest of Israel (see note on Exodus 40:13) were transferred to his son Eleazar. This showed that Eleazar was the legitimate successor to his father in this role.

Eleazar served as high priest for the rest of Moses' life and also for a time after Joshua succeeded Moses as leader of the Israelites. Eleazar assisted in the division of the land of Canaan among the twelve tribes (Joshua 14:1).

The unique clothing of the High Priest helped identify his special role within Israel.

Moab and Chemosh

Chemosh was the national pagan god worshiped by the Moabites and Ammonites, tribal enemies of the Israelites. Hence, the Moabites are referred to in this verse as the "people of Chemosh."

This pagan god may have been associated with worship of the stars. Children were sacrificed to Chemosh as an act of worship (2 Kings 3:27), just as they were to Molech (see note on Leviticus 18:21). The prophet Jeremiah also referred to the Moabites as the "people of Chemosh" (Jeremiah 48:46).

Woe to thee, Moab! thou art undone [destroyed, NIV], O people of Chemosh.
NUMBERS 21:29

Baal Worship

King Balak of Moab enlisted a wizard named Baalam to pronounce a curse against the Israelites. Balak and Baalam went up into the "high places" (see note on Leviticus 26:30) devoted to worship of the pagan god Baal to get a panoramic view of the Israelites as they camped in the valley below.

Balak took Balaam, and brought him up into the high places of Baal.
NUMBERS 22:41

Baal was a major pagan god of the Canaanites that was thought to provide fertility for crops and livestock. Stone carvings discovered by archaeologists show Baal holding a bolt of lightning. This probably shows that he was thought to bring the rain, which caused crops to grow. Baal is also shown in other carvings as a mating bull—another fertility symbol.

After settling in Canaan, some of the Israelites were influenced by their pagan neighbors to worship this false god. During the days of King Ahab of Israel, one of his wives, Jezebel, actually promoted Baal worship throughout the land.

The statuette of the storm god and bull above were both associated with Baal, a major pagan god of the Canaanites thought to provide fertility.

With King Ahab looking on, the prophet Elijah won a decisive victory over the prophets of Baal in a dramatic contest on Mount Carmel (1 Kings 18).

A Localized Baal

The name of the pagan Canaanite god Baal (see note on Numbers 22:41) was often localized by adding a place name to his main name. Thus, *Baal-peor* (or Baal of Peor) refers to Baal worship on the summit of Mount Peor.

Israel joined himself unto Baal-peor: and the anger of the LORD was kindled against Israel.
NUMBERS 25:3

DEUTERONOMY

So the LORD our God delivered into our hands Og also, the king of Bashan, and all his people.
DEUTERONOMY 3:3

Only Og king of Bashan remained of the remnant of giants; behold, his bedstead was a bedstead of iron. . . . Nine cubits [thirteen feet, NIV] was the length thereof, and four cubits [six feet, NIV] the breadth of it.
DEUTERONOMY 3:11

Lest thou lift up thine eyes unto heaven, and when thou seest the sun, and the moon, and the stars, even all the host of heaven [all the heavenly array, NIV], shouldest be driven [enticed, NIV] to worship them, and serve them.
DEUTERONOMY 4:19

LAND OF BASHAN

This event, recounted by Moses, is described in Numbers 21:33–35. Og was an Amorite king who lived in Bashan, a territory east of the Jordan River across from the land of Canaan. After the Israelites conquered Canaan, the territory of Bashan was settled by the half tribe of Manasseh (Joshua 13:29–31).

Bashan is mentioned several times in the Old Testament (Joshua 17:5; 1 Chronicles 5:16; Psalm 68:15; Jeremiah 22:20).

BEDSTEAD OR COFFIN?

King Og was apparently the last of a giant race that once occupied the territory of Bashan. This description of his iron bed leaves no doubt that he was a person of superhuman size.

Some interpreters believe the Hebrew word behind "bedstead" (literally, "resting place") should be translated as "coffin" or "sarcophagus." Thus, Og may have been laid to rest in a huge coffin that reflected his large size as well as his position as the king.

WORSHIP OF THE SUN, MOON, AND STARS

Worship of the sun and other heavenly bodies was common among the pagan nations of the ancient world. For example, the city of Ur in Mesopotamia from which Abraham migrated was a center of moon worship. The Egyptians worshiped the sun god known as Ra (see note on Genesis 12:15). The Lord, speaking through Moses, specifically prohibited this form of idolatry.

The title "the Lord of hosts" applied to God throughout the Old Testament (Psalm 24:10; Isaiah 19:16) is actually a declaration that He is superior to all of the heavenly bodies, since He brought them into being (Genesis 2:1).

Worship of the heavenly bodies is also referred to in Deuteronomy 17:3; 2 Kings 17:16; 21:3; 23:5; and Jeremiah 8:2.

WRITING ON THE DOOR

The Israelites were commanded by the Lord to write passages from His law on the doorframes of their houses after they settled permanently in the land of Canaan. Every time they entered or left their dwellings, they would be reminded of God's Word and their promise to obey His commands.

Thou [Israelites] shalt write them upon the posts [doorframes, NIV] of thy house, and on thy gates.
DEUTERONOMY 6:9

IRRIGATION OF EGYPTIAN CROPS

This verse contrasts the land of Egypt, where the Israelites had been enslaved, with the land of Canaan, which God had promised to His people. Egyptians crops grew in the

Mezuzah fixed to a door frame. This small box contains a passage from God's law in obedience to God's command in Deuteronomy 6:9.

fertile floodplain along the Nile River (see note on Genesis 41:1). But Canaan was a land of hills and valleys. Here the crops of the Israelites would flourish from the "water of the rain of heaven" (Deuteronomy 11:11).

Watering crops "with thy foot" in Egypt probably refers to the small waterwheels that were turned by foot to pump water from the Nile River into irrigation canals. This artificial watering system was essential for crop production in Egypt's hot, dry climate.

The land, whither thou [Israelites] goest in to possess it, is not as the land of Egypt, from whence ye came out, where thou sowedst thy seed, and wateredst [irrigated, NIV] it with thy foot.
DEUTERONOMY 11:10

EATING BLOOD FORBIDDEN

These verses occur in the context of presenting a sacrificial animal as an offering to the Lord. The Israelites believed the blood of such an animal was sacred, since it carried the very essence of life itself. In a sense, the blood was the ransom price that atoned for their sins. It was to be drained from the animal and poured on the ground at the base of the altar.

The meat from some sacrificial animals could be eaten by the priests (Leviticus 6:19–30). But the blood of such animals was considered sacred and was never to be eaten.

Perhaps another reason for this prohibition against eating blood is that this was practiced in some pagan religious systems. Pagan priests would drink the blood of sacrificial

Be sure that thou [Israelites] eat not the blood: for the blood is the life; and thou mayest not eat the life with the flesh. Thou shalt not eat it; thou shalt pour it upon the earth as water.
DEUTERONOMY 12:23–24

animals to symbolize their devotion to the false gods they worshiped. God made it clear that His people were to avoid such pagan customs.

No Black Magic

The term *divination*, as used in this passage, refers to attempts to control evil spirits, to penetrate the mysteries of the universe, or to foretell the future by using magical acts, pronouncing superstitious incantations, or interpreting natural signs. Today we refer to such practices as "the occult."

"Black magic" was a prominent feature of pagan religious systems in Bible times. But God prohibited the Israelites from participating in these practices. Seven different types of divination are mentioned in this passage.

Observer of times. The Hebrew word behind "observer of times" is translated by the New International Version as one who practices "sorcery." They often made their predictions by "reading" the clouds in the sky. The practitioners of this art specialized in distinguishing lucky days from unlucky days and recommending to people the best times to plant crops, make a purchase, take a trip, and so on.

Enchanter. The New International Version translates the Hebrew word behind "enchanter" as one who "interprets omens." This person predicted the future or told people's fortunes by reading certain signs. One way of doing this was to use a magic cup. The cup of Joseph was referred to as a "divining cup" (see note on Genesis 44:2). Another method was to interpret the pattern formed by birds in flight.

The art of enchantment is referred to several times in the Old Testament (Leviticus 19:26; Numbers 23:23; 24:1; 2 Kings 17:17; 21:6; 2 Chronicles 33:6).

Witch. A witch was a person who cast spells or used other supernatural "black magic" tricks to commit evil or wicked acts. The Hebrew word for "witch" or "witchcraft" is used to describe Jezebel and her associates who promoted the worship of the false god Baal (see note on Numbers 22:41) throughout the Northern Kingdom during the reign of King Ahab (2 Kings 9:22).

Charmer. The Hebrew word behind "charmer" is translated as one who "casts spells" by the New International Version. It is not clear how a charmer differed from a witch. Some interpreters believe charmers practiced their craft by tying magic knots or using a magic ring.

Consulter with familiar spirits. Consulters with familiar spirits claimed to be able to call up the spirits or ghosts of dead people. They did this at the request of friends or loved

There shall not be found among you [Israelites] any one. . .that useth [practices, NIV] divination, or an observer of times, or an enchanter, or a witch, or a charmer, or a consulter with familiar spirits, or a wizard, or a necromancer.

DEUTERONOMY 18:10–11

ones who sought advice or guidance from the deceased.

King Saul sought out "a woman that hath a familiar spirit" (1 Samuel 28:7) when he wanted to communicate with the prophet Samuel, who had died. This woman was shocked when the spirit of Samuel actually appeared and gave the king some bad news about his forthcoming battle with the Philistines (1 Samuel 28:11–19). Her surprise indicates that these consulters with familiar spirits probably used trickery—perhaps ventriloquism—to convince people that they were talking with their departed friends and loved ones.

Wizard. The Hebrew word behind "wizard" means "the knowing one." Thus, a wizard may have been an expert in all of the magical tricks associated with sorcery and divination.

Necromancer. The New International Version translates the Hebrew word behind "necromancer" as one who "consults the dead." This practitioner of the occult apparently claimed to be able to conjure up the spirits of the dead, just like a consulter with familiar spirits. In addition, necromancers may have used corpses to foretell the future. Some interpreters believe they "read" dead people's bones or veins to determine the future of the survivors of the deceased.

ACCIDENTAL DEATH

This verse shows God's desire that cities of refuge be established throughout the land once the Israelites had conquered and settled the land of Canaan. Any person who caused the accidental death of another could seek refuge in one of these cities until it was determined through due process what punishment, if any, should be levied against him.

In Old Testament times, the people lived under a "life for life" rule. Any person who caused the death of another was to be sought out and killed by the relatives of the victim. A city of refuge offered asylum for the perpetrator in cases of accidental death.

Different types of axes were used by the Israelites. The heads of some lighter axes were fastened to the axe handle with strips of leather. But the axe described in this verse must have been a heavy-duty version used for cutting down trees and hewing timbers. The axe head slipped over the end of the handle, much like our modern axes.

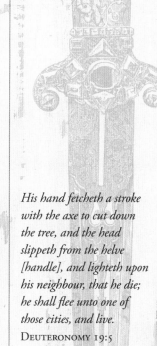

His hand fetcheth a stroke with the axe to cut down the tree, and the head slippeth from the helve [handle], and lighteth upon his neighbour, that he die; he shall flee unto one of those cities, and live.
DEUTERONOMY 19:5

BOUNDARY STONES

Thou [Israelites] shalt not remove thy neighbour's landmark [boundary stone, NIV], which they of old time have set in thine inheritance.

DEUTERONOMY 19:14

After the Israelites settled in Canaan and received their land allotments, they marked their property by placing small stones around the edges of their plots.

Unlike permanent fences, these stones could be moved easily. A dishonest person on an adjoining plot could move these markers and encroach on his neighbor's property. The Lord specifically prohibited this practice because it was a form of stealing (Exodus 20:15). The practice of moving boundary stones is also forbidden in Proverbs 22:28 and 23:10.

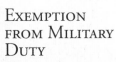

EXEMPTION FROM MILITARY DUTY

The Israelites apparently attached great importance to the dedication of a new house, since a man was exempted from military duty until he had dedicated his newly built house.

In some portions of Israel today, boundary markers like this are still used to mark the boundaries of one's property.

What man is there that hath built a new house, and hath not dedicated it? let him go and return to his house, lest he die in the battle, and another man dedicate it.

DEUTERONOMY 20:5

An exemption was also granted to a man who had planted a new vineyard that had not yet produced grapes (Deuteronomy 20:6). Also exempt was a man whose parents had arranged his marriage (see note on Genesis 24:4) but who had not yet taken the bride as his wife (Deuteronomy 20:7).

JUSTICE AT THE CITY GATE

The gates of ancient walled cities were places where people gathered to conduct business and catch up on the latest news (see note on Genesis 19:1). The elders or rulers of the city also held court at this location, rendering judgments in cases brought before them by the people.

Then shall his father and his mother lay hold on him [a rebellious son], and bring him out unto the elders of his city, and unto the gate of his place [town, NIV].

DEUTERONOMY 21:19

This verse specifies that parents with a rebellious son could bring charges against him before the elders at the city gate. A son who was found guilty of consistent disobedience, gluttony, and drunkenness could actually have the death penalty pronounced against him (Deuteronomy 21:20–21).

No Cross-dressing

In Bible times, both men and women wore long, outer robes or tunics that were very similar. So this prohibition against wearing clothing of the opposite sex probably applied to accessories such as undergarments, jewelry, and hats.

Transvestitism, or the adoption of the clothing and behavior of the opposite sex, was an abomination to God because of its association with the forbidden practice of homosexuality (Leviticus 18:22; 20:13).

Some pagan idols of the ancient world were portrayed with the features of one sex and the dress of the other, perhaps in an attempt to appeal to both sexes. God may have prohibited cross-dressing to show that His people were to avoid any practice that might be associated with idol worship.

Guardrails on the Roof

This verse is something of an ancient "building code." A house was to be built with a guardrail around the edge of the roof to protect people from accidental falls.

In Bible times the roofs of houses were flat. A stairway on the outside of the house allowed the residents to use the roof much like a patio or deck is used today. Particularly at night, the roof was a good place to relax and catch a cooling breeze. Sometimes a family would even sleep on the roof to escape the oppressive heat (2 Samuel 11:2).

Perhaps the most famous "rooftop incident" in the Bible was King David's chance encounter with Bathsheba. The king was tempted to commit adultery with her when he looked down from the roof of his palace and saw her taking a bath (2 Samuel 11:2).

Protection of the Poor

This law, a protection against high-handed search and seizure, is one of many in the Old Testament that preserved the rights and dignity of the poor (see notes on Deuteronomy 24:12–13 and Deuteronomy 24:20).

A person who had lent money or property to a poor man could not just barge into his house and take what he wanted. He had to stand outside and make a formal request for repayment of the loan.

The Robe as a Blanket

This law also protected the poor (see notes on Deuteronomy 24:10–11 and Deuteronomy 24:20). If a poor man had put up his outer robe as collateral for a loan, the creditor could not hold it overnight. He had to return it to the poor man at sundown so he could use it like a blanket to sleep in.

The woman shall not wear that which pertaineth unto a man, neither shall a man put on a woman's garment [clothing, NIV]: for all that do so are abomination unto the LORD thy God.
DEUTERONOMY 22:5

When thou [Israelites] buildest a new house, then thou shalt make a battlement [parapet, NIV] for thy roof, that thou bring not blood [the guilt of bloodshed, NIV] upon thine house, if any man fall from thence.
DEUTERONOMY 22:8

When thou [Israelites] dost lend thy brother any thing, thou shalt not go into his house to fetch his pledge. Thou shalt stand abroad [outside, NIV], and the man to whom thou dost lend shall bring out the pledge abroad unto thee.
DEUTERONOMY 24:10–11

If the man be poor, thou [Israelites] shalt not sleep with his pledge: in any case thou shalt deliver him the pledge [cloak, NIV] again when the sun goeth down, that he may sleep in his own raiment.
DEUTERONOMY 24:12–13

OLIVES FOR THE POOR

When thou [Israelites] beatest thine olive tree, thou shalt not go over the boughs again [a second time, NIV]: it shall be for the stranger [alien, NIV], for the fatherless, and for the widow.

DEUTERONOMY 24:20

God's concern for the poor is also demonstrated in this law (see notes on Deuteronomy 24:10–11 and Deuteronomy 24:12–13).

Olives (see note on Exodus 27:20) were harvested by beating the branches of the trees with sticks. The ripe olives were gathered when they fell to the ground. This law directed that the trees were not to be beaten a second time. Olives that had ripened since the first beating were to be left for gleaning by the poor and disadvantaged (see note on Ruth 2:3).

METAPHORICAL OLIVES

Olives were an important crop in Palestine since they provided food for the table and fuel for the small oil-burning lamps with which homes were illuminated (see note on Exodus 27:20)

The olive tree is often spoken of metaphorically in the Bible. The psalmist described himself as "a green olive tree" (Psalm 52:8) because he was so richly blessed by the Lord. According to the prophet Hosea, in the future messianic age, the blessings of Israel would be "as the olive tree" (Hosea 14:6).

THRESHING BY OXEN

Thou [Israelites] shalt not muzzle the ox when he treadeth out the corn [grain, NIV].

DEUTERONOMY 25:4

The heads of grain such as wheat and barley were sometimes separated from the stalks by driving an ox or a team of oxen back and forth over the stalks on a flat surface. An unmuzzled ox would be able to eat some of the grain while it worked, thus renewing its strength.

The apostle Paul cited this verse to show that churches have a responsibility to contribute to the financial support of their ministers (1 Corinthians 9:9–14).

MARRIAGE OF A BROTHER'S WIFE

If brethren dwell together, and one of them die, and have no child, the wife of the dead shall not marry without [outside the family, NIV] unto a stranger: her husband's brother shall go in unto her, and take her to him to wife, and perform [fulfill, NIV] the duty of an husband's brother unto her.

DEUTERONOMY 25:5

The custom described in this verse is known as the law of levirate marriage. If a man died and he and his wife had no children, his brother was expected to take his widow as his wife. This would keep the deceased man's property in the family and possibly produce sons who would carry on his family name (Deuteronomy 25:6).

This custom was not binding in an absolute sense on a dead man's brother. But if he refused to marry his brother's widow, he was branded by having one of his sandals removed (Deuteronomy 25:9–10). This signaled to others that he had failed to assume his family responsibilities.

HONEST BUYING AND SELLING

Dishonest merchants of Bible times conducted business by using two different weights on the scales on which they weighed out merchandise. These weights looked alike, and they were marked as if they weighed the same amount.

If a dishonest merchant was buying from a supplier, he used the heavier weight in order to get more than he paid for. But if he was selling merchandise, he used the lighter weight to deliver less than the customer actually paid for. Of course, the unsuspecting suppliers and customers never realized they were being cheated.

The Lord made it clear that He expected His people to exercise honesty and integrity in their business practices.

Thou [Israelites] shalt not have in thy bag divers weights [two differing weights, NIV], a great [one heavy, NIV] and a small [one light, NIV].
DEUTERONOMY 25:13

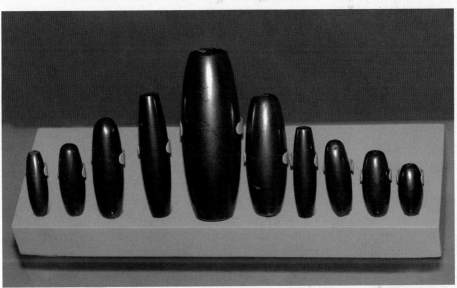

Some merchants carried two sets of weights to measure goods, one for buying and one for selling. God required His people to buy and sell with the same set of weights.

CRUSHING OLIVES

Before his death, Moses predicted the future of each of the tribes of Israel after they settled in the land of Canaan (Deuteronomy 32:1–25). The tribe of Asher would be known for its olive oil production. "Dipping" or "bathing" the foot in oil refers to the ancient practice of crushing olives by foot to expel the oil.

Olive oil was used as fuel in oil-burning lamps (Exodus 27:20; see note on Mark 4:21) and as an anointing agent (Leviticus 2:1).

Of Asher he [Moses] said. . .let him be acceptable to his brethren [favored by his brothers, NIV], and let him dip [bathe, NIV] his foot in oil.
DEUTERONOMY 33:24

JOSHUA

ROOFS USED FOR STORAGE

Rahab was a Canaanite woman who lived in the city of Jericho. When Israelite spies came to scout the city, she hid them under stalks of flax on the roof of her house.

Houses of Bible times had flat roofs that were used as sleeping areas (see note on Deuteronomy 22:8), as well as for storage. The flax under which the spies hid had probably been placed there in the sun for drying.

A HOUSE ON A WALL

Some walled cities of Bible times had an inner wall and an outer wall for maximum protection (see note on 2 Samuel 18:24). To strengthen these walls, the space between them was filled with dirt and rubble at selected points. Houses were sometimes built right into the city wall by placing them on top of these piles of rubble.

Since Rahab "dwelt upon the wall" of Jericho, she must have lived in one of these "wall houses." She helped the Israelite spies escape over the city wall (see note on Joshua 2:6) by lowering them with a rope from her window.

Another similar escape was made in New Testament times by the apostle Paul. Believers in the city of Damascus delivered him from his enemies, who were watching the city gates "day and night to kill him" (Acts 9:24). They placed Paul in a basket and lowered him over the city wall.

CIRCUMCISION KNIVES

The Lord issued this command to Joshua when the Israelites were camped at Gilgal after they had crossed the Jordan River into Canaan.

They had wandered in the wilderness for forty years, and all of the adults who had rebelled against the Lord had died. The rite of circumcision (see note on Genesis 17:11) had apparently not been performed on the new generation of males, so God directed that this be done before they set out to conquer the land.

Knives fashioned from flint, an extremely hard stone, were used for this circumcision ritual. In various periods of biblical history, knives were made from bone, copper, iron, and steel.

Monument to a Crime

Achan was executed because he kept some of the spoils of war taken in battles against the Canaanites for himself (Joshua 7:20–21). This was a violation of the Lord's command (Joshua 6:19).

To commemorate Achan's crime, Joshua and other Israelite leaders piled stones on his grave. This makeshift monument served as a constant reminder to others of the seriousness of disobeying God.

Throughout Israel's history, stones were also heaped up to serve as memorials of positive events in the life of the nation (Exodus 24:4; Joshua 4:3–9; 24:26; 1 Samuel 7:12).

Trickery of the Gibeonites

The Gibeonites were Canaanites, just like the other tribal groups that Joshua was defeating and executing. But the Gibeonites were smart. They used trickery to save their lives.

By wearing worn-out clothes and carrying torn wineskins and stale bread, the Gibeonites pretended that they were travelers from a distant country rather than residents of Canaan. Fooled by their trickery, Joshua agreed to grant them asylum and to let them live in peace in the land (Joshua 9:15).

After he discovered the truth, Joshua honored the covenant he had made with the Gibeonites. But he sentenced them to a life of servitude as woodcutters and water carriers

They [all Israel] raised [heaped, NIV] over him [Achan] a great heap of stones.
Joshua 7:26

When the inhabitants of Gibeon heard what Joshua had done unto Jericho and to Ai, they did work wilily [resorted to a ruse, NIV], and went and made as if they had been ambassadors, and took old sacks upon their asses [donkeys, NIV], and wine bottles [wineskins, NIV], old, and rent, and bound up; and old shoes and clouted upon their feet, and old garments upon them; and all the bread of their provision was dry and mouldy.
Joshua 9:3–5

The Gibeonites who lived on the hill in the foreground used trickery to save their lives in the face of Joshua's army.

for the Israelites (Joshua 9:21–23).

The task of carrying water must have been particularly degrading to the Gibeonites. This chore was normally done by women (see note on Genesis 24:11).

FEET ON THE NECKS OF ENEMIES

When they [Israelite warriors] brought out those kings unto Joshua. . .Joshua. . . said unto the captains [commanders, NIV] of the men of war. . .Come near, put your feet upon the necks of these kings.
JOSHUA 10:24

Joshua directed that this action be taken against the five Amorite kings whom his military forces had defeated (Joshua 10:5–10).

Putting one's foot on the neck of an enemy was not an act of hostility or violence but a symbolic action that showed total subjection. There was no doubt that these kings and their people were now under Israel's control.

JUDGES

MUTILATION OF CAPTIVES

They [the tribe of Judah] pursued after him [King Adoni-bezek], and caught him, and cut off his thumbs and his great [big, NIV] toes.
JUDGES 1:6

Adoni-bezek, a Canaanite king, was defeated by warriors from the tribe of Judah. In ancient warfare captive soldiers were sometimes mutilated as Adoni-bezek was to take away their fighting abilities. With both thumbs and both big toes missing, the king would not be able to move quickly or handle a bow or spear.

The ancient Assyrians were known to mutilate captives just for sport, cutting off body parts that had nothing to do with waging war. One monument left by an Assyrian king testifies to their military cruelty: "Their men, young and old, I took prisoners. Of some I cut off the feet and hands; of others I cut off the noses, ears, and lips; of the young men's ears I made a heap."

BAAL AND ASHERAH

The word *Baalim* in this verse is the plural form of Baal, the fertility god of the Canaanites (see note on Numbers 22:41). The worshipers of this pagan god may have referred to him in the plural to emphasize his prestige and importance in their eyes.

The Hebrew word translated in the King James Version as "the groves" is *Asherahs*. This is the plural form of Asherah, mother god of the Canaanite religious system who gave birth to seventy pagan gods—the most important of which was Baal. During the days of the judges, the Israelites were enticed into worship of these two false gods.

Wooden images of Asherah are sometimes referred to as "Asherah poles" in modern translations of the Bible (2 Kings 23:6 NIV). The name of this goddess is usually spelled "Ashtaroth" (Judges 2:13) or "Ashtoreth" (1 Kings 11:5) in the King James Version.

UNDER LOCK AND KEY

A door lock of Bible times consisted of a sliding piece of wood that was pushed into a slot in the doorframe. A catch in the frame clamped down on the lock to hold it in place.

This lock was mounted on the inside of the door. It could be opened easily from that side with a wooden key that released the catch in the doorframe. But how was a locked door opened from the outside?

The door had a hole near the lock that made this possible. A person put his hand through the hole from the outside and inserted the key in the doorframe to open the door. This is how Eglon's servants opened a locked door to check on their master.

This locking system is also described by Solomon's bride: "My lover thrust his hand through the latch-opening; my heart began to pound for him" (Song of Solomon 5:4 NIV).

AN OX GOAD AS A WEAPON

As one of the judges, or military deliverers, of Israel, Shamgar used an ox goad as an efficient weapon against the Philistines. An ox goad was a pole about eight feet long and two inches in diameter. It was sharpened to a point on one end. A farmer used this end when plowing with an ox to prod him into a faster gait. The other end had a metal blade that he used to clean roots or clay from the tip of the plow.

Jesus referred to an ox goad when He appeared to the apostle Paul on the road to Damascus: "Saul, Saul, why persecutest thou me? it is hard for thee to kick against the pricks [goads, NIV]" (Acts 26:14).

The children of Israel did evil in the sight of the LORD, and forgat the LORD their God, and served Baalim and the groves [Asherahs, NIV].

JUDGES 3:7

Asherah figurine. Asherah was the mother god of the Canaanite religious system.

Then Ehud went forth through the porch, and shut the doors of the parlour [upper room, NIV] upon him [Eglon], and locked them. . . . Behold, he [Eglon] opened not the doors of the parlour: therefore they [Eglon's servants] took a key, and opened [unlocked, NIV] them.

JUDGES 3:23–25

After him [Ehud] was Shamgar the son of Anath, which slew of the Philistines six hundred men with an ox goad.

JUDGES 3:31

*Speak, ye that ride on
white asses [donkeys, NIV],
ye that sit in judgment,
and walk by the way
[along the road, NIV].*
JUDGES 5:10

*The mother of Sisera
looked out at a window,
and cried through
the lattice, Why is
his [Sisera's] chariot
so long in coming?*
JUDGES 5:28

VICTORY OVER THE POWERFUL

This verse appears in the Song of Deborah (Judges 5:1–31) after she led the Israelites to victory over the forces of a Canaanite king.

White donkeys were rare and expensive. Anyone who rode one was rich and influential—a member of the elite class of society. This was Deborah's poetic way of saying that the Lord had overthrown the proud and powerful and given the Israelites a decisive victory over their enemies.

A CRY FROM A WINDOW

This phrase from the Song of Deborah (see note on Judges 5:10) pictures Sisera's mother wondering why her son had not returned from a battle with the Israelites. But Sisera would not return; he had been killed by a woman named Jael, who drove a tent peg through his head while he was asleep (Judges 4:21).

The windows of houses in Bible times were nothing like our modern glass windows. They were crude openings in exterior walls covered with wooden shutters. A person could open these shutters to look outside or to let in a cool breeze.

A Phoenician ivory that has been entitled, "The Woman at the Window." Judges 5 places Sisera's mother in just such a pose, longing for the return of her fallen son.

BIBLICAL WINDOWS

1. Michal looked out a window and saw King David dancing before the ark of the covenant as it was brought into Jerusalem (2 Samuel 6:16).
2. Jezebel watched from a window as Jehu entered Jezreel to begin his reign as the new king of Israel (the Northern Kingdom) (2 Kings 9:30).
3. The prophet Daniel prayed three times a day with his windows opened toward Jerusalem (Daniel 6:10).
4. Eutychus fell asleep and fell to his death from a window during a long sermon by Paul. The apostle restored him to life (Acts 20:7-12).

Beautiful Cloth

This phrase from the Song of Deborah (see note on Judges 5:10) has the servants of Sisera's mother assuring her that he has not returned from battle because he is gathering spoils of war from the Israelites. Of course, this was not true, since Sisera had been killed (see note on Judges 5:28).

The spoils of war mentioned here probably consisted of cloth of many beautiful colors with designs or figures either woven into the cloth or produced by an embroidery technique. Clothes made from cloth like this were highly prized in the ancient world. The prophet Ezekiel referred to the Assyrians' fondness for costly clothing (Ezekiel 23:12).

Gideon's Secret Weapons

Gideon relied on the Lord, as well as shock and surprise, to defeat the huge Midianite army with a force of only three hundred warriors. He and his men advanced on the enemy camp at night while most of the Midianites were still asleep. Then, at Gideon's signal, they blew their trumpets and broke their pitchers with torches inside, suddenly bathing the camp in light.

All of the noise and light convinced the Midianites that they were being attacked by a huge army. In the shock and confusion, they "set every man's sword against his fellow" (Judges 7:22) and fled into the night. Their disorganization made them easy prey for the pursuing Israelites.

Decorated Camels

Zeba and Zalmunna were Midianite kings whom Gideon pursued and executed after he and his warriors had defeated their army (see note on Judges 7:16).

The Hebrew word behind "ornament" in this verse is rendered in Isaiah 3:18 as "round tires like the moon [crescent necklaces, NIV]." Judges 8:26 describes these ornaments as "chains" around the necks of the camels.

Thus, these ornaments must have been gold chains that contained emblems of the moon. These Midianaite kings probably placed them there as charms to protect their camels from evil or injury. Worship of the heavenly bodies, including the moon, was widespread throughout the ancient

To Sisera a prey [plunder, NIV] of divers colours, a prey of divers colours of needlework, of divers colours of needlework on both sides.

JUDGES 5:30

Gideon sounded his shofar, signaling his soldiers to begin their surprise attack on the Midianites.

He [Gideon] divided the three hundred men into three companies, and he put a trumpet in every man's hand, with empty pitchers [jars, NIV], and lamps [torches, NIV] within the pitchers.

JUDGES 7:16

Gideon arose, and slew Zebah and Zalmunna, and took away the ornaments that were on their camels' necks.

JUDGES 8:21

73

*Thou [Manoah's wife]
shalt conceive, and bear
a son; and no razor shall
come on his head:
for the child shall be a
Nazarite unto God from
the womb.*

JUDGES 13:5

world (see note on Deuteronomy 4:19).

When Gideon removed these ornaments, he was taking away objects of Midianite idolatry.

SAMSON THE NAZARITE

A Nazarite was a person who took an oath known as the Nazarite vow. He promised to avoid worldly things and to devote himself totally to the Lord. As evidence of this commitment, a Nazarite was not to drink wine or any intoxicating beverages and was not to cut his hair (Numbers 6:5).

The Nazarite vow was voluntary, and it was generally taken for a limited time, perhaps thirty or sixty days. But Samson was designated as a Nazarite for life; this choice was made for him by the Lord and his parents even before he was born.

Samson failed to live up to the vow that others had made for him. He indulged in worldly pleasures and sinned against the Lord. When Delilah succeeded in cutting his hair, the Spirit of the Lord left him and his great strength was taken away (Judges 16:19).

OTHER NAZARITES

Like Samson, the prophet Samuel was probably also a Nazarite. His mother, Hannah, made a vow before he was born that "there shall no razor come upon his head" (1 Samuel 1:11). And the refusal of John the Baptist, forerunner of Jesus, to drink wine indicates that he had probably taken the Nazarite vow, as well (Matthew 11:18–19).

SAMSON'S RIDDLE

In an age without television or other leisure-time pursuits, the people of Bible times often used riddles as a form of entertainment. Like Samson, they would pose a puzzling or mystifying question or problem and see who could figure it out.

Some of these riddle games were long-term deals. Samson gave his friends seven days to solve his riddle.

The Queen of Sheba tested Solomon, an Israelite king who was known for his wisdom, with riddles (1 Kings 10:1). The Hebrew word behind "riddle" in this passage is translated elsewhere in the King James Version as "hard questions" (1 Kings 10:1; 2 Chronicles 9:1).

*Samson said unto them
[thirty friends], I will now
put forth a riddle unto
you.*

JUDGES 14:12

SAMSON'S DEGRADING LABOR

After Samson's strength left him (see note on Judges 13:5), he was captured, blinded, and reduced to the status of a slave in a Philistine prison.

Samson is often portrayed in books and movies pushing against a long pole to turn a huge mill around which he walks like a donkey or a mule. But this would have been difficult, since his strength had left him and he was placed in shackles.

*The Philistines. . .bound
him [Samson] with fetters
of brass [bronze shackles,
NIV]; and he did grind in
the prison house.*

JUDGES 16:21

The most likely scenario is that he was put to work grinding grain with a hand mill (see note on Matthew 18:6). This was considered woman's work, so the Philistines added insult to injury by assigning their enemy the lowest kind of slave labor.

DAGON OF THE PHILISTINES

This pagan god to whom the Philistines attributed such power was their primary, national god. They must have gathered often in ceremonies such as this—probably in a temple devoted to Dagon—to worship and pay tribute to him.

Stone carvings of Dagon portray him with the head, hands, and upper body of a man and with the lower body of a fish. The Hebrew word for "Dagon" actually means "little fish." This pagan god represented the reproductive powers of nature. The fish was an appropriate image because of its ability to reproduce rapidly and in great numbers.

The Philistines boasted that Dagon had delivered their enemy Samson into their hands. But when he pushed down the pillars that held up Dagon's temple (Judges 16:29–30), he proved that Israel's God was superior to this pagan idol.

The lords [rulers, NIV] of the Philistines gathered them [the Philistines] together for to offer a great sacrifice unto Dagon their god, and to rejoice [celebrate, NIV]: for they said, Our god hath delivered Samson our enemy into our hand.
JUDGES 16:23

RUTH

GLEANING IN THE FIELDS OF BOAZ

Ruth's gathering of grain in the fields of Boaz is the best example in the Bible of the practice of gleaning. After crops had been harvested, poor people were allowed in the fields and orchards to pick up any grain or fruit that had been left behind (see note on Deuteronomy 24:20).

Old Testament law specified that the corners of fields were not to be harvested by landowners. Grain in these spots was to be left for the poor (Leviticus 23:22). Likewise, a sheaf of grain left accidentally in the field was to remain there as provision for the poor (Deuteronomy 24:19).

Some generous landowners went beyond the letter of the law and deliberately left part of the harvest in the fields for the

She [Ruth] went, and came, and gleaned in the field after the reapers [harvesters, NIV].
RUTH 2:3

poor. For example, when Boaz learned about Ruth gleaning on his property, he instructed his workers, "Pull out some stalks for her from the bundles [of grain] and leave them for her to pick up" (Ruth 2:16 NIV).

MUTUAL GREETINGS

These greetings exchanged by Boaz and the workers in his field seem ornate and flowery by modern standards, but they were customary and routine in Bible times. Boaz greeted and blessed his workers, and they returned his salutation with a blessing of their own. This type of greeting is referred to in Psalm 129:8.

SOUR WINE AND ROASTED GRAIN

The "vinegar" that Boaz offered Ruth was probably a drink similar to wine that had been fermented longer than usual until it developed a sour taste. This is the same type of drink that was offered to Jesus on the cross (Matthew 27:34, 48).

Behold, Boaz came from Bethlehem, and said unto the reapers [harvesters, NIV], The LORD be with you. And they answered him, The LORD bless thee.
RUTH 2:4

Boaz said unto her [Ruth], At mealtime come thou hither, and eat of the bread, and dip thy morsel in the vinegar [wine vinegar, NIV]. And she sat beside the reapers: and he reached [offered, NIV] her parched corn [roasted grain, NIV], and she did eat.
RUTH 2:14

EATING ROASTED GRAIN

1. Jesse sent roasted grain and other food to his sons who were serving in King Saul's army (1 Samuel 17:17).
2. The Israelites ate roasted grain in Canaan soon after occupying the land. This brought an end to God's provision of manna, which they had eaten in the wilderness (Joshua 5:11 – 12).
3. Abigail brought roasted grain, along with other food, to David's hungry warriors after her stingy husband, Nabal, refused to give them provisions (1 Samuel 25:10 – 11, 18).
4. King David's supporters brought roasted grain and other food to him and his aides after they were forced to flee Jerusalem during Absalom's rebellion (2 Samuel 17:27 – 29).

The parched corn or roasted grain eaten by Ruth consisted of whole grains of roasted wheat or barley. Roasted in a pan or over an open fire, it served as a good bread substitute. Regular bread was made from wheat or barley that had been ground into a fine flour.

MAKESHIFT THRESHING

Landowners with a lot of wheat or barley to thresh separated the grain from the stalks by driving threshing sledges behind oxen over the stalks on a flat surface (see note on Deuteronomy 25:4).

Ruth was forced to perform this task by beating the stalks with a rock or a stick. This shows that she and her mother-in-law, Naomi, were living a precarious existence—gathering enough grain in one day (see note on Ruth 2:3) to make enough bread to last them for just a few days.

WINNOWING AT NIGHT

Ruth's mother-in-law, Naomi, told Ruth that she would find Boaz, Naomi's distant relative, winnowing grain at night on the spot where he had threshed the grain, or separated it from the stalks.

Winnowing was the process of separating the grain from the chaff, or waste material, by tossing both of them together into the air (see note on Luke 3:17). The wind blew the lighter chaff away, allowing the heavier grain to fall at the winnower's feet. The grain was then ready to be stored or ground into flour.

Boaz was probably winnowing at night because stronger night breezes were needed for this task.

She [Ruth] gleaned in the field until even [evening, NIV], and beat out [threshed, NIV] that [which] she had gleaned.
RUTH 2:17

Is not Boaz of our kindred. . . ? Behold, he winnoweth barley to night in the threshingfloor.
RUTH 3:2

Winnowing involved throwing the mixture of grain and chaff into the air, allowing the wind to carry away the chaff.

GUARDING THE GRAIN

A threshing floor was located out in the open. And stealing must have been a problem in Bible times, just as it is today. At night Boaz guarded his valuable threshed and winnowed grain by sleeping right in the middle of it.

SIGN OF THE SHOE

Naomi's deceased husband, Elimelech, had some land in Bethlehem that she had been forced to sell because of her poverty conditions (Ruth 4:3). Elimelech had a relative who, as his next of kin, had the right to buy back or redeem this property to keep it in the family.

But this unnamed relative gave up that right by removing his sandal. Only the owner of a plot of land had the right to walk on it. Removal of his sandal symbolized that he was giving up his ownership rights and transferring them to Boaz, who could then proceed to buy back the property from the current owner.

I SAMUEL

ELI'S SEAT OF JUDGMENT

Since Eli was the high priest of Israel, the seat on which he sat was probably a "seat of judgment" from which he advised the people. As the final judge in religious matters, he helped people solve their problems by subjecting themselves to the Lord's will. Hannah, a godly woman who had been unable to have children, brought this problem before Eli for his advice and counsel.

Eli told Hannah, "Go in peace: and the God of Israel grant thee thy petition" (1 Samuel 1:17). She eventually did give birth to a son—the prophet Samuel.

Hannah's Song of Praise

After Hannah gave birth to a son (see note on 1 Samuel 1:9), she thanked the Lord for His goodness in a beautiful song of praise (1 Samuel 2:1–10). This song is similar to the Magnificat, the virgin Mary's song of praise, when she learned that she would give birth to the Messiah (Luke 1:46–55).

In Bible times an animal's lifting his horn high in the air was a symbol of power and dignity. Hannah's exclamation, "Mine horn is exalted in the Lord," was her poetic way of saying that God had lifted her out of her despair at not being able to have children and had blessed her beyond all expectations.

Hannah prayed, and said, My heart rejoiceth in the LORD, mine horn is exalted [lifted high, NIV] in the LORD.

1 SAMUEL 2:1

Pagan Charms

The Philistines captured the ark of the covenant (see note on Exodus 40:3) from the Israelites and carried it to the city of Ashdod (1 Samuel 5:1). God punished the Philistines by sending swarms of mice throughout their land. These mice apparently carried a disease that caused the Philistines to break out in sores, or tumors.

Pagan priests among the Philistines recommended that they send the ark back to the Israelites, along with images of the mice and tumors that were caus- ing their suffering. They thought these images would serve as magic charms to cure their sores and ward off evil spirits.

Ye [Philistines] shall make images [models, NIV] of your emerods [tumors, NIV], and images of your mice that mar [are destroying, NIV] the land.

1 SAMUEL 6:5

The mouse or sand rat is very common in the Middle East. God may have used swarms of such mice to punish the Philistines.

Goliath's Battle Gear

Goliath, the Philistine giant whom David faced in battle, was equipped for close-quarter combat. Several implements of attack and defense are mentioned in these three verses.

Helmet. Goliath's helmet was designed to protect him from blows by a sword in hand-to-hand fighting. Some ancient helmets were made from wood, closely woven tree branches, or tough animal hide. But the Philistine army was well equipped with helmets of bronze, a hard metal that was probably an alloy of copper and zinc. Helmets are also mentioned in 2 Chronicles 26:14; Jeremiah 46:4; and Ezekiel 23:24; 27:10; 38:5.

Body armor. Goliath also wore scale armor, or body armor—probably from his neck to his waist—to protect himself in battle. Scale armor was made of small pieces of metal attached to a solid piece of linen or felt. These small metal pieces moved independently of one another, giving

He [Goliath] had an helmet of brass [bronze, NIV] upon his head, and he was armed with a coat of mail [scale armor, NIV]. . . . He had greaves of brass upon his legs, and a target of brass [bronze javelin, NIV] between his shoulders. . . . The staff [shaft, NIV] of his spear was like a weaver's beam [rod, NIV]; and his spear's head weighed six hundred shekels of iron: and one bearing a shield went before him.

1 SAMUEL 17:5–7

79

a warrior greater mobility in combat. Body armor like this must have been heavy, cumbersome, and clumsy to someone who wasn't accustomed to wearing it. When King Saul put his armor on David to send him out to fight Goliath, David took it off with the words, "I cannot go in these. . .because I am not used to them" (1 Samuel 17:39 NIV).

Greaves. To protect his lower legs, Goliath wore greaves, or leg armor, from his knees down to his feet. These were usually made of leather or wood, but Goliath had heavy-duty greaves of brass, or bronze.

Javelin. The Hebrew word behind "target" is more correctly translated as "javelin." As a matter of fact, this word is rendered as "spear" (Job 41:29) and "lance" (Jeremiah 50:42) in other places in the King James Version. A javelin was a shorter and lighter version of the spear. Slung over a soldier's back so it could be reached quickly, it was particularly useful in hand-to-hand battles.

Spear. Goliath carried both a javelin and a spear—the javelin for close-quarter combat and the spear for thrusting close in as well as throwing from a distance. A spear's sharp point was not the only thing that made it a formidable weapon. Apparently its butt end was sharpened or strengthened so it could also be used in battle. Abner killed Asahel with the "hinder end" ("butt," NIV) of his spear by thrusting it through his stomach (2 Samuel 2:23).

Shield. The final piece of Goliath's battle gear was a large shield that a carrier held in front of the giant. This protected Goliath from arrows or spears that might be shot or hurled by the enemy. The Hebrew word behind "shield" in this verse makes it clear that it provided full-body protection. This word is also rendered as "buckler" (1 Chronicles 5:18). These shields were about five feet tall for a normal man, but Goliath's may have been bigger because of his giant size. Made of wood and covered with animal skin, shields like this provided good protection when warriors knelt behind them. They were often pulled together in tight formation to serve as movable breastworks.

CHEESE FOR DAVID'S BROTHERS

The food sent by David's father, Jesse, to his sons in King Saul's army included cheese, as well as bread and roasted grain (1 Samuel 17:17; see note on Ruth 2:14). The cheese of Bible times was made of curdled, or soured, milk. This was the only way to preserve milk for future use, since refrigeration was unknown.

Carry these ten cheeses unto the captain [commander, NIV] of their [David's brothers'] thousand, and look how thy brethren fare [see how your brothers are, NIV].
1 SAMUEL 17:18

David's Battle Gear

The battle gear that David carried into battle against Goliath seemed ridiculous when compared to the giant's weapons. Several items in David's arsenal are mentioned in these verses.

Sword. King Saul wanted David to carry his sword into battle against the Philistine giant Goliath (see note on 1 Samuel 17:5–7). But David refused it after he decided it did not fit his battle style. Fashioned from heavy metal, a typical sword of Bible times was about three feet long. Its double-edged blade allowed a warrior to slash right or left and up or down in hand-to-hand engagement of the enemy. The sword was the main weapon of the Israelite army. A man was identified as a soldier by the fact that he "drew the sword" (2 Samuel 24:9).

Staff. A staff was a slender stick about five or six feet long that a shepherd used for balance and support when walking over the rough terrain where his sheep grazed. He also found it useful for nudging stray sheep back to the flock and beating the undergrowth to drive away snakes. Some staffs had a crook on one end that the shepherd used like a hook to pull sheep away from danger or to rescue them from pits or crevices into which they had fallen. Why did David carry his staff into battle, since he never used it against Goliath? Perhaps he wanted to lull the giant into feeling overconfident and letting down his guard. When Goliath saw David's staff, he declared, "Am I a dog, that thou comest to me with staves [sticks, NIV]?" (1 Samuel 17:43).

Bag. The bag where David put five stones for his sling was probably a goatskin container in which he kept his food supply. Travelers and shepherds often carried such bags when on extended trips or work assignments.

Sling. The sling that David carried was a simple but effective weapon used by shepherds, farmers, and even soldiers in Bible times. It was similar to the slingshot in its design and use. Like a slingshot, the sling had a pocket in which a

> *David girded [fastened, NIV] his [King Saul's] sword upon his armour. . . . He took his staff in his hand, and chose him five smooth stones out of the brook, and put them in a shepherd's bag which he had, even in a scrip; and his sling was in his hand: and he drew near to the Philistine [Goliath].*
> 1 SAMUEL 17:39–40

An Assyrian sling and sling stones. David killed Goliath using this simple but effective weapon.

A SHEPHERD'S STAFF

A shepherd's staff, like the one that David carried into battle against Goliath, is mentioned metaphorically several times in the Bible.

1. Jacob declared to his brother, Esau, "With my staff I passed over this Jordan; and now I am become two bands" (Genesis 32:10). This was his way of saying that he had grown from a humble shepherd into a man of means during his years in Haran with his father-in-law, Laban.

2. The psalmist declared that God was always with him, like a shepherd with his sheep, gently leading with His rod and staff (Psalm 23:4).

David put his hand in his bag, and took thence a stone, and slang it, and smote [struck, NIV] the Philistine [Goliath] in his forehead, that the stone sunk into his forehead; and he fell upon his face to the earth.

1 SAMUEL 17:49

Jonathan stripped himself of the robe that was upon him, and gave it to David, and his garments, even to his sword, and to his bow, and to his girdle [belt, NIV].

1 SAMUEL 18:4

When David was returned from the slaughter of the Philistine [Goliath]. . . the women came out of all cities of Israel, singing and dancing.

1 SAMUEL 18:6

small stone was placed. Attached to this pocket were two leather straps. The slinger grasped the ends of the straps, twirled the stone around several times in a circular motion, then released one of the straps at just the right time to hurl the stone toward its target. In skilled hands, the sling was a formidable weapon. The force of the stone was strong enough to kill wild animals and—in Goliath's case—even a giant of a man (1 Samuel 17:49).

During the time of the judges, the tribe of Benjamin had a unit of seven hundred soldiers who specialized in use of the sling. All of the slingers in this elite corps were left-handed, and they "could sling a stone at a hair and not miss" (Judges 20:16 NIV).

HOW DAVID DEFEATED GOLIATH

David defeated Goliath for two reasons: He trusted God to give him the victory (1 Samuel 17:45–47), and he outsmarted the giant.

Goliath was equipped and trained for hand-to-hand combat (see note on 1 Samuel 17:5–7). David knew he would be no match for the giant in a battle of this type, so he fought him at a distance. He appeared before Goliath as a simple shepherd, lulling him into overconfidence and carelessness (see note on 1 Samuel 17:39–40). Then David felled him with a stone from his sling before he had a chance to draw his weapons.

CLOTHES OF HONOR

As a token of his friendship with David, Jonathan took off his own clothes and gave them to David to wear. As King Saul's son, Jonathan was the prince who would succeed his father on the throne. The robe he gave David probably signified his royal status.

In Bible times it was considered a special honor to wear clothes that had belonged to a king or any member of the royal family (see note on Esther 6:8–9). These clothes were thought to convey honor and power to the new owner.

CELEBRATION OF VICTORY

When warriors returned following victory on the battlefield—as David did in this case—it was customary for the women to greet them with singing and dancing. Miriam and other Israelite women also danced and sang to celebrate the destruction of the Egyptian army at the Red Sea (see note on Exodus 15:20).

Responsive Singing

This verse describes the ancient practice of responsive singing. One group of these women sang, "Saul hath slain his thousands," and the others responded, "and David his ten thousands."

When Saul heard these choruses, he grew jealous of David. From that day on, he tried to kill the popular young military leader.

Another example of responsive singing is Miriam's response to the Song of Moses after the Israelites were delivered from the Egyptian army at the Red Sea (Exodus 15:21).

Not Quite Naked

The basic dress for both men and women of Bible times was a full-length outer garment, or robe, along with a full-length undergarment of lighter material. Thus, the term *naked* as rendered by the King James Version in this verse does not mean totally nude. A person who took off his outer robe was considered "naked," although he might still be wearing his undergarment.

This is the sense in which the prophet Isaiah went around "naked" (Isaiah 20:2) at the Lord's command to symbolize the fate of the people of Judah unless they turned from their idolatry. The New International Version says that Isaiah went around "stripped"—without his outer robe.

A Greater Insult

King Saul condemned and insulted his son Jonathan because Jonathan was protecting his friend David. But Saul strengthened his insult by directing it at Jonathan's mother.

This type of abuse is still practiced in modern times, perhaps because some people believe that an insult against a person's relatives will cause more pain and suffering than a direct assault.

Wrapped in a Cloth

David was forced to flee when King Saul sought to kill him (see note on 1 Samuel 18:7). He had left hurriedly with no weapons. A priest named Ahimelech befriended David by giving him the sword that David had taken from the giant Goliath (1 Samuel 17:50–51).

The priest had wrapped the sword in a cloth and was apparently keeping it in a holy place. Items that were especially valuable or sacred were kept hidden away and wrapped in this fashion.

Samuel died; and all the Israelites were gathered together, and lamented [mourned for, NIV] him, and buried him in his house at Ramah.

1 SAMUEL 25:1

SAMUEL'S TOMB

Some interpreters believe this verse means that Samuel was buried in a tomb in the house he lived in at Ramah. But it is likely that the term *house* was just a poetic way of referring to a tomb. Job spoke of the grave as a "house appointed for all living" (Job 30:23).

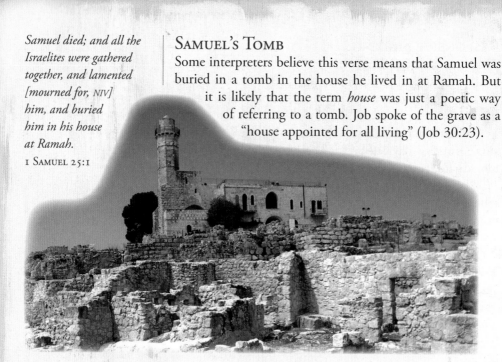

Nevi Samuel, the traditional tomb of the prophet Samuel.

2 SAMUEL

I [a soldier from Saul's camp] took the crown that was upon his [Saul's] head, and the bracelet [band, NIV] that was on his arm.

2 SAMUEL 1:10

KING SAUL'S BRACELET

After King Saul was killed in a battle with the Philistines, a warrior removed his crown and bracelet and brought a report to David about his death. The bracelet worn by Saul probably signified his royal status, just like his crown. Common among kings of the ancient world, these royal arm bands were often decorated with jewels and precious stones.

Murder in the Gate

Abner was the commander of King Saul's army. After Saul's death, David became king. Joab, a military leader who was loyal to David, killed Abner because Abner had tried to install one of Saul's sons as the new king.

Joab took Abner "aside in the gate" of the city of Hebron, supposedly for a private talk. The vaulted openings through the massive walls of some ancient cities were ten to twelve feet thick. This dark passageway was an ideal place for Joab to commit this crime.

When Abner was returned to Hebron, Joab took him aside in the gate [gateway, NIV] to speak with him quietly [privately, NIV], and smote him there. . . that he died.
2 Samuel 3:27

David's Lament for Abner

This verse is part of King David's lament for Abner, who had been murdered by Joab (see note on 2 Samuel 3:27).

Even though Abner had supported David's rival for the throne, David had great respect for Abner. The king made it clear that Abner was different from criminals and prisoners of war who were shackled and bound as they were carried away for execution or imprisonment.

Thy [Abner's] hands were not bound, nor thy feet put into fetters.
2 Samuel 3:34

Playing the Sistrum

The Hebrew word behind "cornets" is rendered more accurately by the New International Version as "sistrums." This is the only place in the Bible where this musical instrument is mentioned.

Like the tambourine (see note on Genesis 31:27), the sistrum was a handheld percussion instrument. It was made up of several thin bands of brass. When shaken, these bands moved apart and then struck against one another, creating a distinctive rustling sound.

David and all the house of Israel played before the LORD on all manner of instruments made of fir wood, even on. . .cornets [sistrums, NIV].
2 Samuel 6:5

A Dead Dog

King David summoned Mephibosheth, the lame son of his deceased friend Jonathan, to his palace. This verse describes how Mephibosheth responded when the king offered to take care of him.

To the Israelites, dogs were worthless and despised animals (1 Samuel 17:43; Psalm 22:16). Mephibosheth's description of himself as a "dead dog" indicates that he thought he was unworthy of King David's kindness and compassion.

He [Mephibosheth] bowed himself, and said, What is thy servant, that thou [David] shouldest look upon such a dead dog as I am?
2 Samuel 9:8

A DOUBLE INSULT

King David sent several ambassadors to Hanun, king of the Ammonites, to express his sympathy at the death of his father (2 Samuel 10:1–2).

Convinced these messengers were spies, Hanun humiliated them by cutting off their beards on one side of their faces. Israelite men were fond of their beards and considered them a symbol of manhood. To have only half a beard made these messengers objects of ridicule and scorn.

Israelite men also wore long outer robes and full-length undergarments (see note on 1 Samuel 19:24). To have these clothes cut off below the waist so their lower bodies were exposed added to the embarrassment they had already endured. When David learned about these actions by Hanun, he took military action against the Ammonites (2 Samuel 10:7–9).

Israelite men typically wore a long outer robe. Hanun trimmed the robes of David's servants so as to embarrass them.

TEMPTATION ON THE ROOF

In Bible times the roofs of houses were flat. People used these rooftops, particularly in the evening, to catch a cooling breeze (see note on Deuteronomy 22:8).

This is probably what King David was doing when he looked down and saw Bathsheba taking a bath. His casual "rooftop glance" turned to lust. He committed adultery with her and eventually arranged for her warrior husband to be killed in battle to cover up his sin (2 Samuel 11:4–27).

OTHER ROOFTOP EVENTS

1. Rahab the prostitute hid the Israelite spies under stalks of flax on her roof (Joshua 2:1–6).
2. In Ezra's time the people reinstituted the celebration of the Feast of Tabernacles (see note on John 7:37) by building booths, or shelters made from the branches of trees, on the roofs of their houses (Nehemiah 8:13–17).
3. Four friends of a disabled man tore through the roof of a house and lowered him down to Jesus for healing (Mark 2:1–4).
4. Peter was praying on the roof of Simon the tanner's house when he was shown through a vision that God is no respecter of persons (Acts 10:9–15).

David's Bereavement Pattern

The newborn child whom King David's servants referred to had been conceived during his adulterous affair with Bathsheba (see note on 2 Samuel 11:2).

David's servants were amazed because he reversed the normal pattern of grieving in Israelite culture. Following the death of a loved one, the survivors would stop all of their normal activities and mourn and fast for a period of several days. Then they would be persuaded by other family members to return to their daily routine.

But David mourned for his newborn child for seven days before he died. He knew this child would die because the prophet Nathan had told him so (2 Samuel 12:13–17). He returned to his routine activities as soon as the child died.

Then said his servants unto him [David], What thing is this that thou hast done [Why are you acting this way, NIV]? thou didst fast and weep for the child, while it was alive; but when the child was dead, thou didst rise and eat bread.
2 SAMUEL 12:21

Signs of Distress

Covering the head, as well as taking off one's sandals and going barefoot, was a sign of great distress. The head was probably covered by pulling up a fold of the outer robe or tunic. In this way David showed his desperation and fear as he fled Jerusalem. His son Absalom had led a rebellion and declared himself king (2 Samuel 15:13–14).

The custom of covering the head in distress is also referred to in Esther 6:12 and Jeremiah 14:4.

David went up by the ascent of mount Olivet, and wept as he went up, and had his head covered, and he went barefoot.
2 SAMUEL 15:30

Dust on the Head

Hushai was a friend and supporter of King David. During Absalom's rebellion (see note on 2 Samuel 15:30), Hushai expressed his sorrow over David's exile by tearing his clothes (see note on Genesis 37:34) and throwing dust on his head.

Adam, the first man, was created by the Lord from "the dust of the ground" (Genesis 2:7), one of the most common substances on earth. Putting dust on one's head may have been a way of showing humility and helplessness in the face of sorrow.

The custom of putting dust on the head is also referred to in several other passages in the Bible (Joshua 7:6; 1 Samuel 4:12; 2 Samuel 1:2; 13:19; Nehemiah 9:1; Job 2:12; Lamentations 2:10; Ezekiel 27:30; Revelation 18:19).

Hushai the Archite came to meet him [David] with his coat rent [torn, NIV], and earth [dust, NIV] upon his head.
2 SAMUEL 15:32

Throwing Dirt at Others

This encounter between David and Shimei happened as the king fled Jerusalem to escape his son Absalom (see note on 2 Samuel 15:30).

As David and his men went by the way, Shimei went along on the hill's side over against him, and cursed as he went, and threw stones at him, and cast dust [dirt, NIV].
2 SAMUEL 16:13

Throwing dust or dirt at a person was a way of expressing anger and contempt. A member of Saul's family (2 Samuel 16:5–13), Shimei was probably bitter because David had taken the throne after Saul's death.

There may be a connection between the practice of throwing dust at an enemy and the custom of putting dust on one's own head to express grief and sorrow (see note on 2 Samuel 15:32). Perhaps throwing dust at others was a symbolic way of wishing them trouble and misfortune.

HIDDEN IN A CISTERN

They [Jonathan and Ahimaaz]. . .came to a man's house. . .which had a well in his court; whither they went down. And the woman took and spread a covering over the well's mouth [opening, NIV], and spread ground corn [grain, NIV] thereon; and the thing was not known.

2 SAMUEL 17:18–19

Jonathan and Ahimaaz were spies who reported on Absalom's activities to King David while David was in exile during Absalom's rebellion (see note on 2 Samuel 15:30).

The "well" in which Jonathan and Ahimaaz were hidden was probably a cistern that was used to collect rain water (see note on Genesis 37:24). It must have been dry at this time. With containers of grain or flour placed on top of its cover, this cistern was an ideal hiding place.

DOUBLE GATES IN THE CITY WALL

After David fled Jerusalem to escape Absalom's rebellion (see note on 2 Samuel 15:30), he gathered his forces at the city of Mahanaim on the eastern side of the Jordan River (2 Samuel 17:24).

David sat between the two gates [the inner and outer gates, NIV]: and the watchman went up to the roof over the gate.

2 SAMUEL 18:24

Since the king "sat between the two gates" of the city, Mahanaim may have had an inner wall and an outer wall (see note on Joshua 2:15). Or, the city's defenses may have been strengthened by building two walls around the gate area. This would force an enemy to break down two gates before gaining entrance to the city.

Large cities of the ancient world were often defended by a thick double wall (called a casemate wall) like the one pictured here at Megiddo.

David sat in the space between these double gates of Mahanaim. A watchman was stationed above him to relay news about the battle against Absalom's forces.

WATCHMEN AND PORTERS

This watchman had been posted on the city wall above the gates of Mahanaim to relay news about the battle against Absalom to King David (see note on 2 Samuel 18:24).

Watchmen were key elements in the defense system of ancient walled cities. This assignment was rotated so fresh watchmen were at their posts around the clock. They sounded the alarm to the city's defenders when they spotted suspicious activity.

Watchmen are mentioned several times in the Old Testament (2 Kings 9:17–20; Isaiah 21:5–12; 62:6; Ezekiel 33:2, 6–7; Habakkuk 2:1).

The porter's task was to listen for signals from the watchman and to open and close the gate into the city. In 2 Kings 7:10 this person is called "the porter of the city." Porters are also mentioned in connection with the rebuilding of the wall around Jerusalem in Nehemiah's time (Nehemiah 7:1).

The watchman saw another man running: and the watchman called unto the porter [gatekeeper, NIV].
2 SAMUEL 18:26

ROOM OVER THE GATEWAY

This verse describes King David's reaction when he received word that his son Absalom had been killed. The room where he expressed his grief was built above the city gateway in the space between the outer gate and the inner gate (see note on 2 Samuel 18:24).

Rooms and even houses were sometimes built right into the massive defensive walls of ancient cities (see note on Joshua 2:15).

The king [David] was much moved, and went up to the chamber [room, NIV] over the gate, and wept.
2 SAMUEL 18:33

DAVID'S SAD LAMENT

David's outpouring of grief over his son Absalom is one of the saddest passages in the entire Bible. Apparently such expressions of sorrow over deceased loved ones were common in Bible times.

The king [David] cried with a loud voice, O my son Absalom, O Absalom, my son, my son!
2 SAMUEL 19:4

BIBLICAL LAMENTS

1. After Jacob died, his family "mourned with a great and very sore lamentation" (Genesis 50:10).
2. A prophet lamented the death of a fellow prophet who had not obeyed the Lord's commands. "Alas, my brother!" he mourned as he laid him in his own tomb (1 Kings 13:30).
3. Isaiah's vision of the holy God on His throne caused him to lament about his sins: "Woe is me! for I am undone; because I am a man of unclean lips" (Isaiah 6:5).

CROSSING THE JORDAN RIVER

There went over a ferry boat to carry over the king's [David's] household.

2 SAMUEL 19:18

This verse describes David's return from exile to take up his duties as king over Israel after Absalom's rebellion had been put down. David and the rest of the royal household crossed over the Jordan River back into Israelite territory.

Many interpreters question the King James Version's use of the term *ferry boat* to describe this crossing. The Jordan River is not very deep in most places. It is generally crossed at shallow places known as fords by just wading across.

The New International Version's rendering of this verse ("They crossed at the ford to take the king's household over") is probably a better translation.

GRASPING THE BEARD

Joab said to Amasa, Art thou in health, my brother? And Joab took Amasa by the beard with the right hand to kiss him.

2 SAMUEL 20:9

Grasping a person's beard and kissing his cheek (see note on Genesis 29:13) was a customary greeting among men of Bible times. But Joab used it as a cover to assassinate Amasa (2 Samuel 20:10) because Amasa had supported Absalom's rebellion.

1 KINGS

PLAYING THE FLUTE

All the people came up after him [Solomon], and the people piped with pipes [flutes, NIV], and rejoiced with great joy.

1 KINGS 1:40

David was succeeded as king of Israel by his son Solomon. This verse refers to the festivities associated with Solomon's accession to the throne.

The pipe played during this celebration was similar to the modern flute. It created a distinctive sound when a musician blew on its mouthpiece to direct the wind through a series of holes along its length.

Pipes were played during times of joy and celebration (1 Samuel 10:5; Isaiah 5:12; Luke 7:32). But they could also produce a soft, wailing sound that was appropriate at funerals (Jeremiah 48:36; Matthew 9:23).

Safety at the Altar

Adonijah, a son of David, had hoped to succeed his father as king of Israel (1 Kings 1:11). But this honor went to Adonijah's brother Solomon (see note on 1 Kings 1:40).

Adonijah sought protection from Solomon's wrath by grasping the four corners, or horns, of the altar in the tabernacle. This provided temporary asylum or protection for a person who had committed a crime until the charges against him were thoroughly investigated.

This same protection could be sought in one of the cities of refuge throughout the land (Deuteronomy 4:41–42).

Buried with Honors

When King David died, he was accorded the great honor of being buried in the city of Jerusalem. The dead were usually buried outside the cities of Bible times.

Several successors of David as kings of Judah were also honored with burials inside Jerusalem: Solomon (1 Kings 11:43), Ahaz (2 Chronicles 28:27), Hezekiah (2 Chronicles 32:33), Manasseh (2 Kings 21:18), and Amon (2 Kings 21:26).

The location of David's tomb was apparently known in New Testament times (Acts 2:29), but the site is a mystery today.

Supplies for Solomon

Taxes are nothing new. They existed as early as King Solomon's time (about 950 BC). He needed revenue to support his lavish building projects and the huge army and staff that he assembled.

For taxation purposes, Solomon divided the nation into twelve administrative districts. Each of these districts supplied the king with what he needed to run the central government for one month out of the year.

Each district had a governor or administrator appointed by the king. This official was responsible for gathering needed supplies from the people in his district.

Adonijah feared because of Solomon, and arose, and went, and caught hold on the horns of the altar.

1 Kings 1:50

This replica of the altar unearthed at Beersheba has "horns" on each of the four corners. Adonijah tried to escape the wrath of Solomon by grasping the horns of the altar in the Tabernacle.

David slept [rested, NIV] with his fathers, and was buried in the city of David.

1 Kings 2:10

Solomon had twelve officers [district governors, NIV] over all Israel, which provided victuals [supplied provisions, NIV] for the king and his household: each man his month in a year made provision [had to provide supplies, NIV].

1 Kings 4:7

HIRAM'S RAFTS

Solomon contracted with King Hiram of Tyre to supply cedar logs for use in building the temple in Jerusalem. Hiram proposed to send these logs by rafts on the Mediterranean Sea. They would be received by Solomon's workmen at a coastal location, then transported overland to Jerusalem.

Hiram's "floats" or rafts may have been the logs themselves that were tied together for shipment. Logs have been transported like this on rivers and lakes since ancient times.

SOLOMON'S TEMPLE

The idea of the temple did not originate with Solomon, but with David, who was not permitted to build it because he had been a man of war (1 Chronicles 28:2–3).

God gave David a plan for the temple, just as He had given Moses the plan for the tabernacle (see note on Exodus 40:2). David communicated this plan to Solomon, directing him to construct the building (1 Chronicles 28:11–19).

The temple was built on Mount Moriah, on the site of the altar that David raised up on the threshing floor of Araunah the Jebusite (2 Samuel 24:21–25). It had the same general arrangements as the tabernacle, since it was a place where God would meet with His people and where they would worship Him.

The dimensions of the temple were double those of the tabernacle. Using eighteen inches as the length of a cubit (see note on Exodus 25:10), the temple was ninety feet long, thirty feet wide, and forty-five feet high.

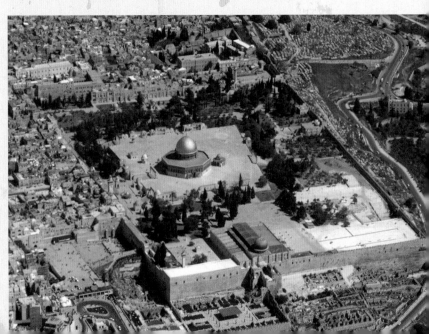

King Solmon built his temple on Mount Moriah in the approximate location occupied by the golden-roofed Dome of the Rock.

The Month of Zif

The "fourth year" in this verse refers to the fourth year of King Solomon's reign (see 1 Kings 6:1). Zif, the second month of the year, parallels our April/May. This Hebrew word means "splendor." It probably referred to the beautiful spring flowers that bloomed during this month.

The Month of Bul

The "eleventh year" in this verse refers to the eleventh year of King Solomon's reign. This verse, when compared with 1 Kings 6:37 (see note there), tells us that it took seven years and six months to build the temple. Bul, the eighth month in the Hebrew calendar, parallels our October/November.

The Month of Ethanim

The "feast" referred to in this verse is the Feast of Tabernacles (see note on Exodus 23:15–16). Solomon chose this important celebration as the perfect time to dedicate the newly constructed temple. The month of Ethanim parallels our September/October.

Hands Lifted in Prayer

When King Solomon dedicated the newly constructed temple with a prayer to the Lord, he stood with his hands open and his palms lifted toward heaven. This stance was often taken when praying, especially in Old Testament times.

OTHERS WHO LIFTED THEIR HANDS TO GOD

1. Moses: to stop the plague of thunder and hail against Egypt (Exodus 9:33).
2. Ezra: to intercede for the people of Israel who had sinned against the Lord (Ezra 9:5–6).
3. The people who had returned to Judah after the Babylonian exile: to show their eagerness to hear and obey God's Word as it was read aloud by Ezra (Nehemiah 8:5–6).
4. The psalmist: to ask God to deliver him from his troubles (Psalm 88:9).

Solomon's Ornamental Shields

Lavish household decorations are nothing new. This verse tells us they go back at least to the time of King Solomon (950 BC).

Shields were generally made for use in warfare (see note

In the fourth year was the foundation of the house of the LORD laid, in the month Zif [Ziv, NIV].
1 KINGS 6:37

In the eleventh year, in the month Bul, which is the eighth month, was the house [temple, NIV] finished.
1 KINGS 6:38

All the men of Israel assembled themselves unto king Solomon at the feast in the month Ethanim, which is the seventh month.
1 KINGS 8:2

Solomon stood before the altar of the LORD in the presence of all the congregation of Israel, and spread forth his hands toward heaven.
1 KINGS 8:22

King Solomon made two hundred targets [large shields, NIV] of beaten [hammered, NIV] gold: six hundred shekels [bekas, NIV] of gold went to one target [shield, NIV].
1 KINGS 10:16

on 1 Samuel 17:5–7). But Solomon was so wealthy that he had shields made from gold—or perhaps gold-plated—apparently for ornamental use in one of his houses (1 Kings 10:17).

SOLOMON'S THRONE

The king [Solomon] made a great throne of ivory [inlaid with ivory, NIV], and overlaid it with the best gold.
1 KINGS 10:18

King Solomon's lavish throne was probably made of wood, then overlaid with ivory and accented with gold trim.

Ivory, made from the tusks of elephants, was a rare and expensive item generally found only in palaces of kings and homes of the very wealthy. The prophet Amos condemned the dishonest wealthy class of Samaria who lived in houses of ivory and slept in beds of ivory (Amos 3:15; 6:4).

Solomon's throne, built on a platform, was reached by climbing six steps. Statues of twelve lions, representing royalty and majesty, stood on the sides of these six steps (1 Kings 10:19–20).

FOOD FOR A JOURNEY

Take with thee [King Jeroboam's wife] ten loaves, and cracknels [cakes, NIV], and a cruse [jar, NIV] of honey, and go to him [the prophet Ahijah].
1 KINGS 14:3

When King Jeroboam's son became sick, he sent his wife to ask the prophet Ahijah whether his son would get well. The journey to Ahijah's house must have been long, since the king's wife carried enough food for several days.

Cracknels were bread that had been baked into thin, hard biscuits. They probably held up under traveling conditions better than soft-baked bread.

FLOUR IN A JAR

She [the widow of Zarephath] said [to Elijah], As the LORD thy God liveth, I have not a cake, but [only, NIV] an handful of meal [flour, NIV] in a barrel [jar, NIV].
1 KINGS 17:12

Elijah asked the widow of Zarephath for some bread to eat. She replied that she had only a little flour in a jar—just enough to make a final meal for her and her son.

Jars made of clay were the most common containers in households of Bible times. They were used to store water, grain, flour, and other foodstuffs. The Hebrew word behind "jar" is also translated as "pitcher" in other places in the Bible.

The widow did agree to bake bread for Elijah from her meager supply of flour. Her faithfulness was rewarded. From that day on, "the jar of flour was not used up" (1 Kings 17:16 NIV). It was replenished miraculously by the Lord every time she baked bread.

A miracle similar to this was performed by Jesus when He multiplied a boy's lunch to feed a crowd of several thousand people (John 6:1–14).

A God Who Hears and Acts

The prophet Elijah challenged the prophets of the pagan god Baal to a contest on Mount Carmel. They laid a sacrificial animal on a pile of wood. The prophets of Baal would call on their god, and Elijah would call on his. The god who answered by sending fire to consume the sacrifice would be declared the superior god (1 Kings 18:22–25).

This statue on Mount Carmel recalls the great victory of Elijah over the prophets of Baal at this location.

Elijah ridiculed Baal because he did not answer the cry of his priests, even though they called to him for several hours. Perhaps he was silent, Elijah suggested, because he was preoccupied with other matters, was away on a journey, or was taking a nap.

When Elijah called on the Lord, fire fell immediately from heaven and consumed the sacrificial animal on the altar (1 Kings 18:38). This proved that God heard the prayers of His people and was superior to Baal.

Elijah mocked them [the prophets of Baal], and said, Cry aloud: for he [Baal] is a god; either he is talking, or he is pursuing, or he is in a journey, or peradventure [maybe, NIV] he sleepeth, and must be awaked.

1 Kings 18:27

Pagan Self-Mutilation

Cutting themselves to draw blood was a desperate attempt by the prophets of Baal to get his attention and cause him to send fire to consume the sacrificial animal (see note on 1 Kings 18:27).

Bloodletting through self-mutilation was a pagan custom that was specifically prohibited among God's people (see note on Leviticus 19:28). God is the sovereign ruler of the universe; He cannot be coerced into action by such practices.

They [the prophets of Baal] cried aloud, and cut themselves after their manner with knives and lancets [spears, NIV], till the blood gushed out upon them.

1 Kings 18:28

It came to pass at the
time of the offering of the
evening sacrifice, that
Elijah the prophet
came near.
1 KINGS 18:36

EVENING SACRIFICE

The priests of Israel were directed by the Lord to offer two sacrificial animals every day to atone for the sins of the people—one lamb in the morning and another lamb "at even" (Exodus 29:39), or evening. This second offering of the day was known as the evening sacrifice.

The precise time when this offering was made is not known. It may have been shortly after sunset. According to the Jewish way of reckoning time in Old Testament times, a new day began at sunset (Nehemiah 13:19; see note on John 11:9).

FACE BETWEEN THE KNEES

He [Elijah] cast himself
down upon the earth, and
put his face between his
knees.
1 KINGS 18:42

Elijah's position in this verse was a stance for deep meditation. He was probably thinking about the victory of the Lord over the priests of the pagan god Baal (see note on 1 Kings 18:27) and praising Him for His awesome power.

In this meditative position, a person sat on the ground with his knees drawn up to his chin. Elijah also pushed his head forward until his face was literally "between his knees."

TUCKING IN THE CLOAK

He [Elijah] girded up his
loins [tucking his cloak
into his belt, NIV], and
ran before Ahab to the
entrance of Jezreel.
1 KINGS 18:46

Both men and women of Bible times wore outer robes or cloaks that extended almost to the feet (see notes on Genesis 37:3; Deuteronomy 22:5; and 1 Samuel 19:24). These loose-fitting gowns were held tight against the body by a belt or sash (generally referred to as a "girdle" by the King James Version) around the person's waist.

If a person needed to run or do strenuous work, he would tuck the bottom part of his robe into the belt or sash. This gave him greater freedom of movement.

This practice is described by the King James Version—as in Elijah's case—as "girding up one's loins." This custom is sometimes referred to in the Bible in a figurative sense to denote strength and determination (Job 40:7; Psalms 65:6; 93:1).

Running in front of Ahab's chariot all the way to the city of Jezreel was Elijah's way of expressing respect for the king. The prophet did not agree with Ahab's policy of promoting Baal worship throughout Israel (1 Kings 18:17–18). But he did have respect for the office of the king and Ahab's authority.

The practice of running in front of the chariots of kings and other dignitaries is also referred to in 1 Samuel 8:11; 2 Samuel 15:1; and 1 Kings 1:5.

When threatened by Jezebel, Elijah fled south into the wilderness of Beersheba.

A Day's Journey

Threatened by the evil queen Jezebel, the prophet Elijah fled into the wilderness. He probably traveled about twenty-five miles, since a day's journey was the distance that a person could travel on foot in one day.

In the New Testament, a Sabbath day's journey was the distance that a person could travel on the Sabbath without breaking the prohibition against working on this day (see note on Acts 1:12).

He [Elijah] himself went a day's journey into the wilderness [desert, NIV].

1 KINGS 19:4

BIBLICAL JOURNEYS OF A DAY OR MORE

1. Moses asked Pharaoh to let the Hebrew slaves take a three-day journey into the desert to make sacrifices to the Lord (Exodus 3:18; 5:1–3; 8:27).
2. Laban pursued Jacob on a seven-day journey before he overtook him near Mount Gilead (Genesis 31:22–23).
3. In Jonah's time the city of Nineveh, Assyria, was "an exceeding great city of three days' journey" (Jonah 3:3), probably indicating it took this long to walk through it and the outlying towns, or to walk around it.
4. Joseph and Mary traveled a day's journey toward Nazareth before they realized the boy Jesus had been left behind in Jerusalem (Luke 2:42–44).

A Sign of Reverence

Elijah expected to see some awesome display of God's power. But the Lord spoke to him instead in "a still small voice" (1 Kings 19:12). This led him to pull his outer robe up over his face in a gesture of reverence and deep respect.

Moses had a similar reaction when the Lord appeared to him in a burning bush. He "hid his face; for he was afraid to look upon God" (Exodus 3:6).

When Elijah heard it [God's voice]. . .he wrapped his face in his mantle [cloak, NIV], and went out, and stood in the entering in [mouth, NIV] of the cave.

1 KINGS 19:13

97

Those living in Israel continued to plow with oxen into the early days of the twentieth century.

PLOWING WITH OXEN

Oxen were the animals of choice for heavy duties such as pulling plows and carts in Bible times. They were slow and clumsy, but their strength and stamina were legendary. The field in which Elisha was plowing must have been huge, since eleven other teams of oxen besides his were working the soil.

At this time in biblical history, Elisha was probably working with a wooden plow. Some agricultural plows of the ancient world were little more than tree trunks that had been sharpened on one end to cut through the soil. But plows of metal were used in later times (Isaiah 2:4).

He [Elijah] departed thence, and found Elisha the son of Shaphat, who was plowing with twelve yoke of oxen before him, and he with the twelfth.
1 KINGS 19:19

PSYCHOLOGICAL WARFARE

This taunt by King Ben-hadad of Syria (1 Kings 20:10) and the reply of his enemy—King Ahab of Israel (1 Kings 20:11)—are good examples of ancient psychological warfare. Opposing armies often used such tactics. They attempted to gain the upper hand even before they drew their swords by intimidating the other side with taunts and threats.

Ben-hadad declared that his army would reduce the city of Samaria, Israel's capital city, to rubble so effectively that his warriors would not be able to pick up handfuls of dust to carry away as souvenirs.

Ahab replied, in effect, "Words don't win battles. Let's see if you are still boasting like this when the battle is over."

Ben-hadad. . .said [to King Ahab of Israel], The gods do so unto me, and more also, if the dust of Samaria shall suffice for handfuls for all the people that follow me. And the king of Israel [Ahab] answered. . . Let not him that girdeth [puts, NIV] on his harness [armor, NIV] boast himself as he that putteth it off.
1 KINGS 20:10–11

BEN-HADAD'S TENTS

King Ben-hadad and the army of Syria were so confident of victory over the Israelites (see note on 1 Kings 20:10–11) that they built temporary huts outside the city walls of Samaria and waited for the battle to begin.

The Hebrew word behind "pavilions" or "tents" is the same word translated as "booths" in other places in the Bible (Genesis 33:17; Job 27:18; Jonah 4:5). Made from the branches of

Ben-hadad was drinking himself drunk in the pavilions [tents, NIV], he and the kings, the thirty and two kings that helped him.
1 KINGS 20:16

trees and shrubs, these crude structures were probably built to shade Ben-hadad and his army from the hot sun.

God of the Hills and Valleys
King Ahab of Israel had won a previous battle against the Syrians (1 Kings 20:21), apparently among the hills and mountains of Israel. This victory gave rise to the Syrian claim that the God of Israel was a god of the high country, not of the level plains. The Syrians reflected the typical pagan belief that different nations and different parts of the earth had their own regional gods.

The next battle against the Syrians would be fought successfully in the plains and valleys (1 Kings 20:29). This would prove that the one true God ruled over the entire earth.

Ropes on the Head
After Israel defeated Syria (see note on 1 Kings 20:28), the servants of the Syrian king appeared before Israel's king and begged for mercy. Putting ropes on the head was a token of their defeat and submission. These ropes may have been bridles, reflecting their submission—like domesticated animals—to the Israelite victors.

No Sale
Naboth's refusal to sell his land in which his vineyard grew shows the dedication of the Israelites to the land they had inherited from their ancestors. By law, Israelites were not to sell their land inheritance, except in cases of extreme poverty or financial hardship (Leviticus 25:23, 25; Numbers 36:7).

King Ahab and Jezebel eventually brought false charges against Naboth, had him killed, and took his land (1 Kings 21:6–16). The Lord sent the prophet Elijah to condemn these brazen acts and to tell the king that he would pay for these crimes with his life (1 Kings 21:17–22).

King Ahab's Seal
The royal seal with which Queen Jezebel signed letters in Ahab's name to condemn Naboth (see note on 1 Kings 21:3) was probably similar to the seal that the pharaoh of Egypt gave to Joseph (see note on Genesis 41:42).

Official royal seals were often engraved into rings worn by kings. Other seals were worn like necklaces. They were used to authenticate royal documents.

Because the Syrians have said, The LORD is God of the hills, but he is not God of the valleys, therefore will I [God] deliver all this great multitude [this vast army, NIV] into thine [Israel's] hand, and ye shall know that I am the LORD.
1 KINGS 20:28

They [Ben-hadad's servants] girded sackcloth on their loins [around their waists, NIV], and put ropes on their heads, and came to the king of Israel.
1 KINGS 20:32

Naboth said to Ahab, The LORD forbid it me, that I should give the inheritance of my fathers unto thee.
1 KINGS 21:3

She [Jezebel] wrote letters in Ahab's name, and sealed them with his seal.
1 KINGS 21:8

A Sumerian seal from Ur. The seal was used by members of the royal family, like Jezebel, to authorize action on behalf of the king.

2 KINGS

AN ELEVATED ROYAL BED

Thou [King Ahaziah] shalt not come down from that bed on which thou art gone up, but shalt surely die.

2 KINGS 1:4

These are the words of the prophet Elijah to King Ahaziah of Israel, who was seriously injured in a fall from the balcony of his palace.

The prophet spoke of the bed on which the king had "gone up" because rulers like Ahaziah usually slept on elevated beds known as divans. These beds had to be entered by climbing two or three steps. King David of Judah also spoke of going "up" to his bed (Psalm 132:3).

SONS OF THE PROPHETS

The sons [company, NIV] of the prophets that were at Bethel came forth to Elisha.

2 KINGS 2:3

These "sons of the prophets" knew that Elisha had been chosen as Elijah's successor, so they came out to see the two prophets together when Elijah and Elisha approached the city of Bethel.

Several different groups of "sons of the prophets" are mentioned in the book of 2 Kings (2:5, 7; 4:38, 43; 6:1–2). They were apparently disciples or followers of prophets such as Elijah and Elisha who assisted the prophets in their work and learned from their example and instruction.

A "company of prophets" is also mentioned in connection with the ministry of the prophet Samuel (1 Samuel 19:19–20). Samuel may have been the founder of this prophetic guild.

WASHING HANDS AFTER MEALS

Here is Elisha the son of Shaphat, which poured water on the hands of Elijah.

2 KINGS 3:11

In modern times we wash our hands before eating, but people of Bible times did just the opposite. This verse probably refers to the biblical practice of washing one's hands after a meal.

Forks and spoons were not available in the ancient world. People ate by hand, using pieces of bread to scoop up meat and vegetables and popping them into their mouths. This was a messy process, so the hands had to be washed when the meal was over.

Water was a precious commodity in Bible times (see note on Genesis 26:15). Hand-washing water may have been caught in a basin and used several times.

A SHOCKING SACRIFICE

Moab was about to be overrun by the army of Israel. The Moabite king used this desperate measure—the sacrifice of his own son—to win the favor of his gods.

Child sacrifice was common among the pagan nations surrounding Israel (see note on Leviticus 18:21). But the Lord distinctly prohibited the practice among His people.

The king of Moab probably also hoped this detestable act would shock the Israelites into retreating. The sacrifice was made "upon the wall" of the city so everyone would be sure to see it. It must have worked: "There was great indignation against Israel: and they departed from him, and returned to their own land" (2 Kings 3:27).

Then he [the king of Moab] took his eldest [firstborn, NIV] son that should have reigned in his stead, and offered him for a burnt offering [sacrifice, NIV] upon the wall [city wall, NIV].

2 KINGS 3:27

SHOWING OFF WITH GIFTS

Hazael was a servant of Ben-hadad, king of Syria. When the prophet Elisha visited Damascus, Ben-hadad sent Hazael to meet him with royal gifts. Since the king was sick, he may have been trying to get Elisha to exercise his healing powers on his behalf.

In Old Testament times, even small gifts were often accompanied by great pomp and ceremony. The forty camels that greeted Elisha were probably not loaded down with all they could carry. Each camel may have carried only a small part of the total gift. Perhaps the king wanted to impress Elisha with an extravagant outward display.

So Hazael went to meet him [Elisha], and took a present with him, even of every good thing of Damascus, forty camels' burden, and came and stood before him.

2 KINGS 8:9

BEAUTIFYING THE EYES

When Queen Jezebel heard that her husband, King Ahab, had been assassinated by Jehu, she knew her days were numbered. But she showed great composure by putting on her makeup and fixing her hair to prepare for Jehu's arrival.

This verse shows that beauty aids for the eyes of women have existed for centuries. To put it in modern terms, we would say that Queen Jezebel "put on her eye shadow and applied her mascara."

The eye-beautification aid of Queen Jezebel's time was a black powder known as kohl. It served the same purpose as modern cosmetics. When applied, it contrasted with the white of the eyes, causing them to look brighter and wider.

The custom of beautifying the eyes is also referred to in Ezekiel 23:40 and perhaps Proverbs 6:25.

When Jehu was come to Jezreel, Jezebel heard of it; and she painted her face [eyes, NIV], and tired her head [arranged her hair, NIV], and looked out at a window.

2 KINGS 9:30

Cosmetic dish from Ur (600–700 BC). Women of the ancient world would apply their cosmetic treatments from such a dish.

EXECUTION BY DECAPITATION

There came a messenger, and told him [King Jehu], saying, They have brought the heads of the king's sons. And he said, Lay ye them in two heaps [Put them in two piles, NIV] at the entering in of the gate until the morning.

2 KINGS 10:8

Jehu assassinated King Ahab and assumed the kingship of Israel. Then he had all of Ahab's sons killed to eliminate all claimants to the throne. These sons were beheaded, and their heads were piled in a heap outside the entrance to the city of Jezreel. King Ahab's palace was located at Jezreel. This was probably Jehu's way of sending a message that anyone who remained loyal to Ahab and opposed Jehu's accession to the throne would suffer the same fate.

Execution by decapitation was common in Old Testament times. David killed Goliath by cutting off his head (1 Samuel 17:51). King Saul was beheaded by the Philistines (1 Samuel 31:9). But the masters of decapitation were the Assyrians. Monuments discovered in excavations at their capital city of Nineveh depict the heads of hundreds of captives piled up outside the city gate.

A ROYAL CORONATION

He [Jehoiada] brought forth the king's son [Joash], and put the crown upon him, and gave him the testimony [presented him with a copy of the covenant, NIV]; and they [the people] made him king, and anointed him; and they clapped their hands, and said, God save [Long live, NIV] the king.

2 KINGS 11:12

This verse gives us insight into a royal coronation ceremony in Old Testament times. After the royal crown was placed on Joash's head, the king was presented with a copy of God's law. This was to serve as his guide in governing the people. He was then formally anointed for his task by having oil poured on his head.

A royal coronation must have been a public affair. The people showed their approval of Joash's coronation with applause and shouts of joy.

OTHER ROYAL ANOINTINGS

1. Samuel anointed Saul as the first king of Israel (1 Samuel 10:1).
2. Samuel anointed David as Saul's successor because of Saul's disobedience of the Lord, even while Saul was still on the throne (1 Samuel 16:1–13).
3. David's appointment to the kingship by Samuel was later recognized when he was anointed by the tribe of Judah (2 Samuel 2:4) and then by the rest of the tribes (2 Samuel 5:1–3).
4. King David directed that his son Solomon was to be anointed as his successor (1 Kings 1:33–39).

DECLARING WAR

Then Elisha said, Shoot. And he [King Joash] shot.

2 KINGS 13:17

The prophet Elisha instructed the king of Israel to open a window toward Syria and to shoot an arrow in that direction. This was a symbolic way of declaring war against this enemy nation. Elisha also assured the king that the Lord would give Israel victory over the Syrians.

A Miracle from the Grave

This verse leaves no doubt that the prophet Elisha was the most amazing "miracle man" of the Old Testament. Fourteen miracles are attributed to him, including this one that happened after he had been dead for several years.

Elisha's body had probably been wrapped in bands of cloth and placed in a tomb hewed out of solid rock, similar to the tomb in which Jesus was buried (Mark 15:46). When another body was placed hurriedly in Elisha's tomb, it touched the prophet's bones (indicating he had been dead for some time). But God showed how much He honored this dead prophet by filling his bones with the power to bring this dead man back to life.

As they [a group of Israelites] were burying a man. . .they spied a band of men [raiders, NIV]; and they cast the man into the sepulchre [tomb, NIV] of Elisha: and when the man. . .touched the bones of Elisha, he revived [came to life, NIV], and stood up on his feet.

2 KINGS 13:21

Deportation to Assyria

The Northern Kingdom of Israel was overrun by the Assyrians in about 722 BC The Assyrians were generally cruel and inhumane to enemy soldiers (see note on 2 Kings 10:8). But they used a different approach with the civilian populations of the nations they conquered. The skilled workers and other members of the privileged classes were carried away to Assyria, where they were put to work in the king's service as administrators, craftsmen, and farmers.

Conquered territories were also resettled with people of different ethnic stock who were loyal to the Assyrian king (2 Kings 17:24). This was done to keep down rebellion and hostility toward the Assyrian government among the poor people of the land who were left behind.

The king of Assyria did carry away Israel unto Assyria, and put them in Halah and in Habor by the river of Gozan, and in the cities of the Medes.

2 KINGS 18:11

The exile of the Northern Kingdom is captured in this dramatic scene from an Assyrian relief that shows the Israelites being led into captivity.

A Serious Miscalculation

Soon after the Northern Kingdom (Israel) fell to the Assyrians (see note on 2 Kings 18:11), Judah faced an Assyrian invasion. The king's ambassadors tried to talk Judah into surrendering by reminding them that the gods of all the territories they had conquered had proved ineffective against the Assyrian threat. Why should the Jews of Judah expect their God to deliver them?

But the Assyrians had underestimated the might of the Lord. Judah's all-powerful God wiped out 185,000 Assyrian soldiers with a mysterious plague, and the army withdrew without pressing the attack against Judah (2 Kings 19:35–36).

Blinding of Prisoners

Zedekiah was serving as king of Judah when the nation fell to the Babylonians in 587 BC. The last thing he saw before being blinded by his captors was the death of his sons.

The blinding of prisoners was a cruel punishment often meted out by the Babylonians, Assyrians, and Persians. This was done by searing the pupils with a hot copper plate or by thrusting a sword or dagger into the eyes.

Samson also was blinded when he was captured by the Philistines (Judges 16:21).

1 CHRONICLES

God Knows the News

When the Philistines defeated King Saul and his army, they notified their fellow citizens to carry news about their victory to their pagan gods. This shows the weakness of idols and the superiority of the one true God, who sees all and knows all: "The eyes of the LORD are in every place, beholding the evil and the good" (Proverbs 15:3).

David's Mighty Men

These "mighty men" were the most loyal and courageous soldiers in David's army. Known for their bravery in battle, many risked their lives for their commander.

A listing of their names here (1 Chronicles 11:11–47) and in 2 Samuel 23:8–39 acknowleges that David could not have risen from his humble beginnings as a shepherd boy to become the powerful king of Judah without the support of these valiant warriors.

This is the number of the mighty men whom David had.

1 CHRONICLES 11:11

CRIPPLING WARHORSES

David extended his kingdom as far north as Syria by defeating Hadarezer, king of Zobah. He weakened Hadarezer's ability to wage war by capturing his chariots and crippling his chariot horses, probably by cutting a muscle or tendon in their legs.

Since David did not take the horses as booty, he probably had little use for chariots and horses in his own army. Chariots would have been impractical in the rocky and hilly terrain of Palestine.

David also houghed [hamstrung, NIV] all the chariot horses.

1 CHRONICLES 18:4

MUSIC FOR WORSHIP

David organized the priests and Levites into several different groups to serve at the tabernacle on a rotating basis. The Levites descended from Heman were to provide music for worship—specifically to play the horn, or trumpet.

Other Levite musicians were assigned to play different instruments, including cymbals, psalteries [lyres, NIV], and harps (1 Chronicles 25:6).

All these were the sons of Heman the king's [David's] seer in the words of God, to lift up the horn.

1 CHRONICLES 25:5

2 CHRONICLES

WALLED CITIES

Cities of Bible times—like the twin cities of Upper and Lower Beth Horon—were surrounded by massive stone walls. Some of these structures were more than thirty feet high and ten to twelve feet thick. Residents of the city would retreat behind these walls when under attack by an enemy.

The attacking army would either scale the wall by using ladders or try to break down the city gate. The gate was made of heavy timbers, reinforced with iron. When closed, the gate would be secured by sliding heavy timbers or iron bars across its surface from the inside.

Also he [King Solomon] built Beth-horon the upper [Upper Beth Horon, NIV], and Beth-horon the nether [Lower Beth Horon, NIV], fenced [fortified, NIV] cities, with walls, gates, and bars.

2 CHRONICLES 8:5

This Assyrian relief depicts scaling ladders at work in the siege of a fortified city.

They [the Israelites]. . . laid him [King Asa] in the bed [bier, NIV] which was filled with sweet odours and divers kinds of spices prepared by the apothecaries' art: and they made a very great burning for him [made a huge fire in his honor, NIV].
2 Chronicles 16:14

The children of Judah. . . brought them [the Seirites] unto the top of the rock [cliff, NIV], and cast them down. . .that they all were broken in pieces.
2 Chronicles 25:12

He [King Uzziah] built towers in the desert. . .for he had much cattle.
2 Chronicles 26:10

When in full lock-down mode, a heavily fortified or "fenced" city was an effective defense against an army of superior numbers. Often the besieging force would camp around the city for months and starve its citizens into submission (see note on Jeremiah 52:5).

Was King Asa Cremated?

Was the body of King Asa of Judah cremated by being burned on a platform, or bier, sprinkled with spices? Some interpreters say yes; others say no.

Some believe the spices were first burned as an offering and then the king's body was laid in a coffin on top of the ashes from these spices. Others believe the king's body was actually burned along with the spices. This verse lends itself to either interpretation.

What is certain is that cremation was practiced on occasion among the Jews in Old Testament times. The bodies of King Saul and his sons were burned (1 Samuel 31:12). The prophets Jeremiah (Jeremiah 34:5) and Amos (Amos 6:10) also mentioned the practice of cremation.

Execution by Being Thrown from a Cliff

These Seirites killed by King Amaziah of Judah were actually Edomites, who lived in the barren, mountainous territory around the Dead Sea. This method of execution was practiced by several nations of the ancient world. It was a quick and efficient way to get rid of a large number of prisoners of war.

Watchtowers in the Desert

These towers in the desert were probably built by King Uzziah of Judah as watchtowers. These enabled the shepherds who were taking care of his sheep to be forewarned about predators or thieves who threatened the flock. Watchtowers were built in vineyards for the same reason (see note on Matthew 21:33).

UZZIAH'S WAR MACHINES

King Uzziah of Judah made Jerusalem's city wall defenses even more effective by increasing the firepower of the warriors on the wall. In the defense towers on top of the wall, he placed mechanical war machines that were capable of hurling huge stones and shooting arrows in bulk on the enemy below.

These "engines" were probably similar to the catapults used so effectively by the Roman army in later centuries.

He [King Uzziah] made in Jerusalem engines [machines, NIV], invented by cunning [skillful, NIV] men, to be on the towers and upon the bulwarks [corner defenses, NIV], to shoot arrows and great stones.

2 CHRONICLES 26:15

Wooden catapults like these were capable of hurling stones and arrows over great distances.

BIBLICAL NAME CHANGES

1. Abram was changed to Abraham to indicate that God would make him the father of many nations (Genesis 17:5).
2. Sarai was changed to Sarah to show that she would become the mother of many nations through the son of her old age (Genesis 17:15–16).
3. Jacob was changed to Israel to indicate that he had found favor with God and that his offspring would become the twelve tribes of Israel (Genesis 32:28; 35:9–12).
4. Joseph was changed to Zaphnath-paaneah, a name of uncertain meaning, by the pharaoh of Egypt (Genesis 41:45).
5. After defeating the nation of Judah, the king of Babylon placed Mattaniah on Judah's throne and changed his name to Zedekiah (2 Kings 24:11–17).
6. The Jewish names of Daniel and his three friends were changed when they were selected for service in the administration of King Nebuchadnezzar of Babylon: Daniel to Belteshazzar, Hananiah to Shadrach, Mishael to Meshach, and Azariah to Abed-nego (Daniel 1:1–7).

FROM ELIAKIM TO JEHOIAKIM

Egypt seized control of Judah, deposed King Jehoahaz, and installed Jehoahaz's brother Eliakim as king in his place. Then the Egyptian authorities changed the new king's name to Jehoiakim.

This renaming of the king sent a message to all of the people that a new era in the life of their nation had begun—their subjection to Egypt. The power to change their king's name symbolized Egypt's supreme authority.

The king of Egypt made Eliakim his [Jehoahaz's] brother king over Judah and Jerusalem, and turned [changed, NIV] his name to Jehoiakim.

2 CHRONICLES 36:4

EZRA

TEMPLE SERVANTS

This verse begins a listing of all of the Nethinims, or temple servants, who returned to Jerusalem under Zerubbabel after the Babylonian captivity. The Nethinims were a distinct class of people of non-Jewish background. Many were captives of war or former Canaanites such as the Gibeonites (see note on Joshua 9:3–5) who had been made lowly servants.

The Nethinims assisted the Levites in the temple by doing such menial jobs as cleaning sacrificial utensils and carrying water and wood to the altar.

NEW MOON SACRIFICES

The Jewish people who returned to their homeland after their period of exile in Babylonia and Persia restored their worship rituals. These included the celebration of each new moon, which marked the beginning of a new month in their calendar. Offerings and sacrifices were made to atone for their sins committed during the previous month. The new moon celebration is also referred to in Numbers 10:10.

ZERUBBABEL'S TEMPLE

One of the reasons King Cyrus of Persia allowed the Jewish exiles to return to Jerusalem was to rebuild the temple. This central place of worship for the Jewish people had been destroyed by the Babylonian army about sixty years before.

Work on this temple began under Zerubbabel, the Persian-appointed governor of Jerusalem. Thus, it is known as Zerubbabel's Temple. It was built on the site of the first temple, known as Solomon's Temple (1 Kings 6).

NEHEMIAH

A ROYAL CUPBEARER

A cupbearer was one of the most important servants in the household of a king. His task was to taste the king's wine before he drank it to make sure it had not been poisoned by his enemies.

Although Nehemiah was a Jew, he had risen to a position of prominence in the Persian court. Artaxerxes, the king, trusted him and allowed him to return to Jerusalem to rebuild the walls of the city (Nehemiah 2:3–7).

> *For I [Nehemiah] was the king's cupbearer.*
> NEHEMIAH 1:11

LETTERS OF RECOMMENDATION

Nehemiah wanted to make sure he was not arrested or detained for questioning during his long trip to Jerusalem (see note on Nehemiah 1:11). As a Jew, he would be traveling through several Persian territories between the Euphrates River and his homeland of Judah. So he asked King Artaxerxes to give him letters of recommendation that would guarantee him safe passage throughout the Persian Empire.

This is a good example of Nehemiah's remarkable foresight and leadership ability. His planning and attention to detail contributed to his success.

> *I [Nehemiah] said unto the king. . . Let letters be given me to the governors beyond the river, that they may convey me over [provide me safe-conduct, NIV] till I come into Judah.*
> NEHEMIAH 2:7

AN EMPTY POCKET

The "lap" in this passage was a pocket in the loose outer robe where people carried items such as money or important papers. It served the same purpose as a man's wallet in modern times.

Nehemiah had just received a promise from the wealthy Jews of Jerusalem that they would no longer mistreat and defraud their poorer fellow Jews. When he shook out the pocket in his robe, he was saying to the wealthy, "God will make you just as empty as this pocket if you fail to keep the promise you have made."

> *I [Nehemiah] shook my lap [shook out the folds of my robe, NIV], and said, So God shake out every man from his house, and from his labour, that performeth not this promise, even thus be he shaken out, and emptied.*
> NEHEMIAH 5:13

A Gesture of Contempt

Then sent Sanballat his servant unto me [Nehemiah] in like manner the fifth time with an open [unsealed, NIV] letter in his hand.

NEHEMIAH 6:5

In his efforts to rebuild Jerusalem's walls, Nehemiah was opposed by Sanballat, an official of the nearby territory of Samaria. Sanballat saw the rebuilding of Jerusalem as a threat to the Samaritan people.

To show his contempt for Nehemiah, Sanballat sent him a letter that was left unsealed. Official documents of that era were generally rolled up in a scroll and enclosed in a bag. Then the bag was sealed with sealing wax. Sanballat declared by this act that he viewed Nehemiah as a person of inferior rank and status—a nobody who could not succeed at the task of rebuilding Jerusalem's walls.

But Nehemiah and the God whom he served had the last word. The work went forward in spite of opposition and was completed in just fifty-two days (Nehemiah 6:15).

Wood for the Altar

We cast the lots among the priests, the Levites, and the people, for the wood offering, to bring it into the house of our God, after the houses of our fathers, at times appointed year by year, to burn upon the altar of the LORD our God.

NEHEMIAH 10:34

Supplying wood for priests to use in offering burnt sacrifices on the altar was a task assigned to the Nethinims, or temple servants (see note on Ezra 2:43). But not enough of these servants returned from the exile in Babylonia and Persia to handle this task.

Nehemiah solved the problem by assigning other people from among the Levites and the general population to do this work. He cast lots to set up a rotating system under which wood would be supplied for this purpose throughout the year.

A Severe Punishment

I [Nehemiah] contended with them [Jewish men who had married pagan women], and cursed them, and smote [beat, NIV] certain of them, and plucked off [pulled out, NIV] their hair.

NEHEMIAH 13:25

In addition to rebuilding Jerusalem in a physical sense, Nehemiah was also concerned for the spiritual rebuilding of his people. He was so angry toward the Jewish men who had married pagan women—a flagrant disobedience of God's command (Joshua 23:12–13)—that he beat some of them and pulled out their hair. This violent and serious punishment showed the severity of their sin.

People sometimes pulled out their own hair as an expression of mourning (Ezra 9:3). Sometimes the act was committed against others as an act of extreme persecution (Isaiah 50:6).

ESTHER

No-Rules Drinking

King Ahasuerus (also known as Xerxes I) of Persia threw a banquet for all of his royal officials. What's interesting about this particular banquet is that it lasted seven days (Esther 1:5). The king also threw out the rules about drinking wine and let every person drink as little or as much as he wished. This was a departure from the norm, which required the guests to follow specific drinking guidelines.

Separation of Persian Women

While Ahasuerus was entertaining his royal officials (see note on Esther 1:8), his queen, Vashti, was serving as hostess at a feast for the wives of these men. Separation of men and women at such royal events must have been the normal practice in the Persian court.

When King Ahasuerus ordered Vashti to come to his banquet to show off her beauty to his male guests, she refused (Esther 1:11–12). Did she do so because she had too much self-respect to play the role of a "trophy wife"? Did she think the king was drunk and didn't know what he was doing? Was she repulsed at the prospect of being

The drinking was according to the law [each guest was allowed to drink in his own way, NIV]. . .for so the king had appointed to all the officers of his house [had instructed all the wine stewards, NIV], that they should do according to every man's pleasure [to serve each man what he wished, NIV].

Esther 1:8

An inscribed bowl of Artaxerxes, a Persian king from the time of Esther. The inscription on the rim reads: "Artaxerxes, the great king, king of kings, king of countries, son of Xerxes the king, of Xerxes son of Darius the king, the Achaemenian, in whose house this drinking-cup made of silver was made."

Also Vashti the queen made a feast for the women in the royal house which belonged to king Ahasuerus.

Esther 1:9

stared at by a group of drunken men? Vashti may have felt it was inappropriate for a woman to appear at a men-only event—even if this meant defying the king.

HAREM CARETAKERS

A chamberlain was a male servant in a king's court who was responsible for the king's harem. To minimize the danger to these women, a chamberlain was emasculated. King Ahasuerus of Persia must have had a large harem, because he had seven of these servants.

Sometimes these male servants rose to positions of prominence as advisers in the king's administration. This must have been the case with two chamberlains of King Ahasuerus, since they participated in a plot to assassinate the king (Esther 2:21–23).

Other references to chamberlains or eunuchs include 2 Kings 9:32; Jeremiah 29:2; and Daniel 1:10.

PRIVILEGES OF A PERSIAN QUEEN

King Ahasuerus had many wives and concubines in his harem, but the wife on whom he bestowed the title of queen—first Vashti, then Esther—occupied a more privileged position than all the others.

The queen performed certain official royal duties, such as entertaining the wives of the king's officials (see note on Esther 1:9). She had an income or stipend of her own, established by Persian law. And she had special access to the king by virtue of her position as his favorite (Esther 5:1–2). Queen Esther used her influence with the king to save her people, the Jews, from annihilation by the scheming Haman (Esther 7:1–10).

MORDECAI'S EXTREME DISTRESS

Haman, an aide to King Ahasuerus of Persia, convinced the king to order the destruction of all of the Jewish people in his empire. When Mordecai heard the news, he expressed his distress with these four actions: tearing his clothes, wearing a rough cloth known as sackcloth (see note on Genesis 37:34), throwing ashes on his head, and lamenting with a bitter cry.

Any one of these actions by itself would have been enough to show that Mordecai was distraught. But he used all four to demonstrate that he was at rock bottom in grief and despair.

The seven chamberlains [eunuchs, NIV] that served in the presence of Ahasuerus the king.
ESTHER 1:10

The king [Ahaseurus] loved [was attracted to, NIV] Esther above all the women, and she obtained grace and favour in his sight [won his favor and approval, NIV] more than all the virgins; so that he set the royal crown upon her head, and made her queen instead of Vashti.
ESTHER 2:17

Mordecai rent [tore, NIV] his clothes, and put on sackcloth with ashes. . . and cried with a loud and a bitter cry.
ESTHER 4:1

Don't Bother the King

Mordecai asked Esther to seek an audience with King Ahasuerus of Persia to plead for the Jewish people. In this verse, Esther reminded Mordecai that anyone who approached the king without a personal invitation ran the risk of immediate execution.

The purpose of this harsh law may have been to keep the king from being pestered by grumblers and favor-seekers. He had the option of granting an audience to uninvited visitors by touching them with his royal scepter.

Esther did decide to approach the king—uninvited—on behalf of her people, the Jews. The king touched her with his scepter and agreed to hear her request (Esther 5:1–2).

> *Whosoever. . .shall come unto the king. . .who is not called, there is one law. . .to put him to death, except such to whom the king shall hold out [extend, NIV] the golden sceptre.*
> Esther 4:11

Eating with the King

Haman was referring to a "banquet," or a royal meal that Queen Esther had arranged and to which Haman had been invited. It was a rare privilege for a citizen of Persia—even someone of high rank such as Haman—to be invited to eat with the king.

Unknown to Haman, Esther planned to reveal to the king at this event Haman's underhanded plot to wipe out the Jews. It would be one of Haman's last meals (Esther 7:1–10).

> *To morrow am I [Haman] invited unto her [Esther] also with the king [Ahasuerus].*
> Esther 5:12

The Ultimate Honor

This was Haman's response to the king when he asked how to honor one of his subjects. Haman outlined the highest royal recognition possible because he thought the king intended to honor him.

To be allowed to ride the king's horse while dressed in a royal robe that had been worn by the king himself was almost as great a privilege as to sit upon the king's throne. And to be paraded through the streets of the capital city so everyone could see how important you were made the recognition even sweeter.

Did this honor involve wearing the king's crown? Probably not. The reference to the "crown royal" in the King James Version is probably to the royal crest engraved on the bridle or headdress of the horse. The New International Version translates this passage as "a horse the king has ridden, one with a royal crest placed on its head" (Esther 6:8).

The irony of Haman's suggested recognition is that it was carried out to the letter—but it was accorded not to him but to his enemy, Mordecai the Jew. And Haman was assigned the responsibility of seeing that it was done (Esther 6:10–11).

> *Let the royal apparel be brought which the king useth to wear, and the horse that the king rideth upon, and the crown royal which is set upon his head. . .array the man withal whom the king delighteth to honour, and bring him on horseback through the street of the city.*
> Esther 6:8–9

A CELEBRATION OF DELIVERANCE

The Jewish people celebrated their deliverance from the death edict issued by Haman (Esther 3:5–18) with a special holiday known as the Feast of Purim.

The Hebrew word *purim* means "lots." The feast was named for the lots that Haman cast to determine the time when the Jews would be annihilated (Esther 3:7). Thanks to the brave actions of Esther and Mordecai, Haman was annihilated and the Jewish people prospered throughout the land.

Wherefore they [the Jews] called these days Purim after the name of Pur.

ESTHER 9:26

JOB

A MAN OF MEANS

In Old Testament times, a man's wealth was measured by the size of his flocks and herds. Job was a rich man by these standards. Female donkeys are mentioned in this passage because they were more valuable than male donkeys. The milk produced by females was a valuable food substance.

His [Job's] substance also was seven thousand sheep, and three thousand camels, and five hundred yoke of oxen, and five hundred she asses [female donkeys, NKJV].

JOB 1:3

Like other people of his day, Job's wealth was measured by the size of his flocks and herds.

GRAIN AMONG THORNS

In this verse Job complained that trouble comes to everyone, even the righteous. People who work hard to grow food for their families often have it stolen by the lazy and shiftless.

Harvesters in Bible times would sometimes cover piles of threshed grain with thornbushes on the threshing floor. This was a temporary measure to keep the grain from being carried away or eaten by animals until it could be stored in a secure place. Thieves who stole grain from these piles literally took it "out of the thorns."

Whose harvest the hungry eateth up, and taketh it even out of [from among, NIV] the thorns, and the robber swalloweth up their substance.
JOB 5:5

LETHAL ARROWS

Job complained throughout his book that God was "out to get him." He thought he was being punished for sins that he had not committed. Here he charged that God was shooting him with poisoned arrows. In ancient warfare the tips of arrows were often coated with a poisonous substance to give them more killing power.

For the arrows of the Almighty are within me, the poison whereof drinketh up my spirit.
JOB 6:4

LENGTHENING SHADOWS

Job longed for death to put him out of his misery. He eagerly awaited his demise, much as a tired worker in the field watched for the lengthening shadows to signal the end of the workday.

In ancient times farm workers could tell time by the length of their own shadows. A laborer would stand up straight and note where his shadow ended. By stepping off the distance to that point, he could tell the hour of the day with amazing accuracy.

As a servant [slave, NIV] earnestly desireth the shadow [evening shadows, NIV], and as an hireling [hired man, NIV] looketh for the reward of his work.
JOB 7:2

MESSAGES ON FOOT

Job complained about the brevity of human life by declaring that his days went by faster than a swift runner. He was probably referring to the fleet-footed messengers used by Old Testament kings to carry important messages to distant places.

King Hezekiah of Judah restored several important religious practices, including observance of the Passover, which had been neglected by the people. He sent "posts [couriers, NIV]. . .with. . .letters. . .throughout all Israel and Judah" (2 Chronicles 30:6), summoning all citizens to gather at Jerusalem for this solemn occasion.

My [Job's] days are swifter than a post [runner, NIV]: they flee away, they see no good.
JOB 9:25

PROSPEROUS THIEVES

Job had lost his livestock to bands of robbers (Job 1:15, 17), so he knew what he was talking about when he lamented the fact that thieves and other wicked people sometimes seem to be more prosperous than honest, God-fearing people.

Robbery is a crime that has existed since ancient times. The Bible gives evidence that sometimes entire clans or tribes made their living by stealing from the unwary. During the period of the judges, one such group was associated with the city of Shechem: "The men of Shechem. . .robbed all that came along that way" (Judges 9:25).

Thieves and robbers may prosper for a while, but ultimately they will be caught and punished. God commanded His people, "Thou shalt not steal" (Exodus 20:15).

A FUTILE ATTACK

A "buckler" or shield was used by a warrior for protection in hand-to-hand combat (see note on 1 Samuel 17:5–7). The "boss" of the shield was the thickest and strongest point on its outer edge that offered maximum protection against an enemy arrow or sword.

Thus, Eliphaz in this verse was pointing out the futility of a wicked man's attack against God. It would be like a warrior trying to break through the strongest point of his opponent's shield.

UNSTABLE HOUSES

Eliphaz continues his diatribe against the wicked (see note on Job 15:26) by comparing them to people living in houses that are about to cave in.

Houses of Bible times were built of flimsy materials that would break down through exposure to the weather unless they were carefully maintained. For example, the roof of a typical house was overlaid with tree branches that were coated over with clay (see note on Mark 2:4). If the roof began to leak, it was not long before the walls—made of mud bricks dried in the sun—would begin to crumble and fall.

LIGHT AND DARKNESS

These words of Bildad compare God's blessings on His people with the light, and the calamity He brings on the wicked with the darkness. This is an important theme that appears throughout the Bible.

For example, David declared, "Thou wilt light my candle [lamp, NIV]: the LORD will enlighten my darkness" (Psalm 18:28). Jesus used this light/darkness metaphor when He referred to the destiny of unbelievers: They will be "cast out into outer darkness" (Matthew 8:12).

CAUGHT IN GOD'S NET

Birds and other animals were often trapped with nets (see note on Psalm 91:3). These were also effective weapons in combat. A warrior would restrain an enemy by throwing a thick net around him. Then he would finish him off with a sword or spear.

In his suffering and struggles with God, Job compared himself to an animal or a man trapped in a net. He believed God was wielding the net. As an innocent sufferer, he thought he was being punished by God for no reason.

ANCIENT WRITTEN RECORDS

Job's desire that his words be recorded for future generations shows three different ways that ancient records were written down. According to the New International Version, these methods were (1) writing on scrolls, (2) writing on lead tablets, and (3) writing on stone monuments.

1. *Scrolls.* The most common form of writing was that done on scrolls by using primitive pens and ink (see note on Jeremiah 36:18). These scrolls were continuous rolls of papyrus or animal skins, each end of which was wound around a stick. They had to be unrolled for reading.

2. *Lead tablets.* Tablets made of lead were inscribed with an iron stylus. Tablets make of soft clay were also written on, then baked to make them hard and durable (see note on Ezekiel 4:1). Archaeologists have found many tablets of both lead and clay that shed light on ancient Middle Eastern customs and traditions.

3. *Stone monuments.* These monuments, much like modern monuments, recorded important events in a nation's history. Many ancient stone monuments have been discovered. Perhaps the most significant for Bible students is the Moabite Stone, which describes the rebellion of King Mesha of Moab against King Jehoram of Israel, confirming the biblical account (2 Kings 3:4–27).

Job got his wish. His words were written down, probably on a scroll. They have been preserved in the Bible for our edification and instruction.

The Moabite Stone mentions the revolt led by King Mesha of Moab that won his country's freedom from Israel.

Houses with Clay Walls

In the dark they [the wicked] dig through houses, which they had marked for themselves in the daytime.

Job 24:16

This verse reminds us of modern burglars. They drive through neighborhoods in the daytime, taking note of houses that should be an "easy pick." Then they come back at night to break in when no one is home.

Compared to modern houses, dwellings of Bible times were easy to burglarize. Their walls consisted of layers of clay or bricks made of mud that had been dried in the sun (see note on Job 15:28). A determined thief could easily "dig through" these flimsy walls.

Sealing with Clay

It [the earth] is turned as clay to the seal.

Job 38:14

This verse is part of God's response to Job's charge against Him that He was unjust and unfair in causing Job to suffer.

In Bible times clay tablets or clay bricks were often stamped or sealed with a symbol that identified their owner or creator. God declared to Job that He was the all-powerful, omnipotent Lord who had created the earth and stamped it with His own seal. He did not owe Job an explanation for His actions.

PSALMS

A Picture of Abundance

He [the righteous man] shall be like a tree planted by the rivers [streams, NIV] of water, that bringeth forth [yields, NIV] his fruit in his season.

Psalm 1:3

This verse compares the righteous person to a tree that flourishes in an irrigated orchard. The dry Middle East today uses irrigation for many of its crops. Artificial watering was also practiced in many countries of the ancient world.

For example, Egypt used the vast water resources of the Nile River to improve its crop production. Through a series of canals, the waters of the Nile were conveyed to every part of the rich alluvial valley through which the river flowed (see note on Deuteronomy 11:10).

The prophets Isaiah and Jeremiah predicted that Israel would be like a "watered garden" because of the future blessings of the Lord (Isaiah 58:11; Jeremiah 31:12).

KISSING THE SON

A kiss was a customary way of greeting someone in Bible times, just as a handshake is today (see notes on Genesis 29:13 and 2 Samuel 20:9). But the kiss described in this verse expresses the idea of paying homage to someone—perhaps a king—because of his authority and supremacy.

Many interpreters see this verse as a reference to the Messiah. We are to bow down before God's Son in worship and submission.

Kiss the Son, lest he be angry, and ye perish from the way, when his wrath is kindled but a little [for his wrath can flare up in a moment, NIV].

PSALM 2:12

GOD'S ABUNDANT BLESSINGS

Kings were anointed by having olive oil poured on their heads (2 Kings 11:12). This was also an act of courtesy and hospitality performed by hosts for their guests.

David the psalmist compared God's grace to such an anointing. He felt as if God had held nothing back—that He had blessed him beyond measure with His love and mercy.

Like David, another psalmist in the book of Psalms also praised the Lord, comparing His blessings to being "anointed with fresh oil" (Psalm 92:10).

Thou [God] anointest my head with oil; my cup runneth over.

PSALM 23:5

OVERHEAD GATES

This messianic psalm describes the Messiah, the King of glory, entering Jerusalem, the holy city. The gates of the city are ordered to "lift up" to allow the Messiah to enter.

Ancient walled cities had massive gates that could be closed and secured from the inside to provide protection against enemy attacks (see notes on 2 Samuel 18:24 and 2 Chronicles 8:5). In addition to gates that swung on hinges to a closed position, overhead gates also may have been used. These would have been dropped quickly into place in slots in the city wall, providing an extra measure of protection.

Lift up your heads, O ye gates; and be ye lift up, ye everlasting [ancient, NIV] doors; and the King of glory shall come in.

PSALM 24:7

This full-scale reconstruction of the Assyrian gate at Balawat demonstrates the massiveness of the gate structures that protected ancient cities.

David's Clean Hands

I will wash mine hands in innocency: so will I compass thine altar, O Lord.
Psalm 26:6

In this psalm David cried out against the unjust criticism of his enemies. He declared that he was innocent of all the charges they had made against him.

To show his innocence, David stated that he would wash his hands before approaching the altar of the Lord. Symbolic or ritualistic hand-washing was practiced by the Jewish people to show that they were spiritually clean and thus could stand in God's presence.

Pilate, the Roman governor before whom Jesus appeared, picked up on this Jewish practice to show that he could not be blamed for the death of Jesus, whom he considered innocent of the charges against Him (Matthew 27:24).

Psaltery = Harp = Lyre

Praise the Lord with harp: sing unto him with the psaltery and an instrument of ten strings.
Psalm 33:2

The King James Version translation of this verse seems to refer to three different musical instruments: the harp, the psaltery, and an instrument of ten strings. But the New International Version interprets it as a reference to only one instrument—the harp: "Praise the Lord with the harp; make music to him on the ten-stringed lyre."

The words *harp*, *psaltery*, and *lyre* refer to the same thing—a musical instrument similar to the modern harp that was played by plucking its strings (see notes on Genesis 31:27 and 1 Chronicles 25:5).

Harps were probably made in different sizes with different string configurations. Thus, the psalmist tells us in this verse that he is referring to a specific type of harp—one with "ten strings."

Pierced Ears of a Servant

Mine ears hast thou [God] opened [pierced, NIV].
Psalm 40:6

In Old Testament times, an indentured servant might decide to stay with his master for the rest of his life. This lifetime commitment was signified by the piercing of the servant's ear (Exodus 21:2–6; Deuteronomy 15:12–17).

David in this psalm referred to this custom to show that he was a willing servant of the Lord. He was ready to do whatever God asked of him.

Sweet-Smelling Clothes

All thy garments smell of myrrh, and aloes, and cassia.
Psalm 45:8

People of Bible times often sprinkled their clothes with fragrant oils and sewed spices into the folds of their garments, probably to offset body odor. This psalm, a hymn of praise to the future Messiah, refers to this custom to show that the coming King is worthy of all honor and praise.

Myrrh, a fragrant substance extracted from a tree, was included among the gifts presented to the baby Jesus by the wise men from the east (Matthew 2:11). Aloes and cassia were spices used to make perfume.

CLEANSED WITH HYSSOP

Hyssop was a plant of the mint family. It grew to about three feet tall and produced clusters of yellow flowers. Bunches of this plant were used to sprinkle blood on the doorposts of Israelite houses in Egypt to keep them safe from the death angel (Exodus 12:22). Hyssop was also used in purification ceremonies.

In Psalm 51 David prayed for the Lord to take away the guilt of his sins of adultery with Bathsheba and the murder of her husband (2 Samuel 11:1–27). Just as hyssop was used by priests to sprinkle lepers to show that they were free of their disease (Leviticus 14:1–8), so David needed the Lord's cleansing forgiveness.

Purge [cleanse, NIV] me with hyssop, and I shall be clean.
PSALM 51:7

GOD KNOWS OUR TEARS

David may have been referring in this psalm to an ancient custom observed by mourners at funerals. They would collect the tears they shed for departed loved ones in small flasks and place them in their tombs as memorials of their love. The New International Version renders this phrase as "list my tears on your scroll." But in a marginal note, it cites "put my tears in your wineskin" as a possible reading.

This was David's way of saying that God knows all about us. He even keeps a record of the tears we shed in our moments of sorrow and sadness. Jesus expressed the same truth when He declared, "The very hairs of your head are all numbered" (Matthew 10:30).

Thou [God] tellest my wanderings: put thou my tears into thy bottle: are they not in thy book?
PSALM 56:8

The tears of mourners were often collected in small glass vases.

THE BITE OF THE WICKED

Psalm 58 declares that wicked people may seem to be flaunting the Lord and getting by with it, but eventually they will pay for their evil deeds.

The psalmist compared the wicked to a snake that refused to be charmed by a snake charmer. Like these uncontrollable snakes, the wicked are always ready to bite the righteous, since they will not give in to the Lord's control.

Snake charming was like a circus act in Bible times. People paid magicians and wizards to see them practice this

Their [the wicked's] poison is like the poison of a serpent [snake, NIV]: they are like the deaf adder [cobra, NIV] that stoppeth her ear; which will not hearken to the voice of charmers.
PSALM 58:4–5

121

ancient art. Solomon observed, "If a snake bites before it is charmed, there is no profit for the charmer" (Ecclesiastes 10:11 NIV).

THORNS FOR FUEL

Thorny shrubs and plants were plentiful in Palestine, and they were gathered and used as fuel under cooking pots (2 Samuel 23:6–7; Ecclesiastes 7:6; Isaiah 9:18; Nahum 1:10). They made a quick, hot fire. The psalmist declared that the Lord would destroy the wicked faster than the heat from a fire of thorns could reach the cooking pot.

Much of Palestine is rocky and barren, so firewood was scarce. In addition to thorns, the people used grass (Matthew 6:30), sticks (1 Kings 17:10), and dried manure (Ezekiel 4:12–15) for fuel.

LIFTING UP THE HORN

This psalm condemns the wicked for their part in flaunting the authority of the Lord. The horn of an animal symbolized its strength (Deuteronomy 33:17; Zechariah 1:18–21). The phrase "lift up the horn" referred to a stubborn animal, such as an ox, that held its head high to keep a yoke from being placed on its shoulders. Thus, the phrase expresses rebellion and stubbornness.

HONORABLE TREATMENT OF THE DEAD

For a corpse to go unburied was one of the greatest dishonors imaginable. To have the body ravaged by vultures and other wild animals made the horror even worse.

When the Philistines killed King Saul and his sons, they insulted the entire nation of Israel by hanging their bodies on the defensive wall of the city of Beth-shan. A group of brave Israelite warriors retrieved the bodies, cremated them, and gave their bones a decent burial (1 Samuel 31:9–13).

ALONE IN THE PIT

Psalm 88 is the saddest psalm in the entire book of Psalms. Feeling depressed and alone, the psalmist cried out that God had forgotten him and was ignoring his pleas for help.

To "go down into the pit" was the psalmist's way of saying that he felt as though he had died and gone to the realm of the dead. To make matters worse, no one seemed to care that he had disappeared.

Some people wonder why God would allow such a depressing psalm to appear in the book of Psalms. Perhaps

---

Before your pots can feel the thorns, he [the Lord] shall take them [the wicked] away as with a whirlwind.
PSALM 58:9

I said unto. . .the wicked [arrogant, NIV], Lift not up the horn.
PSALM 75:4

The dead bodies of thy servants have they given to be meat unto the fowls [birds, NIV] of the heaven, the flesh of thy saints unto the beasts of the earth.
PSALM 79:2

I am counted with them that go down into the pit.
PSALM 88:4

it is included to show that depression and discouragement are as much a part of the human experience as joy and exhilaration. God does not reject us when we are feeling down and out. He wants to lift us up and restore the joy of our salvation. Notice the psalmist did begin this psalm with these words: "O Lord God of my salvation" (Psalm 88:1).

Trapping Birds

This psalm celebrates God's promise that He will deliver and watch over His people, keeping them safe from danger. According to the psalmist, the Lord will not allow His people to fall into the snare, or trap, of the fowler. A fowler was a hunter who trapped birds for a living. Once a bird was caught in a fowler's net, it could not free itself, no matter how hard it struggled (see note on Job 19:6). It was destined to wind up as a meal on someone's table.

Surely he [God] shall deliver thee from the snare [trap] of the fowler.
Psalm 91:3

In the Old Testament, the perils that people face are often compared to the net of a bird trapper (Job 18:8; Psalm 141:9–10; Proverbs 7:23). Only God is able to deliver us from such danger.

God Gives the Victory

A footstool was a piece of furniture, similar to a modern ottoman, on which a person rested his feet while in a reclining or resting position. To treat one's enemies as a footstool was to defeat them and bring them into total subjection. Thus, God assured the psalmist that he would be victorious over his enemies if he trusted in the Lord.

Sit thou at my [God's] right hand, until I make thine enemies thy footstool.
Psalm 110:1

This passage has been interpreted as a reference to the Messiah. Following His victory over death and the grave, Jesus is now seated at God's right hand as our Savior and Mediator (Acts 2:32–35; 1 Corinthians 15:27; see note on Colossians 3:1).

Finding Joy in the Lord

In Bible times wine and other liquids were stored in containers made of animal skins (see note on Matthew 9:17). These skins would eventually become brittle and develop cracks, particularly when exposed to the smoke given off by fires that burned in the tents and primitive houses of that time.

I am become like a bottle [wineskin, NIV] in the smoke; yet do I not forget thy [God's] statutes [decrees, NIV].
Psalm 119:83

The psalmist compared himself to one of these useless wineskins. But even when he felt burned out and unworthy, he found comfort and joy in the law of the Lord.

WATCHING AND ANTICIPATING

As the eyes of servants look unto the hand of their masters. . .so our eyes wait upon [look to, NIV] the LORD our God.
PSALM 123:2

Servants and slaves of Bible times were trained to anticipate the needs of their masters. Over many years they became so sensitive to what their masters wanted that they would not have to be told or commanded. A glance or a hand gesture would be enough to send them into action.

The point of the psalmist in this verse is that we as believers should be just as sensitive to the Lord's will as these household servants are to their human masters. We should be ready and willing to do the Lord's bidding, even anticipating what He desires of His servants.

GRASS GROWING ON THE ROOF

Let them all be confounded and turned back that hate Zion. Let them be as the grass upon the housetops, which withereth afore it groweth up.
PSALM 129:5–6

The psalmist describes wicked people or those who oppose God as haters of Zion, or Jerusalem (see note on Isaiah 1:8). He hopes they will be as short-lived as grass that springs up on the roof of a house.

Houses of Bible times had flat roofs sealed with clay (see notes on Deuteronomy 22:8; Mark 2:4; and Acts 10:9). Grass would sometimes sprout and begin to grow on a flat roof. But it would wither quickly when subjected to heat, foot traffic, and the regular smoothing of the roof with a stone roller.

FLUTE, BAGPIPE, OR HARMONICA?

Praise him [God] with the timbrel [tambourine, NIV] and dance: praise him with stringed instruments and organs [flute, NIV].
PSALM 150:4

The exact nature of the third musical instrument mentioned in this verse is uncertain. The King James Version describes it as an "organ," while the New International Version uses the word "flute." A third translation prefers "woodwinds" (CEV).

It certainly was not an instrument as sophisticated as the modern pipe organ. It probably was a wind instrument of some type, perhaps similar to the flute, the bagpipe, or the harmonica. Whatever it was, the psalmist declared that it was to be played in joyful praise to the Lord.

PROVERBS

From Naughty to Worthless

The word translated as "naughty person" or "scoundrel" in this verse literally means "son of Belial." In the Hebrew language, *Belial* means "worthless" or "useless." Thus, one mark of a worthless person is the evil or corrupt speech that comes from his mouth.

People in the Bible who were called "worthless" or "son of Belial" include the evil sons of Eli the priest (1 Samuel 2:12), those who supported Jeroboam's rebellion against the southern tribes of Israel (2 Chronicles 13:7), and those who gave false testimony against Naboth at the urging of Jezebel (1 Kings 21:11–13).

> *A naughty person [scoundrel, NIV], a wicked man [villain, NIV], walketh with a froward [corrupt, NIV] mouth.*
> Proverbs 6:12

Shifty Signs

We would call the person whom Solomon describes in these verses a "con man." Rather than speaking openly and forthrightly, he goes behind others' backs to cheat and deceive by using eye motions and hand signals that are understood only by his accomplices.

These tactics may have been used by dishonest merchants of Solomon's time. Unfortunately, people like this are still in business today. We should be on guard against their deceptive practices.

> *He [a wicked man] winketh with his eyes, he speaketh [signals, NIV] with his feet, he teacheth [motions, NIV] with his fingers.*
> Proverbs 6:13

Wisdom's Meal

This verse portrays wisdom as preparing a meal that it invites people to eat. The message is that we can achieve wisdom and understanding if only we will partake of the wisdom that God has provided for His people.

The "mingled wine" or "mixed wine" was prepared by mixing two kinds of wine together—possibly an older, stronger wine with a weaker wine of more recent vintage.

> *She [wisdom] hath killed her beasts [prepared her meat, NIV]; she hath mingled [mixed, NIV] her wine; she hath also furnished [set, NIV] her table.*
> Proverbs 9:2

A Hand-to-Hand Agreement

The phrase "hand join in hand" describes the ancient custom of shaking hands—or perhaps striking hands back to back—to seal an agreement between two parties. The handshake is still used this way in modern times.

The New International Version translates the verse like this: "Be sure of this: The wicked will not go unpunished." "Hand join to hand" was often used in the Hebrew language in an idiomatic sense to express certainty or agreement.

Though hand join in hand, the wicked shall not be unpunished.

PROVERBS 11:21

Keep the Gate Low

The typical house of Bible times consisted of four to six rooms built around a central courtyard. This courtyard was similar to a modern hallway. First you entered the courtyard through the front door, or gateway. Then you used the courtyard to gain access to all of the rooms in the house.

The gateway into a house was normally only about four feet high. These low entrances may have been designed to keep thieves from riding horses into the courtyard. Thus, the writer of Proverbs states that anyone who built his gate high was asking for trouble. This was a symbolic way of saying that pride or self-exaltation leads to destruction.

He that exalteth his gate [builds a high gate, NIV] seeketh destruction.

PROVERBS 17:19

This reconstruction of a four-room house illustrates how the Israelites built their homes around a central courtyard.

Making Decisions by Lot

This verse refers to the ancient custom of casting lots to settle disputes or make important decisions (see note on Jonah 1:7). We might compare the practice to flipping a coin or drawing straws in modern times.

The Bible does not give us any details about the materials used in casting lots. But we can speculate that colored stones or pieces of wood may have been placed in a bag or jug. These items were then rolled around inside the container and cast out on the ground. The order in which the stones or pieces of wood lined up may have determined the course of action to follow.

The lot causeth contentions to cease, and parteth between the mighty.
Proverbs 18:18

LOT-CASTING EVENTS

1. The high priest cast lots to determine which one of two sacrificial goats would become the scapegoat (see note on Leviticus 16:10).
2. After the conquest of Canaan, lots were cast to determine the division of the land among the tribes of Israel (Joshua 14:1-2).
3. In David's time Levite gatekeepers were assigned to duties at specific gates of Jerusalem and the temple by the casting of lots (1 Chronicles 26:12-19).
4. At the crucifixion Roman soldiers cast lots to determine how Jesus' clothes would be divided among them (Matthew 27:35).
5. The apostles cast lots to select Matthias as Judas's successor (Acts 1:24-26).

A Hut on the Roof

This verse uses humor to show that no house is big enough to accommodate two people who don't get along. If the husband and wife are always quarreling, each one could say with equal justification to the other, "I would rather be living up on the roof than in this house with you."

People in Bible times sometimes built booths, or temporary shelters, on the flat roofs of their houses to provide relief from the heat during the summertime. Those huts would be cold and uncomfortable during rainy weather and the winter months. But constant squabbling in the main part of the house would tempt the residents to turn a rooftop shelter into a permanent dwelling.

It is better to dwell in a corner of the housetop, than with a brawling woman [quarrelsome wife, NIV] in a wide house.
Proverbs 21:9

Beautiful Words

This verse refers to the beautiful metal engravings that were displayed in the homes of kings and the wealthy in Bible times. "Apples of gold" were probably carvings of apples that were made from gold or painted to look like gold. These were placed in a highly polished silver frame to give the

A word fitly [aptly, NIV] spoken is like apples of gold in pictures [settings, NIV] of silver.
Proverbs 25:11

entire work of art an ornate appearance.

The point of this proverb is that an appropriate word spoken at just the right time is a thing of beauty. Or to put it another way, "A wholesome tongue is a tree of life" (Proverbs 15:4).

A Picture of Laziness

As the door turneth upon his hinges, so doth the slothful [sluggard, NIV] upon his bed.
Proverbs 26:14

This proverb compares a lazy or "slothful" person to a door hinge. He turns back and forth on his bed, but he never makes any effort to get up and go to work.

A door hinge of Bible times consisted of a pin that fit into sockets above and below the pin. The door opened and closed by turning on this pin.

Hinges are also mentioned in connection with Solomon's temple. The main hall in the temple and the doors of the Most Holy Place or Holy of Holies turned on gold hinges (1 Kings 7:50).

Foolish to the Bone

Though thou shouldest bray [grind, NIV] a fool in a mortar among wheat with a pestle, yet will not his foolishness depart from him.
Proverbs 27:22

A mortar was a huge jar or stone container in which a substance such as grain was crushed. This was done by pulverizing the grain in an up-and-down motion with a long, heavy stick known as a pestle. This mortar-and-pestle technique was a primitive way of grinding grain if a hand-turned stone mill was not available (see note on Matthew 18:6).

This proverb shows how futile it is to try to talk sense into a fool. Even grinding him like wheat in a mortar with a pestle will not turn him from his senseless ways.

Churning Up Anger

The churning of milk bringeth forth butter. . . so the forcing of wrath [stirring up anger, NIV] bringeth forth strife.
Proverbs 30:33

In Bible times butter was produced by placing milk in a bag made from an animal skin (see notes on Psalm 119:83 and Matthew 9:17) and shaking it vigorously back and forth until the butter fat separated from the milk.

This proverb has a "just as" construction. Just as surely as shaking milk produces butter, giving vent to one's anger will cause strife and trouble. The phrase "stirring up anger" suggests that a person can feed his anger until it becomes uncontrollable.

A Bedouin woman vigorously churning milk in an animal skin.

ECCLESIASTES

Dressed in White

In the hot climate of Palestine, white was a sensible color for clothes. So it was only natural for Solomon, the author of Ecclesiastes, to express this wish for others.

The wearing of white clothes was also a symbol of purity and holiness—characteristics of God and those who follow His commands. When Daniel saw God in a vision, He was dressed in white clothes (Daniel 7:9). In the end times, the redeemed are also to be "arrayed in white robes" (Revelation 7:13).

Let thy garments be always white.
ECCLESIASTES 9:8

A Bountiful Return

This verse may refer to sowing grain in flooded areas. Or it could refer to ships that carry goods over the seas to distant places for sale or trade.

Whatever the background of the passage, it has been quoted over the centuries to show that widespread distribution of a good thing will result in a bountiful return at harvesttime.

Cast thy bread upon the waters: for thou shalt find it after many days.
ECCLESIASTES 11:1

SONG OF SOLOMON

*I am black, but comely
[dark. . .yet lovely, NIV],
O ye daughters of
Jerusalem, as the tents
of Kedar.*
SONG OF SOLOMON 1:5

SEEING BENEATH THE SURFACE

Solomon's bride, the Shulamite, is speaking in this verse. In an age when women prized pure white skin, she was a country girl whose skin had been darkened by long exposure to the sun.

She compared her complexion to the "tents of Kedar." Kedar refers to a nomadic tribe that lived in the Arabian Desert. Their tents were made of animal skins that had been turned a dark color by constant exposure to the hot desert sun.

In spite of her dark skin, the Shulamite knew she was still "lovely" in Solomon's eyes. True love always sees beneath the surface to the deeper qualities of the inner person.

The beauty of Solomon's dark-skinned bride is celebrated in the Song of Songs.

RESTING AT MIDDAY

These are the words of King Solomon's bride as she searched for her beloved, the king. She referred to a common practice in Bible times of shepherds protecting their sheep by having them rest at midday in order to avoid the oppressive heat.

David may have referred to this practice when he compared God to a watchful shepherd: "The LORD is my shepherd; I shall not want. He maketh me to lie down in green pastures" (Psalm 23:1–2).

Tell me, O thou whom my soul loveth, where thou feedest, where thou makest thy flock to rest at noon.
SONG OF SOLOMON 1:7

SOLOMON'S PORTABLE CHAIR

The Hebrew word translated as "chariot" in this passage actually refers to a palanquin—a portable couch or chair in which kings were carried from place to place by royal servants. Poles were fastened to each side of the palanquin. Four servants would then hoist the king in his chair and place the poles on their shoulders.

Solomon's gold and silver palanquin had a purple awning or cover to protect him from the sun. Purple was the color that signified royalty.

King Solomon made himself a chariot [carriage, NIV] of the wood of Lebanon. He made the pillars [posts, NIV] thereof of silver, the bottom [base, NIV] thereof of gold, the covering of it of purple.
SONG OF SOLOMON 3:9–10

POLICING THE STREETS

Walled cities of Bible times had guards posted on the walls to warn of approaching danger (see note on 2 Samuel 18:26). These words of Solomon's bride showed that armed guards also policed the area inside the walls, particularly at night. Their job was to patrol the streets and keep order, much as policemen do in today's modern cities.

Solomon's Shulamite bride apparently went into the streets at night to search for the king. She may have been mistreated by the guards because they thought she was a prostitute.

The watchmen that went about the city found me, they smote [beat, NIV] me, they wounded me; the keepers of the walls took away my veil [cloak, NIV] from me.
SONG OF SOLOMON 5:7

ISAIAH

They [the wounds of Judah] have not been closed, neither bound up, neither mollified [soothed, NIV] with ointment.

ISAIAH 1:6

JUDAH'S UNTREATED WOUNDS

Medical treatment was very primitive in Bible times. Even simple surgical procedures such as the suturing of wounds did not exist. Cuts were treated by pouring on soothing oil and wrapping them tightly with a cloth.

The prophet Isaiah described the sin and idolatry of Judah as a wound or sore. But these wounds had been left open and untreated. These sin wounds would lead to infection and death unless the nation turned back to the Lord.

The daughter of Zion is left as a cottage [shelter, NIV] in a vineyard, as a lodge [hut, NIV] in a garden of cucumbers [melons, NIV].

ISAIAH 1:8

BAD NEWS FOR JERUSALEM

Farmers of Bible times had to keep a close watch on their crops to protect them from animals and thieves. They would build crude huts from tree branches in the fields to provide shelter for those who watched the crops. After the harvest these huts would soon fall and rot.

Isaiah compared Jerusalem, referred to in this passage as "the daughter of Zion," to one of these abandoned and useless shelters. He declared that the city would fall to an enemy and become utterly desolate unless the people turned from their worship of false gods and renewed their commitment to the Lord.

They shall beat their swords into plowshares, and their spears into pruninghooks.

ISAIAH 2:4

PEACE AND WAR

In this verse Isaiah referred to a future time of universal peace that would be ushered in with the coming of the Messiah. War will not exist in this age, so the nation of Judah can turn its weapons into agricultural tools to contribute to its economic prosperity.

While these Assyrian swords were used for war, Isaiah talked about a time of universal peace when such swords would be beaten into plowshares (Isaiah 2:4).

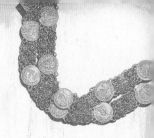

"Beating" these weapons into tools refers to the work of a blacksmith on an anvil. In Bible times, metal was worked by heating it in a fire, then beating it into a specific shape with a heavy hammer.

This weapons-into-tools image was reversed by the prophet Joel. He spoke of the day of the Lord—a time when God would punish His people by sending war and chaos. Then the people would have to "beat your plowshares into swords, and your pruninghooks into spears" (Joel 3:10).

JINGLING FEET

Isaiah compared the proud and rebellious people of Judah with dancing girls who entertained the crowds with seductive movements and rhythmic sounds.

Many female dancers of Bible times used tabrets, or tambourines, to produce rhythmic sounds to enhance their movement (see notes on Genesis 31:27 and Exodus 15:20). The New International Version translation of Isaiah 3:16 makes it clear that anklets or ankle bracelets served the same purpose.

The clinking or jingling sound of these anklets may have been made by striking them together with movements of the feet. Or it may have been produced by small bells or ornaments attached to the anklets.

The daughters [women, NIV] of Zion are haughty, and walk with stretched forth necks and wanton [flirting, NIV] eyes, walking and mincing as they go, and making a tinkling with their feet [with ornaments jingling on their ankles, NIV].
ISAIAH 3:16

PAGAN JEWELRY

This verse continues Isaiah's condemnation of the people of Judah, whom he compared to dancing girls (see note on Isaiah 3:16). He declared that God would take away all evidence of Judah's pride, symbolized by the fine clothes and jewelry worn by these dancing girls.

These items included their headbands and their necklaces with charms in the shape of crescent moons. These "crescent necklaces" may have signified Judah's lapse into pagan worship.

The Lord will take away. . .their tinkling ornaments. . .and their cauls [headbands, NIV], and their round tires like the moon [crescent necklaces, NIV].
ISAIAH 3:18

BALD AND SHABBY

The Jewish people—both men and women—took pride in their full, thick hair (see note on 2 Samuel 10:4). To go from having beautiful, "well set" hair to being bald was a real put-down. But to exchange one's beautiful clothes for sackcloth—a symbol of sorrow and despair (see note on Genesis 37:34)—was the ultimate humiliation. Isaiah declared that this would be the fate of the nation of Judah, unless the people changed their ways.

The Old English word *stomacher* in this verse refers to a fancy robe. The New International Version translates it as "fine clothing."

Instead of well set hair baldness; and instead of a stomacher a girding of sackcloth.
ISAIAH 3:24

SITTING IN DESPAIR

*Her [Jerusalem's] gates
shall lament and mourn;
and she being desolate
[destitute, NIV] shall sit
upon the ground.*
ISAIAH 3:26

Sitting on the ground symbolized sadness and distress. So this is another image from Isaiah that expresses the fate of the nation of Judah if she continued on her present course (see note on Isaiah 3:24).

When Job's friends came to comfort him, they did not say a word for seven days, but "they sat down with him upon the ground. . .for they saw that his grief was very great" (Job 2:13). The same idea of despair is also expressed in these declarations: "Wallow thyself in ashes" (Jeremiah 6:26) and "roll thyself in the dust" (Micah 1:10).

Beehives made from jars show that the people of Bible times not only collected honey from natural hives but also cultivated its production.

A BUTTER AND HONEY SANDWICH

*Butter [curds, NIV] and
honey shall he eat, that
he may know to refuse the
evil, and choose the good.*
ISAIAH 7:15

Butter, or curds, and honey were often mixed together and spread on bread, much as peanut butter and jelly are eaten together as a sandwich in modern times. It may have been a staple in the diet of children, since it is mentioned in this verse as food that a young child would eat.

Honey is mentioned in connection with butter or milk in several other places in the Bible (2 Samuel 17:29; Job 20:17; Song of Solomon 4:11).

HAIRLESS MOABITES

*On all their [Moabites']
heads shall be baldness,
and every beard cut off.*
ISAIAH 15:2

Chapters 15 and 16 of Isaiah contain the prophet's declaration of God's judgment against the Moabites, enemies of the Israelites. The Lord would humiliate these people, Isaiah declared, by making them bald and cutting off their beards. This was a sign of mourning among the Jewish people and other nations of the ancient world.

When Ezra heard that some Israelite men had married pagan wives, he was so upset that he tore the hair off his head and face (Ezra 9:3). Job shaved his head to symbolize his misery and distress (Job 1:20).

No Singing at Work

The people of Bible times sang while working in the fields to escape from the monotony of farmwork. Isaiah declared that the singing and gladness of the Moabites would be taken away when God judged them for their idolatry and disobedience.

Gladness is taken away, and joy out of the plentiful field; and in the vineyards there shall be no singing.
ISAIAH 16:10

Ethiopia's Papyrus Boats

We know that the papyrus plant that grew in abundance in the marshy areas of Lower Egypt was used to make water-proof baskets. The baby Moses was placed in such a basket on the Nile River (see note on Exodus 2:3). But this verse shows that larger sailing vessels were also fashioned from this plant. Perhaps papyrus reeds were woven tightly together and reinforced with harder materials, then coated with tar or bitumen (see note on Genesis 11:3) to make the vessel waterproof.

Ethiopia, also referred to as Cush in the Bible (Isaiah 11:11), was an ancient nation south of Egypt. The Ethiopians used these papyrus vessels to trade with other nations around the Mediterranean Sea.

Woe to the land. . .beyond the rivers of Ethiopia [Cush, NIV]: that sendeth ambassadors [envoys, NIV] by the sea, even in vessels of bulrushes [papyrus boats, NIV] upon the waters.
ISAIAH 18:1–2

Fishing, Egyptian Style

This verse is part of Isaiah's prophecy of doom against Egypt. God's punishment would be so devastating that it would spoil the Egyptian fishing industry. Fish taken from the Nile River and its tributaries were a staple of this ancient nation's diet.

Two types of fishing are mentioned in this verse—with hooks and with nets. Their hooks were probably made of bronze and were baited with live bait, just like fishing hooks today. Nets were cast into the water from the shore or dropped from small boats. Both types of fishing are pictured on stone monuments from Egypt's past.

The fishers [fishermen, NIV] also shall mourn, and all they that cast angle [hooks, NIV] into the brooks shall lament, and they that spread nets upon the waters shall languish.
ISAIAH 19:8

Get Ready for Battle

Isaiah called on the nation of Judah to get prepared for the calamity that God would bring on His people because of their sin and rebellion.

Shields of Bible times were made of thick pieces of wood coated with animal skin (see note on 1 Samuel 17:5–7). This skin needed to be treated with oil occasionally to keep it from becoming dry and brittle. To "anoint" or "oil" the shield was to make immediate preparation for battle.

Watch in the watchtower. . . arise, ye princes [officers, NIV], and anoint [oil, NIV] the shield.
ISAIAH 21:5

QUIVERS AND SHIELD CASES

People from Elam and Kir made up two strong units of the Babylonian army. Thus, Isaiah warned the people of Judah to be prepared for Babylon to invade their territory.

Warriors of Bible times carried their arrows in quivers slung across their backs. Shields used in hand-to-hand combat (see notes on 1 Samuel 17:5–7 and Isaiah 21:5) were kept in cases or covers when not in use to preserve them from dust and the dry climate. The phrase "uncover the shield" expresses the idea of getting ready for battle.

A TOMB IN THE ROCK

Isaiah directed these words to Shebna, an administrator in the court of King Hezekiah of Judah, who was hewing out an elaborate royal tomb in solid rock. Isaiah predicted that the tomb would not be used, since Jerusalem was destined to fall to the Babylonians.

People of means in Bible times were buried in caves (see note on Genesis 23:19) or in tombs carved out of rock in a hillside. Joseph of Arimathea laid the body of Jesus in such a tomb that he had excavated for his own burial (Matthew 27:57–60).

A KEY ON THE SHOULDER

Isaiah predicted that Shebna (see note on Isaiah 22:16) would be deposed from office and that he would be replaced by Eliakim. Carrying a key on his shoulder symbolized his position of power and authority, as well as his trustworthiness.

The primitive locks of Bible times (see note on Judges 3:23–25) had to be opened with long wooden keys. These keys were often slung over the shoulders of those who had the authority to lock and unlock doors in the king's royal buildings.

Ancient door keys doubled as door handles. They were used to reach through the keyhole to lift the locking bolt.

A key on the shoulder as a symbol of authority is probably the image behind Isaiah's famous expression about the Messiah: "The government shall be upon his shoulder" (Isaiah 9:6).

A PEG IN THE WALL

In this verse, Isaiah continued his description of Eliakim, who was named to a place of honor in the king's court (see note on Isaiah 22:22). Eliakim would be like a wooden peg driven into a firm place in the wall of a house.

Houses of Bible times had nails, or pegs, in the walls on which clothes and other household items were hung (see note on Ezekiel 15:3). Ezra referred to these pegs metaphorically when he spoke of God's grace, which gave His people "a nail in his holy place" (Ezra 9:8).

FILTERED WINE

Isaiah referred to a future time when the Lord would restore the faithful remnant of His people and shower them with bountiful blessings. "Wines on the lees" refers to wine that had been stored with particles of grapes left in the liquid. It had to be strained through a cloth to remove the waste before it was ready to drink (see note on Matthew 23:24).

The LORD of hosts [shall] make unto all people. . . a feast of wines on the lees, of fat things full of marrow, of wines on the lees well refined.
ISAIAH 25:6

METHODS OF THRESHING GRAIN

In this verse, Isaiah contrasted two different methods of separating grain from the stalk in Bible times.

Small grains such as caraway and cummin were threshed by beating them with a stick. This method was also used when theshing a small amount of grain (Ruth 2:17). Dragging a stone threshing sledge ("threshing instrument") over the grain was the preferred method for threshing wheat or barley in large quantities.

Isaiah's point is that God knows us, and He knows our needs. He will use whatever method is appropriate as His discipline to keep us focused on Him.

The fitches [caraway, NIV] are not threshed with a threshing instrument [sledge, NIV], neither is a cart wheel turned about upon the cummin; but the fitches [caraway, NIV] are beaten out with a staff [rod, NIV], and the cummin with a rod [stick, NIV].
ISAIAH 28:27

ROLLED LIKE A SCROLL

In the end times, Isaiah declared, the sky will be rolled up like a scroll when God judges the nations for their rebellion and idolatry.

A scroll was the equivalent of a modern book. Writing was done on long rolls of papyrus or animal skins (see notes on Job 19:23–24 and Jeremiah 36:18). The scroll was then rolled up toward the middle from both ends on two sticks.

Some of these scrolls may have been sixty to seventy feet long. To read from a scroll, a person had to unroll it until he found the section he wanted to read. After reading, he rolled it up again.

All the host [stars, NIV] of heaven shall be dissolved, and the heavens shall be rolled together [rolled up, NIV] as a scroll.
ISAIAH 34:4

A fourteenth-century scroll that contains the book of Isaiah in Hebrew.

HOOKED AND BRIDLED PRISONERS

Because thy [Sennacherib's] rage against me, and thy tumult, is come up into mine ears, therefore will I put my hook in thy nose, and my bridle [bit, NIV] in thy lips [mouth, NIV].
ISAIAH 37:29

Sennacherib, king of Assyria, was threatening to overrun Jerusalem. But Isaiah assured the king of Judah that the Lord would deliver them from this threat. God would turn the tables on Sennacherib by putting a hook in his nose and a bit in his mouth.

Hooks and bits were used in Bible times to control draft animals such as oxen and horses. But stone monuments from ancient Assyria show that this technique was also used on prisoners of war. These monuments portray prisoners with iron rings through their lower lips being pulled along by a rope.

GET READY FOR THE KING

Prepare ye the way of the LORD, make straight in the desert a highway for our God. . . . The crooked [rough ground, NIV] shall be made straight [level, NIV], and the rough [rugged, NIV] places plain.
ISAIAH 40:3–4

Roads of Bible times were little more than paths, rough and crude by modern standards. When a king traveled, his servants would go ahead of him, removing stones, filling in low places, and straightening curves so the king's journey would be more pleasant.

Isaiah found in this practice a spiritual principle. The people needed to prepare the way for the coming of the Lord in a new and fresh way—a reference to the future Messiah. In the New Testament, this passage was applied to John the Baptist, who prepared the way for the ministry of Jesus Christ (Luke 3:4–5).

HELPLESS PAGAN GODS

Bel boweth down, Nebo stoopeth, their idols were upon the beasts, and upon the cattle [their idols are borne by beasts of burden, NIV].
ISAIAH 46:1

One of Isaiah's favorite themes was that the pagan gods of his time were powerless, while Yahweh, the supreme God of the Israelites, was all-powerful. Here the prophet portrayed two gods of the Assyrians and Babylonians as so weak and helpless that they had to be carried around by oxen and horses.

Bel, also known as Marduk (Jeremiah 50:2 NIV) and Merodach (Jeremiah 50:2 KJV), was the main god of the Babylonians. Known as the god of war, he was considered the deity who protected the city of Babylon.

Nebo was worshiped by both the Assyrians and the Babylonians as the god of wisdom, science, and the arts. His popularity is verified by the combination of his name with the names of Assyrian and Babylonian kings, such as Nebuchadnezzar of Babylonia.

No Help from Stargazers

The words *astrologers*, *stargazers*, and *monthly prognosticators* refer to people who studied the stars and the movement of the moon in order to foretell the future. This practice was especially popular among the ancient Babylonians.

In Babylonia the astrologers were members of a specific caste. Persons born into this caste continued to practice the stargazing and sign-reading skills inherited from their ancestors. Astrologers were among the people with magical powers summoned by King Nebuchadnezzar of Babylonia to interpret his strange dream (Daniel 2:2).

Isaiah declared that God would judge the people of Judah for their sins and that nothing could thwart His purpose. He—the Creator of the moon and stars—was more powerful than those who read the moon and stars.

Let now the astrologers, the stargazers, the monthly prognosticators, stand up, and save thee from these things that shall come upon thee.
ISAIAH 47:13

A Constant Reminder

A figure or symbol engraved on one's hands would always be in sight and thus a perpetual reminder of a vow or promise.

This is a beautiful picture of God's covenant relationship with His people. He declared through the prophet Isaiah that He would never forget the city of Jerusalem and the people whom He had set apart as His own.

Behold, I [God] have graven [engraved, NIV] thee [Jerusalem] upon the palms of my hands; thy walls are continually before me.
ISAIAH 49:16

God's Power Revealed

People of Bible times wore inner tunics and outer robes that covered the entire body (see notes on 1 Samuel 19:24 and 1 Kings 18:46). The bare arm could be exposed quickly by pulling it from under this loose clothing. "Baring the arm" was a metaphor for swift, decisive action.

When God delivered His people, according to Isaiah in this verse, He would do so by baring His arm—powerfully and forcefully.

The LORD hath made bare his holy arm in the eyes [sight, NIV] of all the nations.
ISAIAH 52:10

Sprinkling of the Nations

The Hebrew word rendered as "sprinkle" in this verse is significant. It is the same word used of the sprinkling by priests of the blood of sacrificial animals to atone for sin (see notes on Leviticus 6:25 and Leviticus 16:34).

When the Messiah comes, according to Isaiah, He will do for the Gentile nations what He has done all along for the Jewish people. He will serve as an atonement for sin for all who receive Him as Savior and Lord.

So shall he [the Messiah] sprinkle many nations.
ISAIAH 52:15

WORSHIP OF STONES?

Some interpreters have speculated that Isaiah in this verse referred to the worship of stones. But it is more likely that he was speaking with sarcasm and irony. Idolatry was so widespread in his time that some people even seemed to worship every rock they passed by!

GOD'S HAND AND EAR

This verse is one of the best examples in the Bible of what theologians call an *anthropomorphism* (Greek *anthropos* [man] + *morphe* [form]). This big word describes the way biblical writers often described God in human terms. Isaiah in this verse said God has a powerful hand that can deliver His people and an ear that is always ready to hear their prayers.

God is a spiritual being (see John 4:24). He does not have human characteristics. So the biblical writers are speaking metaphorically when they speak of God's mouth or eyes. But these metaphors express profound truths in words and images that we humans can understand.

Among the smooth stones of the stream is thy portion. . .even to them hast thou poured a drink offering.
ISAIAH 57:6

The LORD's hand [arm, NIV] is not shortened, that it cannot save; neither his ear heavy [dull, NIV], that it cannot hear.
ISAIAH 59:1

HUMAN CHARACTERISTICS ASSIGNED TO GOD

1. When sin multiplied on the earth, God felt deep sadness in His heart (Genesis 6:6).
2. God declared that no person could look upon His face and live to tell about it (Exodus 33:20).
3. God told Moses that His hand was not short; He had unlimited power to perform miracles on behalf of His people (Numbers 11:23).
4. Moses declared that people are sustained by God's law, or the words "that proceedeth out of the mouth of the LORD" (Deuteronomy 8:3).
5. The psalmist stated that God sees and judges all people with His eyes (Psalm 11:4).

AN OPEN-GATE POLICY

The gates of walled cities (see note on 2 Chronicles 8:5) were closed and bolted at night as a security measure. Residents of the city who didn't make it back inside before darkness fell were forced to spend the night outside.

Isaiah portrayed a future time under the reign of the Messiah when the city gates would never be closed. God would be all the protection His people needed.

Therefore thy gates shall be open continually; they shall not be shut day nor night.
ISAIAH 60:11

MOURNING TURNED TO JOY

Throwing ashes on the head was a sign of deep sorrow and distress (see note on Esther 4:1). But a crown symbolized abundance and joy. Isaiah declares that the mourning of the people will be turned to rejoicing with the arrival of the Messiah, God's servant.

To appoint unto them that mourn in Zion, to give unto them beauty for ashes [a crown of beauty instead of ashes, NIV].
ISAIAH 61:3

JEREMIAH

DRINKING FROM A CISTERN

Cisterns of Bible times were little more than deep pits dug in the ground or shallow reservoirs carved out of limestone rock. Rainwater was directed into these holding tanks and stored for use during the dry season (see notes on Genesis 37:24 and 2 Samuel 17:18–19).

Compared to a spring from which fresh groundwater flowed, a cistern left much to be desired. The water could get contaminated, or the cistern could lose its water supply because of a leak.

Jeremiah criticized the foolish people of Judah for drinking water from a cistern when fresh springwater was available. They had forsaken the living Lord and were worshiping lifeless pagan gods.

They [the people of Judah] have forsaken me [God] the fountain [spring, NIV] of living waters, and hewed them out cisterns, broken cisterns, that can hold no water.

JEREMIAH 2:13

Cistern at Masada. Rain water was directed to underground storage chambers like this for later use.

SORROWFUL HANDS

The prophet Jeremiah predicted that the nation of Judah would be overrun by its enemies because of their sin and rebellion against the Lord. In this verse he portrayed God's people going into captivity with their hands clasped over their heads.

Like throwing dust and ashes on the head (see notes on 2 Samuel 15:32 and Esther 4:1), clasping the hands over one's head symbolized grief and despair. This is how Tamar expressed her sorrow after she was sexually assaulted by Amnon (2 Samuel 13:10–19).

Thou shalt go forth from him, and thine hands upon thine head.

JEREMIAH 2:37

GOD'S HOT JUDGMENT

The bellows are burned [blow fiercely, NIV], the lead is consumed of the fire.

JEREMIAH 6:29

In this verse Jeremiah compared the judgment of God against His sinful people with a fire heated by a blacksmith. The fire was intensified with air from a bellows until it became intense enough to heat metal for shaping by the blacksmith's hammer (see note on Isaiah 2:4).

The bellows of Bible times was a long bag made of animal skin that was placed on the ground in front of the fire. The blacksmith stepped on the bag to expel air into the fire, then pulled it open with a rope to fill it with air again.

WEDDING CELEBRATIONS

Then will I [God] cause to cease from the cities of Judah, and from the streets of Jerusalem, the voice of mirth [joy, NIV], and the voice of gladness, the voice of the bridegroom, and the voice of the bride.

JEREMIAH 7:34

Jeremiah declared that God's judgment would bring an end to the sounds of celebration throughout the nation of Judah. Even the songs of joy associated with weddings would be heard no more.

Weddings of Bible times were events of great celebration that included the entire community (see note on Matthew 25:1–3). The wedding party would march through the streets to sounds of music, singing, and the cheers of the people. Neighbors and friends would be invited to an elaborate wedding feast that lasted for several days.

NO BALM IN GILEAD

Is there no balm in Gilead; is there no physician there?

JEREMIAH 8:22

The word *balm* refers to a spice or soothing ointment that was thought to have healing properties. Gilead was a region not far from Jerusalem where trees and shrubs that produced such ointments were plentiful.

Jeremiah used the phrase "balm in Gilead" to show that God's antidote for the sin of His people was ready and available. All they had to do was reach out and take it, but they refused to do so.

The camel caravan that carried Joseph into slavery in Egypt was carrying some of this healing balm from the region of Gilead (see note on Genesis 37:25).

NOT A RUNAWAY

Oh that I [Jeremiah] had in the wilderness a lodging place of wayfaring men [travelers, NIV]; that I might leave my people, and go from them!

JEREMIAH 9:2

Jeremiah is known as the "weeping prophet" because his heart was broken to see his countrymen rejecting the Lord and following false gods. In this verse he expressed his desire to leave his familiar surroundings, escape to the desert, and live among strangers. Then he would not be exposed every day to the sin and rebellion of the nation of Judah.

But Jeremiah never acted on his desire. For about forty years he stayed at the prophetic task to which God had called him. He is one of the Bible's best examples of faithfulness and obedience to the Lord.

MOURNING FOR PAY

Jeremiah compared the wailing of the people of Judah over God's punishment to laments at a funeral. The Jewish people were known for their loud and bitter mourning over the death of loved ones (see note on 2 Samuel 19:4).

The prophet also referred in this verse to the custom of hiring mourners to contribute to this grieving process. These "professional criers" would weep, shriek, and lament to the rhythm of flutes and tambourines, apparently to heighten the mood of sadness and loss.

Jesus encountered a group of such mourners who were grieving over the death of Jairus's daughter. He sent them away, then raised the girl from the dead (Matthew 9:23–25; Mark 5:38–42).

Call for the mourning women, that they may come; and send for cunning women [the most skillful of them, NIV], that they may come: and let them. . .take up a wailing for us.
JEREMIAH 9:17–18

GONE WITH THE WIND

The phrase "written in the dust" referred to something that would not last long. Like words in the dirt that disappeared with the first strong wind, Jeremiah declared, Judah would be wiped out by her enemies unless the people turned back to God.

All that forsake thee [the LORD] shall be ashamed, and they that depart from me [turn away from you, NIV] shall be written in the earth [dust, NIV].
JEREMIAH 17:13

A LESSON FROM THE POTTER

The Lord instructed Jeremiah to watch a potter at work and He would give the prophet a special message for the people. Ancient potters made pots by shaping wet clay with their hands as it turned on a foot-powered pedestal.

As Jeremiah watched the potter, the vessel he was making collapsed. The potter massaged the clay into a lump and began to form it into another pot. The message for the people was that Judah was like clay in the hands of God. They should allow Him to shape them into a vessel of His own choosing (Jeremiah 18:6).

Then I [Jeremiah] went down to the potter's house, and, behold, he wrought a work on the wheels.
JEREMIAH 18:3

SYMBOLS OF LUXURY

The typical house of Old Testament times was crude by modern standards (see note on Job 15:28). Jeremiah referred in this verse to the luxurious palace built by King Jehoahaz (also known as Shallum) of Judah.

This palace had large rooms with windows. Adorned with red trim, it was "cieled" or paneled with cedar, which had to be imported from Lebanon. To Jeremiah, this luxurious dwelling symbolized the sinful excesses of the king, as well as of the people of Judah. Their pride and rebellion would be judged by the Lord.

I will build me a wide house [great palace, NIV] and large chambers [rooms, NIV], and cutteth him out windows; and it is cieled with cedar, and painted with vermilion [red, NIV].
JEREMIAH 22:14

Jeremiah's Show of Faith

Jeremiah showed faith in the future of Judah, even while Jerusalem, the capital city, was on the verge of falling to the Babylonian army. He bought a plot of land in his hometown of Anathoth, confident that the land would be useful again after the Jewish people returned from the exile in Babylon.

In Jeremiah's time two duplicate deeds to a plot of land were prepared. One copy was buried in a sealed jar in a corner of the property, and the other was left unsealed in a public place for viewing by any interested person.

But the prophet was told by the Lord to place both deeds in a jar for burial on the property. All public records would be destroyed in the Babylonian invasion of Jerusalem. The deeds in the ground would be the only proof of Jeremiah's ownership of the land.

Jeremiah purchased land in his hometown of Anathoth, confident that God would bring Israel back from exile in Babylon.

Cutting a Covenant

In this verse, God charged the people of Judah with violating the covenant they had made with Him. The original covenant that God formed with His people was sealed by Abraham, who cut several animals into two-piece sections and then walked between the sections (see note on Genesis 15:17).

In the Hebrew language, to "make a covenant" was to "cut a covenant," reflecting this ancient custom of walking between the two pieces of an animal carcass. By this action they signified that they agreed on the terms of the covenant. This also may have expressed their wish that if the covenant was broken, the offending party would suffer the same fate as the slaughtered animals.

Baruch's Ink and Paper

Baruch was the faithful scribe of Jeremiah who wrote down the messages of the prophet in order to preserve them for future generations.

The ink used by Baruch and other ancient scribes was made by mixing soot, lampblack, or ground charcoal with water and gum. The scroll on which he wrote Jeremiah's prophecies was probably made from the papyrus plant or from animal skins (see note on Job 19:23–24).

While this writing was primitive by modern standards, it held up well. The manuscripts in the collection known as the Dead Sea Scrolls, discovered in 1947, were still legible, even though they had been written about two thousand years before.

> *Then Baruch answered them, He [Jeremiah] pronounced [dictated, NIV] all these words unto me with his mouth, and I wrote them with ink in the book [scroll, NIV].*
> JEREMIAH 36:18

Buried Food

Ishmael was a Jewish zealot who rebelled against the rule of Babylonia in the chaotic period after Judah fell to the Babylonian army. These ten men agreed to give Ishmael some food supplies that they had hidden in their fields if he would spare their lives.

In Bible times, people often hid their harvested grain in deep pits in the ground. These storage pits were lined with stone and covered with dirt and straw to keep them dry and to conceal them from thieves. Liquids such as oil and honey were sealed in clay jars before being placed in such underground silos.

> *Ten men. . .said unto Ishmael, Slay us not: for we have treasures in the field, of wheat, and of barley, and of oil, and of honey.*
> JEREMIAH 41:8

Amon, God of Thebes

This verse is part of Jeremiah's declaration that God would bring down the Egyptians because of their idol worship. "No" refers to Thebes, the thriving capital of Upper Egypt that was clustered on both sides of the Nile River. The Hebrew word translated as "multitude" by the King James Version actually refers to the Egyptian god Amon, the chief deity of the city of Thebes.

Little is known about Amon. Some think he was a personification of the sun. The Egyptians did practice sun worship, but the name of their sun god was Ra (see note on Genesis 12:15). One theory is that the qualities of Amon and Ra eventually merged into one supreme Egyptian sun god known as Amon-Ra.

> *I [God] will punish the multitude of No [Amon god of Thebes, NIV], and Pharaoh, and Egypt, with their gods, and their kings.*
> JEREMIAH 46:25

Temple at Thebes. Through Jeremiah, God promised that Amon, god of Thebes, would be punished.

JUDGMENT AGAINST MOAB

Moab. . .hath not been emptied from vessel to vessel. . .therefore his taste remained in him, and his scent [aroma, NIV] is not changed.
JEREMIAH 48:11

This verse refers to the step in the process of making wine when it was poured from one jar to another to improve its taste. Jeremiah declared that Israel's enemy, Moab, had not yet experienced devastation by an enemy nation—or been "emptied from vessel to vessel."

But this would change in the future when Moab would be judged by the Lord for its sin. God would "empty his [Moab's] vessels, and break their bottles" (Jeremiah 48:12).

BATTLE AXE OR WAR CLUB?

Thou [Israel] art my [God's] battle axe [war club, NIV] and weapons of war: for with thee will I break in pieces [shatter, NIV] the nations, and with thee will I destroy kingdoms.
JEREMIAH 51:20

The Hebrew word rendered as "battle axe" by the King James Version is probably more accurately translated by the New International Version. A mace, maul, or war club would be used by warriors to "break in pieces" or "shatter" the enemy.

The judge Shamgar used an ox goad as a makeshift war club to defeat a Philistine force of six hundred warriors (see note on Judges 3:31).

AN EIGHTEEN-MONTH SIEGE

So the city [Jerusalem] was besieged unto the eleventh year of king Zedekiah.
JEREMIAH 52:5

Siege warfare was the main tactic used against walled cities of Bible times (see note on 2 Chronicles 8:5). This verse and the surrounding verses tell us how long the Babylonian siege of Jerusalem lasted. The siege began "in the ninth year. . .in the tenth month" (v. 4) of King Zedekiah's reign and ended eighteen months later "in the fourth month" (v. 6) of the eleventh year of his reign.

In siege warfare, the enemy outside the walls always had the upper hand. The army could post sentries to halt the movement of food and water into the city until its inhabitants were starved into submission. This is what happened with Jerusalem: "The famine was sore in the city, so that there was no bread for the people of the land" (v. 6).

About 130 years before Judah (the Southern Kingdom) fell to the Babylonians, the Assyrians overran the city of Samaria and defeated Israel (the Northern Kingdom). Their siege of Samaria lasted three years (2 Kings 17:5).

LAMENTATIONS

Trampled by God's Judgment

Jeremiah referred to the city of Jerusalem as "the virgin, the daughter of Judah." He lamented the destruction of the city by the Babylonian army in 587 BC.

In Bible times, the juice was extracted from grapes to make wine by crushing them underfoot in a vat, or winepress, carved out of solid rock. Jerusalem had been trodden down like grapes in a winepress. God's judgment is also described as a winepress in Isaiah 63:3 and Revelation 14:19–20; 19:15.

The Lord hath trodden [trampled, NIV] the virgin, the daughter of Judah, as in a winepress.

Lamentations 1:15

Rocks for Dinner?

Could any punishment be worse than being forced to eat stones? Jeremiah used this graphic image to show how severely the Lord was punishing the nation of Judah for her sin and idolatry.

The prophet may have drawn this image from the impurities such as sand and gravel that often got mixed in with the bread of Bible times. The methods used to harvest grain (see note on Ruth 3:2) and grind it into flour (see note on Proverbs 27:22) were primitive and unsanitary by modern standards.

He [God] hath also broken my teeth with gravel stones.

Lamentations 3:16

Hanging by the Hand

This verse refers to the humiliation of the nobility of Judah by the army of Babylon after the fall of Jerusalem. Were these princes, or nobles, executed and then hung up by their hands as a public example? Or were they tied and hung up by the hands as a form of torture? We don't know.

What we do know is that the bodies of kings and their sons were sometimes displayed by enemies as a way to celebrate victory and to humiliate and degrade the dead. After the Philistines killed King Saul and his three sons, they hung their bodies on the wall of the city of Beth-shan (1 Samuel 31:8–12).

Princes are hanged up by their hand.

Lamentations 5:12

FOXES IN JERUSALEM

Because of the mountain of Zion, which is desolate, the foxes [jackals, NIV] walk upon it.

LAMENTATIONS 5:18

Jeremiah used this word picture to show the desolation of Jerusalem (referred to as "Zion") after it was captured, plundered, and destroyed by the Babylonians.

The city was virtually empty, since the leading citizens of Judah were carried away to Babylon as captives. Once-thriving Jerusalem was now the haunt of foxes and other wild animals.

The Hebrew word for "foxes" is often rendered as "jackals." These animals, similar to wild dogs, were scavengers. Jackals prowling through Jerusalem gives an even more vivid portrait of the plight of the city.

EZEKIEL

A RECORD IN CLAY

Son of man [Ezekiel], take thee a tile [clay tablet, NIV], and lay it before thee, and pourtray upon it the city, even Jerusalem.

EZEKIEL 4:1

God made a strange request of the prophet Ezekiel. He asked him to draw upon a clay tablet a picture of the city of Jerusalem under siege by the Babylonian army. This was to serve as a warning to the people about the forthcoming judgment of God against Jerusalem and the nation of Judah.

In Bible times, clay tiles or tablets about six by nine inches in size were often used as writing material, just as paper is used today (see note on Job 19:23–24). Characters were etched into these tablets with a metal pen, or stylus, while the clay was soft. When hardened in a kiln, the writing on these tiles was virtually indestructible.

Archaeologists have discovered these clay tablets in the ruins of ancient cities. They shed light on the culture and customs of the ancient world.

Clay, rather than paper, was the material most frequently used for ancient correspondence.

IDOLS IN THE TEMPLE

In a vision the prophet Ezekiel saw the temple of the Jewish people in Jerusalem. He was shocked to see on its walls paintings or sculptures of unclean animals that God's people were not supposed to eat (Leviticus 11:1–19).

But even more shocking were the representations of pagan gods that adorned its walls. This was God's way of showing the prophet that His people were guilty of breaking the first of the Ten Commandments: "Thou shalt have no other gods before me" (Exodus 20:3).

Pagan temples of the ancient world were decorated with images of false gods. God's people had adopted the pagan worship practices of the surrounding nations. They were marked for God's judgment unless they turned back to Him.

FACING TOWARD THE SUN

This was the worst case of idol worship among God's people pointed out to Ezekiel because these twenty-five men were priests. They were supposed to be pointing people toward the one true God. But instead they were sitting in front of the temple, bowing down toward the sun in worship.

Worship of the heavenly bodies, particularly the sun, was practiced by several pagan nations in Bible times (see note on Deuteronomy 4:19). The major deity of the Egyptians was the sun god known as Ra or Amon-Ra (see notes on Genesis 12:15 and Jeremiah 46:25).

A MAN WITH AN INKHORN

In Ezekiel's vision, he saw six men from the north arrive in Jerusalem. They probably represented the Babylonian army, whom God had appointed as His instrument of judgment against His people because of their sin and idolatry.

The prophet also saw a seventh man with a writing kit hanging on his belt. This kit contained quills, or pens, as well as a container of ink. The ink of Bible times consisted of soot or lampblack mixed with water (see note on Jeremiah 36:18). This man's task was to mark the righteous people of Jerusalem with his ink so they would be spared by God's destroyers (Ezekiel 9:4).

> *So I [Ezekiel] went in and saw; and behold every form of creeping [crawling, NIV] things, and abominable [detestable, NIV] beasts, and all the idols of the house of Israel, pourtrayed upon the wall round about.*
> EZEKIEL 8:10

> *At the door of the temple of the LORD. . .were about five and twenty men, with their backs toward the temple of the LORD, and their faces toward the east; and they worshipped the sun.*
> EZEKIEL 8:16

> *Six men came from. . .the north. . .and one man among them was clothed with linen, with a writer's inkhorn [writing kit, NIV] by his side.*
> EZEKIEL 9:2

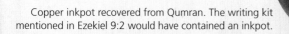

Copper inkpot recovered from Qumran. The writing kit mentioned in Ezekiel 9:2 would have contained an inkpot.

Useless as a Wild Vine

Shall wood be taken thereof [from a vine] to do any work? or will men take a pin [pegs, NIV] of it to hang any vessel thereon?
EZEKIEL 15:3

Ezekiel compared the nation of Judah to a wild vine. Just as a vine of this type yields no lumber—not even as much as a pin or peg to hang a pot on (see note on Isaiah 22:23)—so Judah had become useless to the Lord because of the sin and rebellion of the people.

Domestic vines such as the grape are useful because of the fruit they produce. Throughout their history, the Israelites were often spoken of as a fruitful vine (Genesis 49:22). But even a grapevine is useless if it fails to produce grapes (Jeremiah 2:21). Ezekiel looked in vain for the fruits of righteousness and holiness among the people of his time.

A Lion in a Pit

She [Judah] brought up one of her whelps [cubs, NIV]: it became a young lion. . . . The nations also heard of him; he was taken in their pit.
EZEKIEL 19:3–4

During the final days of the nation of Judah, King Jehoahaz was captured and taken to Egypt (2 Kings 23:31–34). This is probably the event to which Ezekiel referred in this verse. Although the king seemed ferocious like a "young lion," he was at the mercy of the Egyptians once he stumbled into their trap.

In Bible times lions and other large animals were often trapped in pits. The trappers dug a deep hole in the ground and covered it with tree limbs and a layer of dirt. Once the animal fell into the pit, it could be easily captured or killed.

The Royal Scepter

She [Judah] had strong rods for the sceptres of them that bare rule.
EZEKIEL 19:11

In this verse Ezekiel compared the nation of Judah to a vine. At one time this vine had runners so strong that they could have been made into a scepter for a king. But Judah had been reduced to a second-rate nation because of the people's sin and rebellion against the Lord.

A scepter was a rod, staff, or baton carried by a king to symbolize his power and authority. King Ahasuerus of Persia extended his golden scepter to welcome Queen Esther into his presence (see note on Esther 4:11).

The scepter in the hand of the Egyptian Sunusert I symbolized the power and authority of this political leader.

A Solemn Pledge

The Lord commanded His prophet Ezekiel to proclaim God's message to the people of Judah. Striking his hands together was Ezekiel's way of making a solemn pledge and promise: "Yes, Lord, I'll do exactly what you say."

Throughout the book of Ezekiel, God addressed the prophet with the title "son of man." It seems to mean that God had placed His hand on Ezekiel in a special way, empowering him as His designated spokesman to His wayward people.

Son of man, prophesy, and smite [strike, NIV] thine hands together.
EZEKIEL 21:14

Babylonian Sign-Reading

Ezekiel told the people of Judah that the king of Babylonia was coming into their territory on a mission of conquest. He would stop at a fork in the road and decide whether to take the road toward Jerusalem or to go the other way and attack the capital city of the Ammonites (Ezekiel 21:19–20).

To decide which road to take, the king would read the signs by using one of three possible methods. He might cast lots by drawing an arrow out of his quiver and throwing it down to see which way it pointed. He could consult his pagan gods. Or he could have one of his priests "read" the liver of a sacrificial animal and advise him on which city to attack.

Such superstitious sign-reading was practiced by the pagan nations of Bible times. But God declared black magic and divination off-limits to His people (see note on Deuteronomy 18:10–11).

The king of Babylon stood. . .at the head of the two ways [at the junction of the two roads, NIV], to use divination [seek an omen, NIV]: he made his arrows bright, he consulted with images, he looked in the liver.
EZEKIEL 21:21

A Tale of Two Sisters

One of Ezekiel's most famous prophecies is his portrayal of the nations of Israel (the Northern Kingdom) and Judah (the Southern Kingdom) as two adulterous sisters named Aholah and Aholibah (Ezekiel 23).

Both sisters lusted after the "desirable young men" of the surrounding nations. Ezekiel meant by this that both Israel and Judah turned away from the Lord and worshiped the pagan gods of their neighbors. God warned both nations that He would punish them for their sin unless they changed their behavior, but they refused.

Their sin eventually led to the downfall of both sisters. The Northern Kingdom fell to the Assyrians, and Judah was overrun by the Babylonians. Ironically, these were two of the nations or lovers with whom Aholah and Aholibah had committed adultery.

She [Aholibah] doted upon [lusted after, NIV] the Assyrians her neighbours, captains and rulers clothed most gorgeously, horsemen riding upon horses, all of them desirable young men.
EZEKIEL 23:12

BURIED WITH WEAPONS

They [the Egyptians] have laid their swords under their heads.

EZEKIEL 32:27

This verse appears among Ezekiel's prophecy against Egypt. It refers to the Egyptian custom of burying their fallen soldiers with their weapons of war.

Many soldiers of the ancient world slept with their weapons by their side, ready for instant action. So it was natural for the Egyptians to think that their warriors should take their weapons with them into the afterlife.

MESSAGES ON WOOD

The sticks whereon thou [Ezekiel] writest shall be in thine hand before their [Israel's and Judah's] eyes.

EZEKIEL 37:20

God told Ezekiel to write messages on two separate sticks, representing the nations of Judah (the Southern Kingdom) and Israel (the Northern Kingdom). Then he was to place the two sticks together. This represented the time when the two nations would become one again and be ruled over by the messianic king.

Messages were often written on long, narrow strips of wood in Bible times. The practice is referred to as early as the time of Moses (Numbers 17:2–3).

THE BATH

Ye shall have just balances [accurate scales, NIV], and a just ephah, and a just bath.

EZEKIEL 45:10

The bath was the standard unit by which liquids such as oil and wine were measured in Old Testament times. It was equal to about six gallons. The bath was equivalent in liquid measure to the ephah in dry measure (see note on Exodus 16:36).

This command from Ezekiel about honesty in buying and selling affirms the same principle spelled out in the Mosaic law (see note on Deuteronomy 25:13).

DANIEL

LOOTING OF THE TEMPLE

He [King Nebuchadnezzar] brought the vessels into the treasure house of his god.

DANIEL 1:2

When the Babylonian army captured and plundered the city of Jerusalem, King Nebuchadnezzar seized the golden utensils, spices, jewels, and other valuable items that belonged to the Jewish temple. He carried these valuables to Babylon, where he deposited them in the treasure house of a temple devoted to the worship of a pagan Babylonian god.

This fulfilled a prophecy that Isaiah had issued to the people of Judah about one hundred years before: "The days come, that all. . .which thy fathers have laid up in store. . .shall be carried to Babylon" (Isaiah 39:6).

BABYLONIAN GOURMET FOOD

Daniel and his three Jewish friends were in training for positions of responsibility in the court of King Nebuchadnezzar. It was customary for the king to feed such trainees from his own table.

The Babylonian kings were noted for their high living. They ate several different kinds of meat, bread made from finely ground flour, and delicious fruits. They drank the finest wine available. This was quite a contrast to the plain food that Daniel and his friends were accustomed to eating.

The four young Jewish men chose to eat vegetables ("pulse," KJV) and drink water instead of dining on the king's rich food. God blessed their decision by causing them to thrive on their common, everyday diet (Daniel 1:12–16).

The king [Nebuchadnezzar] appointed them [Daniel and other young Jewish men] a daily provision of the king's meat, and of the wine which he drank.
DANIEL 1:5

CRUEL AND UNUSUAL PUNISHMENT

This statement from King Nebuchadnezzar of Babylonia shows how cruel and demanding pagan kings of the ancient world could be. He threatened his own court magicians with this punishment if they could not reconstruct his own dream and tell him what the dream meant.

Execution by being hacked to pieces was a common practice in many nations of Bible times. This savagery was even committed against King Agag of Amalek by the prophet Samuel (1 Samuel 15:32–33).

Tearing down the house of a criminal and placing a curse on it was another method of punishment among the Babylonians and Persians. King Darius of Persia threatened such action against anyone who changed a royal decree (Ezra 6:11).

Ye [Babylonian magicians] shall be cut in pieces, and your houses shall be made a dunghill [piles of rubble, NIV].
DANIEL 2:5

BABYLONIAN MUSICAL INSTRUMENTS

Stone carvings from the ancient city of Babylon show that the Babylonians were fond of music. The six different musical instruments mentioned in this verse were probably part of a royal band that would play on cue to signal that the people should bow down in worship before the golden statue of their king.

The cornet was probably a type of horn. The flute was probably similar to the modern flute. Many scholars think the "harp" in this verse was similar to the modern guitar. The sackbut and psaltery are thought to be two different sizes of the harp, the sackbut being the larger of the two. The dulcimer, according to some authorities, may have given off a shrill sound like the modern bagpipe.

At what time ye hear the sound of the cornet, flute, harp, sackbut, psaltery, dulcimer. . .ye fall down and worship the golden image.
DANIEL 3:5

INTO THE FIRE

This furnace was big enough to hold Daniel's three friends—Shadrach, Meshach, and Abed-nego. It was probably a huge kiln used to cure bricks for the king's ambitious building projects (see note on Genesis 11:3). It was pressed into service as an execution chamber for anyone who refused to bow down and worship King Nebuchadnezzar as a god.

The heat from the fire was so intense that the guards who threw the three men into the furnace were burned to death (Daniel 3:22). But God delivered His three servants without so much as "an hair of their head singed" (Daniel 3:27).

UNCHANGEABLE PERSIAN LAWS

The enemies of Daniel in Persia asked King Darius to issue a law against worshiping any god other than the king himself. They knew this would trap Daniel, since he would refuse to bow down to any god other than the supreme Lord of the universe.

The ancient Medes and Persians considered their laws infallible and irreversible. Once a decree was ordered by the king, it could not be changed or wiped off the books. For example, the Persian law authorizing the extermination of the Jews in Esther's time was not canceled. But the king issued another decree warning the Jews about the death warrant and authorizing them to act in self-defense against their enemies (Esther 8:5–11).

PRAYING TOWARD JERUSALEM

1. In his prayer dedicating the temple, Solomon encouraged the people of Judah to remain faithful to God and always pray toward Jerusalem and the temple (2 Chronicles 6:34–35).
2. The psalmist vowed to God that he would worship "toward thy holy temple" (Psalms 5:7; 138:2).
3. From the stomach of the great fish, the repentant Jonah declared that he would "look toward thy holy temple" (Jonah 2:4).

DANIEL'S PATTERN OF PRAYER

Daniel's enemies succeeded in passing a law against anyone offering prayer to any god other than the Babylonian king, whom they considered divine. But Daniel ignored the law and continued to pray to the one true God.

Daniel prayed toward Jerusalem because that was the site of the Jewish temple, although it had been destroyed by the Babylonian army several years before. And his pattern was to pray three times during the day, probably at morning, noon, and night. This was the procedure followed by David: "Evening, and morning, and at noon, will I pray" (Psalm 55:17).

The Cyrus Cylinder detailing the defeat of Babylon by the Persians. In the days of Daniel, this defeat made Persian law the law of the land.

HOSEA

INDULGENT WORSHIP

The prophet Hosea condemned the people of the Northern Kingdom for their worship of Baal, a pagan fertility god (see note on Numbers 22:41). He described them as indulgent worshipers who loved "flagons of wine."

The Hebrew word rendered as "flagons of wine" by the King James Version is translated as "sacred raisin cakes" by the New International Version. This is probably a more accurate translation, since cakes made of raisins, or dried grapes, were considered a delicacy in Bible times. They may have been eaten in connection with immoral worship ceremonies at the altars of Baal.

The children of Israel. . . look to other gods, and love flagons of wine [sacred raisin cakes, NIV].
HOSEA 3:1

SILLY SUPERSTITIONS

In this verse Hosea condemned God's people for worshiping idols and using black magic and superstition in making decisions. The New International Version translates this verse, "They [God's people] consult a wooden idol and are answered by a stick of wood."

"Wooden idol" may refer to teraphim, or household gods, which people consulted for guidance and direction (see note on Genesis 31:19). "Stick of wood" probably refers to a stick with the bark peeled off on one side. People would toss the stick into the air, similar to flipping a coin, and

My people ask counsel at their stocks, and their staff declareth unto them.
HOSEA 4:12

make a decision based on the side of the stick that faced up when it fell to the ground.

God condemns such silly superstitions. We are to seek His will and direction by praying, reading the Bible, and following the leading of the Holy Spirit.

Relief from the Yoke

In this verse Hosea portrayed the love of God for His special people, the Israelites. Although they had rebelled against Him again and again, He kept pulling them back into His fellowship with "bands of love."

Hosea also compared the love of God to relief given to oxen when they were wearing heavy wooden yokes while working in the fields. These yokes had to be lifted up by their masters to enable the animals to lower their heads so they could eat or drink.

God is the great "yoke lifter" who shows mercy and love to His people (see note on Matthew 11:29–30).

GOOD AND BAD YOKES

1. Solomon's son and successor, Rehoboam, warned the people that he would intensify the yoke of oppression that they had endured during his father's reign. This led to the split of the united kingdom into two factions (1 Kings 12:1-19).
2. The prophet Jeremiah wore a yoke at God's command to signify the coming captivity and oppression of the nation of Judah by the Babylonians (Jeremiah 27:2-8).
3. Jesus declared that His yoke of grace, in comparison to the legalism of the Pharisees, was light and easy to carry (Matthew 11:29-30).
4. Paul admonished the Galatian believers not to return to the "yoke of bondage," or the Old Testament law (Galatians 5:1), because it did not provide salvation from sin.

Smoke through a Window

They [Israel] shall be. . . as the smoke out of the chimney [window, NIV].
HOSEA 13:3

Hosea prophesied the destruction of the Northern Kingdom (Israel) by the Lord, saying it would disappear like smoke from a fire.

In Bible times, cooking was done over an open fire or in a primitive oven (see notes on Genesis 18:6 and Leviticus 7:9). Houses did not have chimneys to let out the smoke. It passed outside through the window, as indicated by the New International Version.

JOEL

DESTRUCTION BY LOCUSTS

A locust plague, such as the one described by Joel in this verse, was one of the worst disasters that could happen in Bible times. Millions of these insects, similar to grasshoppers, would descend on the land and devour the crops. Scarcity of food—and even widespread starvation—could follow.

Joel's account of a swarm of locusts in his time details the four stages in the development of this destructive insect: (1) A hatchling emerges from the egg (palmerworm); (2) it develops wings and begins to fly (locust); (3) it becomes strong enough to begin eating vegetation (cankerworm); and (4) as a fully grown adult, it flies in a swarm with millions of others to do its most destructive work (caterpillar).

The eighth plague that God sent against the Egyptians to convince Pharaoh to release the Hebrew slaves was a swarm of locusts (Exodus 10:12–15).

> *That which the palmerworm hath left hath the locust eaten; and that which the locust hath left hath the cankerworm eaten; and that which the cankerworm hath left hath the caterpiller eaten.*
> JOEL 1:4

AMOS

BAD NEWS FOR THE WEALTHY

Two of God's highest expectations of His people, the Israelites, were that they would practice righteousness and show compassion toward the poor (see notes on Deuteronomy 24:10–11; Deuteronomy 24:12–13; and Deuteronomy 24:20). In this verse, Amos charged the wealthy class of Israel—the Northern Kingdom—with violating both of these commands.

They were so calloused toward righteousness that they

> *They [the wealthy class of Israel] sold the righteous for silver, and the poor for a pair of shoes [sandals, NIV].*
> AMOS 2:6

157

thought they could buy and sell it like any other commodity. Rather than treating the poor with fairness and justice, they were selling them into slavery because they could not pay their debts. Sometimes these debts were no more than the minor sum required to buy a cheap pair of sandals! Amos declared that God would judge the wealthy for such greed and lack of compassion.

OPPRESSION OF THE POOR

In this verse, Amos charged the wealthy class of the nation of Israel (the Northern Kingdom) with oppressing the poor and worshiping pagan gods.

By law, if a poor man put up his outer robe as security for a loan, the garment had to be returned to him by sundown so he could use it for a blanket (see note on Deuteronomy 24:12–13). But the rich were ignoring this law and even using the robes they had taken from the poor as pallets on which they could kneel down to worship in pagan temples.

Judges of Israel were fining the poor by taking their wine, then offering or drinking this wine as an act of worship before their pagan gods. Such flagrant acts of injustice and idolatry would be punished by the Lord.

IVORY HOUSES

They [the wealthy class of Israel] lay themselves down upon clothes laid to pledge by every altar, and they drink the wine of the condemned [wine taken as fines, NIV] in the house of their god.
AMOS 2:8

The houses of ivory [houses adorned with ivory, NIV] shall perish, and the great houses [mansions, NIV] shall have an end [be demolished, NIV], saith the LORD.
AMOS 3:15

Amos declared that the opulent houses of the rich and famous of Samaria would be overthrown when the Lord exercised His judgment against the nation of Israel.

Ivory, from the tusks of elephants, was often used as decorative trim on the houses and household furnishings of kings and the wealthy in Bible times (see note on 1 Kings 10:18).

Ivory decorations. Wealthy Israelites who ignored the needs of the poor and decorated their homes with ivory felt the sting of Amos's criticism.

King Ahab of Israel lived in an "ivory house," or a palace adorned with ivory trim (1 Kings 22:39).

No Place for Horses

The answer to this rhetorical question was obviously "No." Horseshoes to protect a horse's hooves were unknown in Bible times, so horses did not run on rocks. This would cause serious injury to their feet.

Amos was pointing out the foolish actions of the nation of Israel. Their idolatry was senseless, and it would bring them to ruin.

Shall horses run upon the rock?
Amos 6:12

Amos and Sycamore Figs

Amos was a lowly shepherd from the tiny village of Tekoa (Amos 1:1) in Judah (the Southern Kingdom). But he was called to declare God's judgment against the rich people of the neighboring nation, Israel (the Northern Kingdom). This verse shows that he did not claim to be a learned and sophisticated messenger. His only credential was his call from the Lord.

The "sycamore fruit" that Amos mentioned was a type of wild fig that grew in his native Judah. These figs were inferior in quality to the domesticated figs that are mentioned several times in the Bible (Numbers 13:23; 1 Samuel 25:18; Mark 11:12–21). Only the poorest people of the land grew and ate sycamore figs.

I [Amos] was no prophet, neither was I a prophet's son; but I was an herdman [shepherd, NIV], and a gatherer of sycamore fruit.
Amos 7:14

Sycamore tree with figs. God called Amos, a herdsman and gatherer of sycamore figs, to declare God's judgment on Israel.

A Sifting God

Before grain was ground into flour, it was sifted in a sieve to remove any dirt or sand that had become mixed in with the grain during the harvesting process (see note on Ruth 3:2). The larger grain would remain in the sieve while the smaller dirt particles would fall through the sieve to the ground.

Amos used this image to show what God planned to do with the nation of Israel. He would sift out the righteous of the land—the grain—and form them into a remnant that He would restore to the land one day. But the wicked and unrepentant—the dirt—would fall to the ground and experience His wrath and judgment.

I [God] will sift the house of Israel among all nations, like as corn [grain, NIV] is sifted in a sieve, yet shall not the least grain fall upon the earth.
Amos 9:9

OBADIAH

The pride of thine heart hath deceived thee [Edom], thou that dwellest in the clefts of the rock, whose habitation is high; that saith in his heart, Who shall bring me down to the ground?

Obadiah 1:3

BROUGHT LOW BY THE LORD

The prophet Obadiah delivered his brief prophecy against the Edomites, ancient enemies of the Israelites. In 587 BC, the people of Edom had joined in the looting of the city of Jerusalem when it was ransacked by the Babylonian army.

Edomite cities were built on the high cliffs and crags of the mountains around the Dead Sea. They thought they were invincible in these strongholds. But Obadiah declared that they would be brought low by the Lord because of their mistreatment of His people.

The cities of Edom were built in the mountains high above their enemies.

JONAH

A Perilous Storm

The prophet Jonah thought he could get away from God's call by fleeing in a ship to another country. But God stopped him by sending a ferocious storm.

The crew of the ship must have been from many different countries, since they cried out in despair to their own individual gods. They showed how desperate their situation was when they began dumping the cargo overboard. The heavier the ship, the greater the danger that it would be torn apart.

This same action was taken by the sailors on the ship in which Paul was traveling to Rome. They ditched its load of wheat just before it ran aground in a fierce storm (see note on Acts 27:29).

The mariners [sailors, NIV] were afraid, and cried every man unto his god, and cast forth the wares [cargo, NIV] that were in the ship into the sea.
JONAH 1:5

Superstitious Sailors

Sailors of ancient times tended to be very superstitious because of their constant exposure to the dangers of the sea. When a storm struck the ship in which Jonah was escaping from the call of the Lord, they assumed the pagan gods were punishing them because of their displeasure with one person on board.

To find out who this person was, they cast lots—a custom similar to rolling dice or drawing straws in modern times. These lots may have been round stones or flat sticks of various lengths. Exactly what they looked like is not known (see note on Proverbs 18:18).

The casting of lots as a method of decision making is mentioned several times in the Bible (Leviticus 16:8–10; Numbers 33:54; Joshua 14:2; 1 Chronicles 25:8–9; Acts 1:26).

Come, and let us [sailors on Jonah's ship] cast lots, that we may know for whose cause this evil [calamity, NIV] is upon us.
JONAH 1:7

MICAH

Then shall the seers be ashamed, and the diviners confounded [disgraced, NIV]: yea, they shall all cover their lips [faces, NIV]; for there is no answer of God.

MICAH 3:7

They shall sit every man under his vine and under his fig tree; and none shall make them afraid.

MICAH 4:4

A SAD SITUATION

Micah pictured the prophets as calling on God and receiving no answer. Then they covered their faces in a gesture of mourning because of the Lord's silence. Lepers were also required to cover the lower part of their faces as a sign of mourning about their disease (Leviticus 13:45). The prophet Ezekiel also referred to this custom (Ezekiel 24:17, 22).

SITTING IN THE SHADE

Micah used these word pictures to portray the future of God's people. After the coming of the Messiah, they would enjoy peace and prosperity, symbolized by resting in the shade.

In the hot, dry climate of Palestine, people often escaped from the sun's oppressive heat by sitting under a grapevine or fig tree. Its thick branches and broad leaves made the fig tree an ideal shade.

When Philip found Nathanael and brought him to Jesus, Nathanael was sitting under a fig tree. He was probably resting in its shade, perhaps meditating on God's Word (John 1:45–51).

NAHUM

ASSYRIAN DRINKING CUSTOMS

The prophet Nahum declared God's judgment against the nobility of Nineveh, capital city of the Assyrian Empire. In this verse he pictured a wild drinking party for which the Assyrians were well known.

Stone monuments recovered from archaeological sites in ancient Assyria show the king and his aides in drinking scenes at elaborate banquets. They have their wine glasses raised in a toast, while servants stand at a large vat of wine, ready to refill their glasses.

The Persian nobles were also known for their excessive drinking practices (see note on Esther 1:8).

While they [the nobles of Nineveh] are drunken as drunkards, they shall be devoured [consumed, NIV] as stubble fully dry.
NAHUM 1:10

Nahum's description of an Assyrian drinking party is captured in this seventh-century BC relief.

ASSYRIAN TERROR

Nahum's description of Assyrian warriors and their battle gear shows why they struck terror in the hearts of those who faced them in battle.

Their uniforms were scarlet in color, and they carried shields painted red, or perhaps overlaid with copper. They may have used these colors to make the blood from their

The shield of his mighty men is made red, the valiant men [warriors, NIV] are in scarlet: the chariots shall be with flaming torches in the day of his preparation.
NAHUM 2:3

163

wounds hard to see. In hand-to-hand combat, they wanted to give no sign that would infuse the enemy with hope and courage.

The "flaming torches" on their war chariots may have been whirling blades on the axles designed to immobilize the wheels of enemy chariots. Or this could refer to the weapons in their chariots that flashed in the sunlight, giving the appearance of burning torches.

Assyria was noted for its cruelty in warfare. Their warriors would cut off the feet and hands of captives as a terror tactic to intimidate nations into surrendering to their rule (see note on Judges 1:6).

TREADING THE CLAY

In a mocking tone, Nahum called on the citizens of Nineveh to fortify the city with new bricks to prepare for the coming attack. It would be in vain, since God was determined to overthrow the evil city.

To "tread the morter" was to temper the clay to get it ready for making bricks. This was done by laborers who trampled on the clay with their bare feet. Clay for making pottery was tempered in the same way (Isaiah 41:25).

HABAKKUK

WORSHIP OF WEAPONS

They [Babylonian warriors] sacrifice unto their net, and burn incense unto their drag [dragnet, NIV].

HABAKKUK 1:16

This verse apparently refers to the practice among the pagan Babylonians of worshiping and offering sacrifices to their weapons of war. The Babylonians were on a mission of world conquest in Habakkuk's time. Bowing down to these weapons was the Babylonians' way of strengthening and dedicating themselves for this purpose.

This pagan practice made it difficult for Habakkuk to accept the reality that God would use the Babylonians as an instrument of judgment against His own people, the nation of Judah.

God's Naked Bow

The prophet Habakkuk was assured by the Lord that He would deal with the Babylonians after He had used them as an agent of punishment against His own people. He would make His bow "naked," or take it out of its protective case, in order to use it against the Babylonians.

Baring the bow was a symbol of getting ready for war, just like uncovering the shield (see note on Isaiah 22:6).

Thy [God's] bow was made quite naked.
HABAKKUK 3:9

ZEPHANIAH

Mockery and Ridicule

The prophet Zephaniah declared that God would eventually punish the Assyrians for their cruelty and pagan worship (see notes on Judges 1:6 and Nahum 2:3). Their capital city, Nineveh, would become a laughingstock among the nations.

People would express their delight at Nineveh's downfall by heaping contempt on the city. Hissing by passing air through one's teeth and shaking the fist were expressions of mockery and ridicule.

The prophet Jeremiah painted a similar picture of the mockery of Jerusalem after it fell to the Babylonian army in 587 BC (Lamentations 2:15).

Every one that passeth by her [Nineveh] shall hiss [scoff, NIV], and wag his hand [shake their fists, NIV].
ZEPHANIAH 2:15

HAGGAI

THIRTY VESSELS SHORT

When one came to the pressfat [wine vat, NIV] for to draw out fifty vessels out of the press, there were but twenty.
HAGGAI 2:16

The Hebrew word rendered as "pressfat" by the King James Version refers to a winepress or an olive press. These stone presses were used in Bible times to squeeze the oil out of olives for making fuels to burn in lamps or to press the juice out of grapes for making wine.

Haggai declared that God would give the people less harvest than they expected unless they reordered their priorities and resumed the task of rebuilding the temple. Believers can't shirk their responsibility to God and expect Him to shower them with blessings.

ZERUBBABEL AS A SIGNET RING

In that day. . .will I [God] take thee, O Zerubbabel. . .and will make thee as a signet [signet ring, NIV]: for I have chosen thee, saith the LORD of hosts.
HAGGAI 2:23

In ancient times a signet ring functioned much like a personal signature does today. A king or other high official would stamp an official document with the symbol on his ring to establish its legality and show that it was issued under his authority.

God compared Zerubbabel, the Jewish governor of Jerusalem, to a signet ring. He had invested Zerubbabel with the highest honor and would use him as His representative to bring about His purposes in the city of Jerusalem.

When the pharaoh of Egypt appointed Joseph to a high position in his administration, he gave Joseph his signet ring to show that he had the authority to act on his behalf (see note on Genesis 41:42).

Olives were pressed between the vertical and horizontal stones of this limestone press.

ZECHARIAH

THE MONTH OF SEBAT

Zechariah had eight visions that he recorded in his book. In this verse he tells us the exact month and day on which his first vision occurred. The Jewish month of Sebat closely parallels our month of February.

Many scholars believe this vision of the prophet—a man on a red horse among the myrtle trees (Zechariah 1:8)—can be precisely dated at February 24, 519 BC, by using the phrase "the second year of Darius." We know from secular history that King Darius began his reign over Persia in about 521 BC.

> *Upon the four and twentieth day of the eleventh month, which is the month Sebat [Shebat, NIV], in the second year of Darius came the word of the LORD unto Zechariah.*
> ZECHARIAH 1:7

HOLINESS AND HORSES

Zechariah foresaw a future time when all of the nations would worship the one true God. The praise of the Lord would be so widespread that even horses would have "HOLINESS UNTO THE LORD" inscribed on the bells on their harnesses. These are the same words embroidered on the hat worn by the high priest of Israel (Exodus 28:36).

It was customary among the nations of Bible times to hang bells on the harnesses of their warhorses. This gave them a regal military appearance. The noise produced by the bells also may have conditioned the horses for the noise of battle.

> *In that day shall there be upon the bells of the horses, HOLINESS UNTO THE LORD.*
> ZECHARIAH 14:20

MALACHI

He [God] is like a refiner's fire, and like fullers' [launderer's, NIV] soap.
MALACHI 3:2

A Purifying and Cleansing God

Malachi used these images to show that God would purify and cleanse in judgment against the wicked in the end times. A refiner worked metal by heating the ore in a metal pot, then skimming the dross off the top to leave the pure metal. A launderer washed clothes by using a strong alkali soap to remove dirt and stains.

God's Book of Remembrance

A book [scroll, NIV] of remembrance was written before him [God] for them that feared the LORD.
MALACHI 3:16

God promised through Malachi that He would write in a "book of remembrance" the names of all the people who honored and worshiped Him.

This metaphor probably comes from the ancient Persian custom of keeping an official record of those who rendered special service to the king. King Ahasuerus of Persia was looking through such a book when he discovered that Mordecai the Jew had saved him from an assassination plot (Esther 6:1–2).

JOSEPH AND MARY'S BETROTHAL

In Bible times, a marriage was arranged through a legal agreement between the parents of the groom and the bride (see note on Genesis 24:4). The groom's parents selected a woman for their son to marry, then paid the bride's parents a dowry, or bride-price, to compensate them for the loss of her services as a daughter.

The period between the time of this legal agreement and the actual marriage of the couple was known as the betrothal. The future groom and bride were espoused or pledged to each other during this time in a formal agreement that was as legally binding as marriage itself. The betrothal could be broken only by a legal proceeding similar to a divorce.

It was during the time of her betrothal to Joseph that Mary discovered she was pregnant. This was certainly grounds for Joseph and his family to dissolve their marriage agreement with Mary and her parents.

But Joseph was informed by an angel that Mary's pregnancy was due to the miraculous action of the Holy Spirit. This child from her womb would be the Messiah, the Son of God, who would "save his people from their sins" (Matthew 1:21).

Joseph believed this message from the Lord, and he proceeded with his plans to take Mary as his wife (Matthew 1:24).

When as his mother Mary was espoused [pledged to be married, NIV] to Joseph, before they came together, she was found with child of [through, NIV] the Holy Ghost [Holy Spirit, NIV].
MATTHEW 1:18

Fragment of a Palestinian marriage contract. Such a contract would have governed the betrothal of Joseph and Mary.

When Jesus was born in Bethlehem of Judaea in the days of Herod the king, behold, there came wise men [Magi, NIV] from the east to Jerusalem.

MATTHEW 2:1

WORSHIPERS FROM AFAR

These "wise men" were members of a priestly caste known as the Magi who practiced the art of astrology. They believed the sun, moon, and stars gave off periodic signs that foretold future events and the destiny of individuals and nations. They probably came from the territory of ancient Babylonia, since this nation had a prominent class of magicians and wizards who read the signs of the stars (see note on Isaiah 47:13).

This verse shows that Jesus' birth had worldwide implications. Although born a Jew in Jewish territory, He was worshiped from the very beginning by other nations—represented by these pagan magicians—as one who was destined to become a universal king.

A popular Christmas carol ("We Three Kings of Orient Are") that identifies these people as rulers who were three in number has no biblical basis. The number three has been assumed from the number of gifts they presented to the young Jesus (Matthew 2:11).

NO SPECTACULAR STUNTS

The devil taketh him [Jesus] up into the holy city [Jerusalem], and setteth him on a pinnacle [the highest point, NIV] of the temple.

MATTHEW 4:5

Satan tempted Jesus at the beginning of His ministry to cater to the masses with a spectacular performance. He could leap off the highest point of the temple without suffering injury. This would prove without question that He was the Messiah.

This would have been an impressive stunt, since the highest point of the temple was built at the edge of a sheer cliff that plunged 350 feet into the Kidron Valley. But Jesus refused to give in to Satan's temptation. He would not use His divine powers to dazzle the crowds and win them over with cheap tricks.

SALT OF THE EARTH

Ye [followers of Jesus] are the salt of the earth: but if the salt have lost his savour [loses its saltiness, NIV], wherewith shall it be salted? it is thenceforth good for nothing.

MATTHEW 5:13

Salt added flavor to food, and it was also used to preserve meat in a society in which refrigeration and cold storage did not exist.

SIGNIFICANCE OF SALT

1. While fleeing from the cities of Sodom and Gomorrah, Lot's wife looked back and was turned into a pillar of salt (Genesis 19:26).
2. The everlasting covenant, or agreement, between God and His people was called "a covenant of salt" because of its durability and permanence (Numbers 18:19).
3. Because of its salty water, the Dead Sea was also referred to as the "salt sea" (Joshua 12:3).
4. A barren valley south of the Dead Sea where David won a victory over the Syrians was called the valley of salt (2 Samuel 8:13).

Jesus used the imagery of salt to describe His followers. If they did not demonstrate their distinctive purity and holiness as His people, they would have no influence in the world. Christians have no higher calling than to serve as the "salt of the earth" in a sinful and decadent culture.

FULFILLMENT OF THE LAW

The Old Testament law as revealed to Moses was written in the Hebrew language. The "jot" was the Hebrew character known as the *yodh*. Similar to our English apostrophe, it was the smallest letter in the Hebrew alphabet. A "tittle" was a small mark placed on the edge of certain letters to distinguish them from one another.

Thus, Jesus was saying that even the most minute part of the Old Testament law would be fulfilled in Him and the gospel of grace that He came to bring into the world.

One jot or one tittle shall in no wise pass from the law, till all be fulfilled.
MATTHEW 5:18

WATCH YOUR WORDS

The Old Testament law taught that crimes such as slander and murder were wrong. But Jesus went beyond these actions to the thought, motives, or words behind them.

Raca was a term of contempt meaning "empty one" or "vain fellow." Anyone who uttered this word against another person could be charged with slander before the Jewish Council, or the Sanhedrin.

But according to Jesus, to call someone a fool was an even more serious offense. This was a way of uttering a curse against a person and consigning his soul to hell. Anyone who did this was in danger of being sent to the very punishment he wished upon another.

Whosoever shall say to his brother, Raca, shall be in danger of the council: but whosoever shall say, Thou fool, shall be in danger of hell fire.
MATTHEW 5:22

BE QUICK TO ADMIT WRONGDOING

Jesus knew that people tend to justify themselves and defend their actions even when they are wrong. He used this image from Roman law to show that it should be different with believers.

An accused person should try to settle a dispute before it gets to court. Otherwise, the judge's verdict might be severe. In the same way, believers should quickly admit their sin to God and seek His forgiveness day by day. Unconfessed sin can lead a believer farther and farther away from the Lord.

Agree [settle matters, NIV] with thine adversary quickly, whiles thou art in the way with him; lest at any time the adversary deliver thee to the judge.
MATTHEW 5:25

DO NOT RETALIATE

Ye have heard that it hath been said, An eye for an eye, and a tooth for a tooth.
MATTHEW 5:38

The law of retaliation in the Old Testament permitted a person to put out an eye or knock out a tooth of an offender who had inflicted such injuries upon him (Exodus 21:23–25). But Jesus calls for a higher code of behavior from His followers. ("Whosoever shall smite thee on thy right cheek, turn to him the other also," Matthew 5:39.)

Nonretaliation and forgiveness will stop the cycle of retaliation and leave vengeance where it belongs—in the hands of the Lord (Romans 12:19).

GO THE SECOND MILE

Whosoever shall compel thee to go a mile, go with him twain [two, NIV].
MATTHEW 5:41

In New Testament times, Palestine was occupied by Rome. By law, Roman soldiers could press Jewish citizens into service by compelling them to carry their equipment or some other burden for a distance of one mile.

Jesus used this image to show the attitude that should characterize His followers. In the spirit of Christ, the ultimate Servant, we should serve others above and beyond the call of duty.

CUT THE TRUMPETS

When thou doest thine alms [give to the needy, NIV], do not sound a trumpet before thee, as the hypocrites do in the synagogues and in the streets, that they may have glory of men.
MATTHEW 6:2

Giving to the poor was a commendable custom among the Jewish people (Deuteronomy 24:19–22). But the scribes and Pharisees did so with great fanfare so others would notice their generosity.

Jesus condemned this hypocritical attitude in giving. His advice to the people was to "cut the trumpets"—to give quietly and discreetly from a generous heart with no ulterior motives.

There is no evidence that the scribes and Pharisees actually blew trumpets to call attention to their giving. Jesus used this word picture to show how ridiculous their outward display looked to others. Even today, to "blow one's own horn" is to flaunt one's own good deeds and accomplishments.

AUTHENTIC PRAYER

When ye pray, use not vain repetitions [do not keep on babbling, NIV], as the heathen do: for they think that they shall be heard for their much speaking.
MATTHEW 6:7

The word translated as "babbling" by the New International Version means speaking without thinking. Pagan people of the ancient world called on their gods by repeating stock phrases and legalistic formulas over and over again. In their contest with Elijah on Mount Carmel, for example, the prophets of Baal called out "from morning even until noon, saying, O Baal, hear us" (1 Kings 18:26).

What a contrast this is to Jesus' approach to prayer. He taught His disciples to place their daily needs before the

Lord with confidence. Prayer is not heaping up meaning-less words but engaging in sincere communication with our heavenly Father (Matthew 6:9–13).

A HEALING TOUCH

In Bible times, lepers were people with a dreaded skin disease that caused them to be quarantined from the rest of the community. According to the Old Testament law, they were considered unclean, and it was their duty to warn people not to approach them.

Behold, there came a leper and worshipped him [Jesus].
MATTHEW 8:2

This leper who approached Jesus was breaking the law by doing so. This shows how desperately he wanted to be made well. And Jesus also violated social custom by reaching out and touching the man in a compassionate act of healing.

TOTAL PARALYSIS

The word *palsy* is used in the King James Version to describe a person who is totally paralyzed. The Gospels use this word only of the man whose friends let him down through the roof of a house on a blanket so he could be healed by Jesus.

The disabled man's friends did not let the thronging crowds prevent them from getting their friend to Jesus (Matthew 9:6).

Matthew's Gospel eliminates the details about this man's being let down through the roof. But scholars believe this is the same healing miracle—with these details added—reported by Mark and Luke. (Matthew 9:1–6; see also Mark 2:1–12; Luke 5:17–26).

The apostle Peter also healed a man who was totally paralyzed (Acts 9:32–34).

Then saith he [Jesus] to the sick of the palsy [the paralytic, NIV], Arise, take up thy bed.
MATTHEW 9:6

EATING WITH TAX COLLECTORS

Matthew, author of the Gospel of Matthew, was a Jewish citizen who collected taxes from his countrymen for the Roman government. After Jesus called Matthew to become one of His disciples, Matthew invited some of his tax collector friends to his home for a meal with Jesus and His other disciples.

The Pharisees criticized Jesus for associating with tax

As Jesus sat at meat in the house [Matthew's house, NIV], behold, many publicans [tax collectors, NIV] and sinners came and sat down with him and his disciples.
MATTHEW 9:10

173

collectors and other people whom they considered outcasts and sinners. Tax collectors were hated by the Jewish people because they considered them traitors who cooperated with the Romans to drain their country of its resources (see note on Luke 5:27).

But Jesus replied that His mission was to seek and to save people like Matthew and his friends. "They that be whole need not a physician," He said, "but they that are sick" (Matthew 9:12).

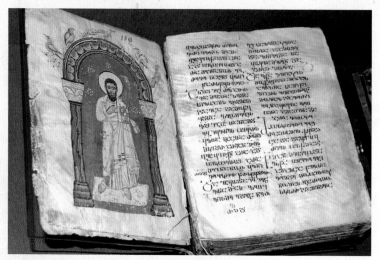

An ancient edition of the Gospel of Matthew with an illustration depicting the Evangelist.

ANIMAL SKIN CONTAINERS

Neither do men put new wine into old bottles [wineskins, NIV]: else the bottles [skins, NIV] break, and the wine runneth out, and the bottles perish [wineskins will be ruined, NIV]: but they put new wine into new bottles [wineskins, NIV], and both are preserved.
MATTHEW 9:17

In Bible times, many containers for liquids such as water, olive oil, and wine were made from the skins of animals, particularly young goats. After the head and feet were cut off, the skin was stripped in one piece from the animal's body. These skins retained the shape of the animal, with the neck sometimes serving as the channel through which the container was filled and emptied.

In this verse Jesus referred to these skin containers to show that the old age of the law was not compatible with the new age of grace that He brought to the world. Just as old, brittle wineskins would burst under the process of fermenting new wine, so His new age of grace demanded a radical departure from the traditions of the past.

SHREWD AND GENTLE

Be ye therefore wise [shrewd, NIV] as serpents, and harmless [innocent, NIV] as doves.
MATTHEW 10:16

With these words, Jesus sent out His twelve disciples on a mission of preaching, teaching, and healing throughout the countryside.

He wanted them to be aware of the dangers they faced and to use their cleverness and ingenuity to secure a hearing for the gospel. But they also were to be blameless and innocent at the same time. As representatives of Christ, they were to treat all whom they met with kindness and respect.

Shout It Out

Jesus had spoken to His disciples in private about many things—repentance, forgiveness, prayer, the kingdom of God, righteousness, and service. Now it was their duty to proclaim these truths openly to others.

Preaching "upon the housetops" is a metaphor for speaking boldly for the Lord. Jesus may have picked up this metaphor from town criers who stood on elevated platforms to read official announcements to the crowds.

What ye hear in the ear [What is whispered in your ear, NIV], that preach ye upon the housetops [from the roofs, NIV].
Matthew 10:27

Valuable to God

Poor people who could not afford a large animal such as a goat or a calf to offer as a sacrifice were allowed to bring two birds instead (Luke 2:24). These common birds could be purchased with a Roman coin known as a farthing.

A farthing was equivalent to one-tenth of a denarius. Since one denarius was the typical wage for a day's work by a common laborer, a farthing was worth about one hour of work.

Jesus used these insignificant items—sparrows and a farthing—to show His disciples that no one is unworthy in God's sight. "Fear ye not therefore," He told them, "ye are of more value than many sparrows" (Matthew 10:31).

Are not two sparrows sold for a farthing [penny, NIV]? and one of them shall not fall on the ground without your Father.
Matthew 10:29

Not in the Game

Children of Bible times, just like kids today, played games of make-believe. These children described by Jesus were pretending to be attending weddings and funerals. They called all their friends to join the fun, but some refused to play.

Jesus compared the scribes and Pharisees to these don't-want-to-play children. He had come to bring God's grace and forgiveness to all people. But these self-righteous religious leaders stood on the sidelines, refusing to accept His offer of abundant life and resenting those who were in the game.

It is like unto children sitting in the markets. . .and saying, We have piped [played the flute, NIV] unto you, and ye have not danced; we have mourned unto you [we sang a dirge, NIV], and ye have not lamented [did not mourn, NIV].
Matthew 11:16–17

An Easy Yoke

A yoke was a wooden collar placed on the neck of an ox to which plows and other farming implements were attached (see note on Hosea 11:4). Jesus used the yoke in this passage as a metaphor for commitment to Him and His teachings.

Compared to the burdensome teachings of the Pharisees,

Take my [Jesus'] yoke upon you, and learn of me. . .and ye shall find rest unto [for, NIV] your souls. For my yoke is easy, and my burden is light.
Matthew 11:29–30

Jesus' yoke was light and easy to wear. It did not chafe or bind, as did their legalistic rules. Anyone who wore His yoke would actually find rest, relief, and hope in His gospel of grace and forgiveness.

EATING GRAIN OFF THE STALK

While passing by a field of wheat or barley on the Sabbath, Jesus' disciples stripped some grain from the stalks. They rubbed it in their hands to remove the outer husks, then popped the grain into their mouths.

Wheat or barley was usually ground into flour, then baked into bread. But when bread was not available, eating grain right off the stalk was a quick way to satisfy one's hunger.

The Old Testament law permitted hungry travelers to pick and eat handfuls of grain from fields along the road (Deuteronomy 23:25).

His [Jesus'] disciples were an hungred, and began to pluck the ears of corn [heads of grain, NIV], and to eat.
MATTHEW 12:1

A STANDING TESTIMONY

In this verse Jesus referred to the repentance of the citizens of Nineveh, the capital city of Assyria, when they heard the prophet Jonah's message of judgment (Jonah 3:5–10). These pagan Gentiles were actually more responsive to God's message than His own people, the Jews, to whom Jesus preached.

The phrase "rise in judgment" may refer to the custom followed in courts of that time. A witness was asked to stand when accusing another person or bearing testimony on his behalf.

The men of Nineveh shall rise in judgment with this generation, and shall condemn it.
MATTHEW 12:41

TARES AMONG THE WHEAT

The tares or weeds described by Jesus in this parable were probably worthless plants known as "darnel." They looked almost exactly like wheat plants. It was difficult to tell them apart until the wheat began to form grain on the stalks.

The message of the parable is that good and evil are often intermingled in this world. It is difficult to distinguish between counterfeit believers and authentic Christian disciples. But they will be separated by the Lord at the final judgment.

But while men slept, his enemy came and sowed tares [weeds, NIV] among the wheat.
MATTHEW 13:25

PRECIOUS TREASURE

Banks did not exist in Bible times. People hid their money and other valuables in their houses and even buried them in waterproof containers on their property.

In this parable, Jesus told about a man who found a

The kingdom of heaven is like unto treasure hid in a field; the which when a man hath found, he. . .selleth all that he hath, and buyeth that field.
MATTHEW 13:44

forgotten treasure that had been buried in a field many years before. He sold everything he owned in order to buy the field and take possession of the treasure.

The message of this parable is that the kingdom of heaven is life's greatest treasure. We should be willing to give up everything in order to become citizens of this heavenly kingdom.

Separating the Fish

The message of this parable is the same as that of the tares and the wheat. In this life it may be difficult to tell the difference between token believers and authentic disciples. But the Lord will separate them out at the final judgment, just as commercial fishermen cull the worthless fish caught in their nets from the good fish.

> *The kingdom of heaven is like unto a net, that was cast into the sea, and gathered of every kind [caught all kinds of fish, NIV].*
> Matthew 13:47

Jesus compared the kingdom of heaven to a cast net.
This net encircled and captured all kinds of fish when it was used.

Delegated Authority

Giving a person a key was a symbol of delegated authority (see note on Isaiah 22:22). Jesus used this metaphor to show that He was delegating to Peter and the other apostles the power and responsibility of carrying on His work after His death, resurrection, and ascension.

This authority to proclaim the gospel and to carry on the work of Christ in the world continues today through the church.

> *I [Jesus] will give unto thee [Peter] the keys of the kingdom of heaven: and whatsoever thou shalt bind on earth shall be bound in heaven: and whatsoever thou shalt loose on earth shall be loosed in heaven.*
> Matthew 16:19

177

A Tax for the Temple

They [the temple officials] that received tribute money came to Peter, and said, Doth not your master [Jesus] pay tribute [the temple tax, NIV]?
MATTHEW
17:24

An annual tax, required of every Jewish male, was designated for maintenance and support of the temple in Jerusalem. Perhaps the temple officials who collected this tax approached Peter about paying it because Jesus and His disciples were hard to pin down. Their teaching and healing ministry kept them moving from place to place.

The New International Version translates the Greek word for "tribute money" in this verse as "two-drachma tax." The standard Greek coin of that time was the drachma. It took two of these coins to pay the tax.

The drachma was roughly equivalent to the Roman coin known as the denarius. A common laborer of Bible times would often be paid one denarius for a full day's work (see note on Matthew 20:2).

A Roman denarius minted in honor of Emperor Tiberias.

Drowning by a Millstone

Jesus specified this punishment for any person who would lead little children astray. He probably had in mind the grinding stones on a hand mill that were used to make wheat or barley into flour.

The grain was crushed by rotating an upper millstone against a stationary lower stone. These millstones were about three feet across, so one could easily be hung around a person's neck.

It were better for him that a millstone were hanged about his neck, and that he were drowned in the depth of the sea.
MATTHEW 18:6

Forced to Pay Up

This verse comes from Jesus' famous parable of the unforgiving servant. This servant's indebtedness to his master was written off. But the servant refused to do the same for people who owed him money. So his master threw him into debtor's prison to force him to pay up.

The "tormentors" in this passage were keepers of the prison who were allowed to torture debtors to force them to pay. This tactic often caused his family or friends to come forward to settle his accounts.

His lord was wroth [in anger, NIV], and delivered him to the tormentors [turned him over to the jailers to be tortured, NIV], till he should pay all that was due unto him.
MATTHEW 18:34

Bless the Children

It was customary among Jewish parents to bring their young children to a rabbi or other noted religious figure for his prayer and blessing. The laying on of hands signified the Lord's favor.

Perhaps the disciples thought Jesus was too busy with

Then were there brought unto him [Jesus] little children, that he should put his hands on them, and pray.
MATTHEW 19:13

other more important matters to be bothered with blessing children. But Jesus welcomed the little ones and "placed his hands on them" (Matthew 19:15) to give them His blessing.

A Denarius a Day

This verse comes from Jesus' parable of the vineyard workers. The vineyard owner hired people at several different times during the day to work in his vineyard. But at the end of the day, he paid each of them the same amount—a denarius—for his work.

The denarius was the main silver coin issued by the Roman government. During New Testament times, one denarius was the wage paid for a day's work by a common laborer.

This coin apparently was engraved with the image of the reigning Roman emperor. When the Pharisees tried to trick Jesus with a question about paying taxes to Rome, He asked them to show Him one of these silver coins. He noted the image of the emperor on the coin, then declared, "Render therefore unto Caesar the things which are Caesar's; and unto God the things that are God's" (Matthew 22:21).

Waiting for Work

This verse is also part of Jesus' parable of the vineyard workers. When the owner of the vineyard wanted to hire more laborers, he went looking for them in the marketplace, probably the place where goods were sold near the main gate of the city (see note on Genesis 19:1).

The marketplace was also the gathering place for laborers who were looking for work. Even today, common laborers will sometimes gather on designated street corners in large cities, hoping to find an employer for the day.

Daily Payment of Wages

Life for most people of Bible times was a hand-to-mouth existence, so it was customary to pay laborers at the end of each workday. They needed the money to buy food for their families for the next day.

This custom was also sanctioned by the law of Moses: "The wages of him that is hired shall not abide with thee all night until the morning" (Leviticus 19:13).

Sitting by the King

This request from the mother of two of Jesus' disciples shows that she minsunderstood the nature of His mission. Jesus had come as a spiritual Savior, but she thought He was establishing an earthly kingdom over which He would

When he [the vineyard owner] had agreed with the labourers for a penny [denarius, NIV] a day, he sent them into his vineyard.
MATTHEW 20:2

He [the vineyard owner] went out about the third hour, and saw others standing idle in the marketplace.
MATTHEW 20:3

When even was come, the lord of the vineyard saith unto his steward, Call the labourers, and give them their hire [wages, NIV].
MATTHEW 20:8

Grant that these my [mother of James and John] two sons may sit, the one on thy [Jesus'] right hand, and the other on the left, in thy kingdom.
MATTHEW 20:21

preside as king. She wanted her two sons to serve as His chief aides and advisers.

Sitting beside a king was a symbol of power and authority. The person at his right side had the post of highest honor (Psalm 80:17). Even today, we refer to a leader's most trusted aide as his "right-hand man."

This imagery even applies to Jesus. He declared that after His resurrection and ascension, He would be seated at His Father's right hand (Luke 22:69; see note on Colossians 3:1).

COMMERCIALISM IN THE TEMPLE

These commercial activities that upset Jesus were being conducted in an outer court of the Jewish temple during the observance of the Passover in Jerusalem.

All male Jews were expected to attend this festival, even if they lived a long distance from Jerusalem (see note on Exodus 23:17). The money changers were probably exchanging foreign coins of these pilgrims for the appropriate coins with which to pay the temple tax (see note on Matthew 17:24).

These pilgrims were also expected to provide animals for sacrifice on the altar of the temple during this celebration. Merchants were selling animals for this purpose as a convenience so pilgrims would not have to bring them along on their trip to the holy city.

Jesus was angry about the crass commercialism of the scene. Temple officials may have been profiting personally from the buying and selling. He quoted Isaiah 56:7, saying, "Mine house shall be called an house of prayer," and accused the merchants of defiling the temple: "But ye have made it a den of thieves" (Matthew 21:13).

Jesus went into the temple. . .and cast out all them that sold and bought in the temple, and overthrew the tables of the moneychangers, and the seats [benches, NIV] of them that sold doves.
MATTHEW 21:12

Jesus overthrew the tables of the moneychangers who were conducting business under the shaded protection of the Royal Stoa.

Caring for a Vineyard

Wine was one of the most valuable agricultural commodities in Bible times. People grew grapes to make their own wine, and many farmers produced wine for sale as a commercial product. This verse, from Jesus' parable of the vineyard owner, gives insight into how grapes were grown and made into wine.

The vines on which grapes grew were planted in rows. These vines were trained to run on stakes, which were pulled over and tied at the tops with the stakes on adjoining rows to form an arch. Harvesting was done by stooping beneath these arches and picking the ripe grapes overhead.

Many vineyards were fenced with a hedge of thornbushes (see note on Job 5:5) or a stone wall (Proverbs 24:30–31) to keep out intruders. A winepress for extracting the juice from the grapes to make wine (see note on Lamentations 1:15) was often located right in the field so the grapes would not have to be carried a long distance after harvesting.

The "tower" mentioned in this verse refers to a watchtower (see note on Isaiah 1:8) that stood in the middle of the vineyard. From this tower, the landowner or his servants stood watch over the grapes while they were ripening to protect them from birds, other animals, and thieves.

Farmers took up residence in towers like this located in the vineyard to protect their ripening harvest from animals and thieves.

There was a certain householder [landowner, NIV], which planted a vineyard, and hedged it round about [put a wall around it, NIV], and digged a winepress in it, and built a tower.

Matthew 21:33

BIBLICAL VINEYARDS

1. The first vineyard mentioned in the Bible was planted by Noah following the Flood. He fell into a drunken stupor after drinking wine produced from its grapes (Genesis 9:20–21).
2. King Ahab and Queen Jezebel of Israel (the Northern Kingdom) plotted to steal a choice vineyard from Naboth. The prophet Elijah pronounced God's judgment against them because of their murder of Naboth (1 Kings 21:1–24).
3. Isaiah described the Israelites metaphorically as a vineyard that belonged to the Lord (Isaiah 5:7).

A Second Invitation

[A king] sent forth his servants to call them that were bidden to the wedding: and they would not come.

MATTHEW 22:3

This verse is part of Jesus' parable about the wedding feast. A king invited people to attend a feast to celebrate the wedding of his son. They agreed to come. Then when the king sent word that everything was ready and the feast was about to begin, they refused to attend.

This is how banquets and parties were staged in Bible times. An invitation well in advance of the event determined how many people to prepare for. Then a second invitation went out on the day of the event to those who had agreed to attend.

With this parable Jesus emphasized that His offer of salvation and eternal life went first to His own people, the Jews. But they refused to accept it. And just like the king in this parable who invited people off the street to replace those who would not attend the wedding, Jesus now issued His invitation to the Gentiles.

Put On the Clothes

When the king came in to see the guests, he saw there a man which had not on a wedding garment.

MATTHEW 22:11

This verse continues Jesus' parable of the wedding feast. The king had invited people off the street to attend the feast. He could not expect them to own the fancy clothes that were considered suitable attire for a royal wedding, so he provided such clothes for these guests. He was surprised to see that one guest had not put on these clothes.

The message of this part of the parable is that Jesus offers salvation to all, just as the king provided generously for all of his guests. But each person must exercise faith through an act of the will and "put on" this salvation for himself before it becomes meaningful and effective in his life.

Jesus and the Pharisees

Then went the Pharisees, and took counsel how they might entangle him [Jesus] in his talk [laid plans to trap him in his words, NIV].

MATTHEW 22:15

Jesus clashed often with the Pharisees during His ministry. They criticized Him for healing on the Sabbath (Luke 14:1–5), associating with people whom they considered sinners (Matthew 9:9–11), and not observing the external rituals that they considered essential for maintaining purity before God (Matthew 15:2).

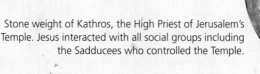

Stone weight of Kathros, the High Priest of Jerusalem's Temple. Jesus interacted with all social groups including the Sadducees who controlled the Temple.

The word *Pharisee* means "separated ones." The Pharisees went to extremes to keep themselves pure in accordance with the ceremonial laws as well as the moral laws of the Old Testament. In addition to the written law of Moses, they also observed the oral law. These were traditions that had been added to the written law over the course of many centuries. To them, these oral traditions were just as binding as the original written law.

Jesus rejected these traditions and charged that the Pharisees often used them to get around the more stringent requirements of the written law: "Why do ye also transgress the commandment of God by your tradition?" (Matthew 15:3).

The Pharisees often used debate and personal confrontation to try to discredit Jesus and His teachings. This verse points out that they also tried to trick Him into making statements that would undermine His influence and popularity with the people.

PHARISEES AND HERODIANS

In Jesus' time, most of the Roman rulers over the Jewish provinces were members of the family of Herod. Herodians were Jewish citizens who supported these Roman rulers and urged others to do so because this was the best way to gain the goodwill of the Roman government. Herodians generally were members of the upper class who had the most to gain from friendly relations with Rome.

The Pharisees' doctrine of separation from sinners meant that they would shun the Herodians under normal circumstances. But they were so opposed to Jesus and His teachings that they allied with the Herodians to try to bring Him down.

They [the Pharisees] sent out unto him [Jesus] their disciples with the Herodians.
MATTHEW 22:16

JESUS AND THE SADDUCEES

Unlike the Pharisees, the Sadducees denied the authority of oral traditions that had been added to the written law. They accepted only the books of the law—Genesis, Exodus, Leviticus, Numbers, and Deuteronomy—as authoritative scripture.

As this verse indicates, the Sadducees were known for their denial of the possibility of bodily resurrection because they could find no evidence for it in the books of the law. Their trick question about the resurrection was turned aside by Jesus with His observation that they were judging heavenly matters with earthly logic.

The same day came to him [Jesus] the Sadducees, which say that there is no resurrection.
MATTHEW 22:23

Two Supreme Commandments

On these two commandments [love for God and love for others] hang all the law and the prophets.

MATTHEW 22:40

A Pharisee asked Jesus to tell Him which commandment in the law of Moses He considered the greatest of all (Matthew 22:36). This was a trick question. No matter which way Jesus answered, He was sure to leave out some commandments that His enemies considered essential.

Jesus didn't restrict His answer to one commandment. He cited two verses from the Old Testament law, declaring that it was important to love God (Deuteronomy 6:5) but that it was just as important to love other people (Leviticus 19:18). These two principles were the font from which all religion and morality flowed.

With this answer Jesus actually charged the Pharisees with blind legalism. Many of the minute commandments that they considered important were empty and meaningless because they were not grounded in love for God and love for others.

Phylacteries and Tassels

They [the Pharisees] make broad their phylacteries, and enlarge the borders [tassels, NIV] of their garments.

MATTHEW 23:5

In this verse Jesus denounced the scribes and Pharisees for their hypocrisy and legalism. The Pharisees were noted for their attempts to keep the Old Testament law in every minute detail.

Phylacteries were little boxes containing strips of parchment on which portions of the law were written. The Pharisees wore these boxes on their foreheads and wrists as a literal obedience of the Lord's command, "Thou shalt bind them [God's laws] for a sign upon thine hand, and they shall be as frontlets between thine eyes" (Deuteronomy 6:8). Tassels were decorative fringes that the Pharisees wore on their clothes to remind them of God's laws (Deuteronomy 22:12).

The phylactery on this man's arm contains verses from the Old Testament.

184

The problem with these displays of piety among the Pharisees is that they were done just for show. Jesus declared that they worked hard to observe the externals of religion while omitting "the weightier matters of the law, judgment, mercy, and faith" (Matthew 23:23).

Pride versus Humility

The twenty-third chapter of Matthew is known as this Gospel's "woe" chapter because Jesus pronounced a series of woes against the Pharisees. He was particularly critical of their desire for status and recognition.

The Pharisees expected to be seated in places of honor at banquets and in the synagogue. They loved the public recognition they received when people called them "Rabbi" or "Teacher" when they walked through the streets. This vain, prideful attitude was the very opposite of the spirit of humility that Jesus taught His disciples to model before others (Matthew 5:5).

[The Pharisees] love the uppermost rooms at feasts [place of honor at banquets, NIV], and the chief seats in the synagogues. . .and to be called of men, Rabbi, Rabbi.
Matthew 23:6–7

The Great Pretenders

The Pharisees were consulted by the people on property matters because of their religious influence in the community. But they often violated this trust and caused the poor and helpless to lose their property. They covered up their dishonesty by praying long, pious prayers.

To Jesus, these Pharisees were nothing but hypocrites. This Greek word referred to an actor in a play who held a mask in front of his face when he changed characters. Pretending to be people of integrity, the Pharisees were actually frauds and con artists.

Woe unto you, scribes and Pharisees, hypocrites! for ye devour widows' houses, and for a pretence make long prayer.
Matthew 23:14

Majoring on Minors

In Bible times people strained their wine before drinking it to remove impurities—even tiny insects (see note on Isaiah 25:6). How ridiculous it would be to strain a tiny gnat out of the wine, only to wind up gulping down a huge animal like the camel!

Jesus used this analogy to show the senseless actions of the Pharisees. They made a big deal out of rituals such as ceremonial washings before eating (Matthew 15:1–2), but they failed to show love, generosity, and justice toward others.

Ye blind guides [Pharisees], which strain at [out, NIV] a gnat, and swallow a camel.
Matthew 23:24

CORRUPT ON THE INSIDE

The Jewish people believed that contact with a grave caused a person to become unclean (Numbers 19:16), so tombs were coated with a white lime solution to make them stand out to keep people from touching them accidently.

Jesus used this image to describe the Pharisees. On the outside they looked pious and religious, like the whitewashed tombs that dotted the countryside. But on the inside, they were full of decay and corruption.

Following the decay of flesh and muscle, the Jews of Jesus day would rebury the deceased in small boxes called ossuaries.

BE PREPARED

These verses are part of Jesus' parable about the wise and foolish virgins who were invited to a wedding celebration. In Bible times the groom went to the home of his bride and took her to his own home, accompanied by his friends as they celebrated along the way. These virgins were probably friends of the bride who were supposed to join the procession at some point as it passed by.

Since the wedding was at night, all ten virgins carried tiny oil-burning lamps (see note on Mark 4:21) to light the path as they walked with the rest of the wedding party. The wise virgins carried an extra supply of oil for their lamps, but the foolish virgins did not. When the wedding procession was delayed, the foolish virgins were unable to join in the celebration of this joyful occasion.

Jesus' message in the parable is this: Be prepared. The second coming of Christ can happen at any moment, and we need to be ready at all times.

Small oil-burning lamps like this were used by the ten virgins in Jesus' parable (Matthew 25:1–3).

Separating the Sheep and Goats

In Bible times, sheep and goats would often graze in the same pasture. But the shepherd would place them at a distance from each other because male goats tended to be hostile and aggressive toward the sheep.

Jesus used this image to show that good and evil might exist together in this life, but they will be separated by the Great Shepherd in the final judgment.

Before him [Jesus] shall be gathered all nations: and he shall separate them one from another, as a shepherd divideth his sheep from the goats.
MATTHEW 25:32

Thirty Pieces of Silver

The Jewish religious leaders wanted to arrest Jesus and have Him tried for blasphemy and treason. But they needed to take him into custody in a secluded place because of His popularity with the common people. They paid Judas to let them know when He could be arrested discreetly and under the cover of darkness.

The exact identity of the thirty silver coins that they paid Judas for providing this information is not known. They may have been the common silver coins issued by the Romans in New Testament times that were approximately equal in value to the Old Testament shekel (see note on Genesis 23:16). The value of a slave was placed at thirty shekels in Old Testament times (Exodus 21:32).

They [the religious leaders] covenanted with him [Judas] for thirty pieces of silver [thirty silver coins, NIV].
MATTHEW 26:15

The Ultimate Sacrificial Lamb

Jesus and His disciples were in Jerusalem for the observance of the Passover. This was the most significant festival of the Jewish people, celebrated each year to memorialize their deliverance from slavery in Egypt (see notes on Exodus 23:15 and Exodus 23:17).

The central event of this celebration was the eating of a lamb. Before this lamb was roasted, its blood was sprinkled by the priests on the base of the altar in the temple. This symbolized the blood sprinkled on the doorposts of Israelite houses in Egypt to ward off the angel of death whom God sent throughout the land (Exodus 12:1–13).

When the disciples "made ready the passover," they probably secured a lamb and had it sacrificed by the priests and prepared it appropriately for eating by Jesus and the other disciples. Little did they know that within a few hours the crucified Jesus would become the ultimate Passover Lamb whose blood would become an everlasting atonement for sin.

The disciples did as Jesus had appointed them; and they made ready the passover.
MATTHEW 26:19

Jesus' Cup of Suffering

He [Jesus]. . .fell on his face, and prayed, saying, O my Father, if it be possible, let this cup pass from me.
MATTHEW 26:39

This verse is part of Jesus' prayer of agony in the Garden of Gethsemane before His arrest and crucifixion. The "cup" to which He referred was the suffering He would endure on the cross as an atoning sacrifice for sin.

The word *cup* is often used in a figurative sense in the Bible to express God's blessings as well as His wrath. For example, the psalmist declared, "I will take the cup of salvation, and call upon the name of the LORD" (Psalm 116:13). But the prophet Isaiah spoke of God's punishment as "the cup of his fury" (Isaiah 51:17).

Chief Priests

Judas, one of the twelve, came, and with him a great multitude [large crowd, NIV]. . .from the chief priests and elders of the people.
MATTHEW 26:47

The phrase "chief priests" in this verse probably refers to the leaders or directors of the twenty-four groups of priests into which the priesthood was divided in David's time (1 Chronicles 24:1–5). These twenty-four divisions of the priesthood probably presided at the altar in the tabernacle or temple on a rotating basis.

In New Testament times, these "chief priests" may have included the high priest as well as priestly members of his immediate family.

OLD TESTAMENT CHIEF PRIESTS

1. Azariah was a chief priest in the days of King Uzziah of Judah (2 Chronicles 26:20–21).
2. Ezra made all of the chief priests and the Levites swear that they would obey the commands of the Lord (Ezra 10:5).
3. Several people are listed as chief priests in the days of Nehemiah (Nehemiah 12:7).
4. Chief priests are also referred to as "princes of the sanctuary" (Isaiah 43:28).

Punishment by Scourging

When he [Pilate] had scourged [flogged, NIV] Jesus, he delivered him to be crucified.
MATTHEW 27:26

It was customary among the Romans to scourge or flog a condemned criminal before he was executed. A scourge was a whip with sharp pieces of metal or bone imbedded in the leather. The back and chest of the criminal were struck repeatedly with this whip until the flesh was severely lacerated, sometimes all the way down to the bone.

This savage beating often led to death from shock or loss of blood. Jesus apparently grew too weak to carry His cross to the crucifixion site after the scourging administered by Pilate's soldiers. A passerby from Cyrene named Simon was pressed into service to carry His cross (Matthew 27:32).

The Jews also practiced scourging, but they were more humane in administering this punishment than the Romans. By Jewish law, a person could not be struck more than forty times (Deuteronomy 25:2–3). To make sure this limit was not exceeded, it was customary to stop at thirty-nine blows (2 Corinthians 11:24). There is no evidence that the Romans placed any limit on this cruel punishment.

PILATE'S ROMAN SOLDIERS

The Praetorium, as recorded by the New International Version, was probably a part of the palace of Pilate, the Roman provincial governor of Judah before whom Jesus appeared.

A special detachment of soldiers was housed in the Praetorium to serve as bodyguards for Pilate and to carry out other duties as assigned by him. These were the soldiers who flogged and mocked Jesus, gambled for His clothes, and carried out Pilate's execution order.

The soldiers of the governor [Pilate] took Jesus into the common hall [Praetorium, NIV], and gathered unto him the whole band [company, NIV] of soldiers.
MATTHEW 27:27

THE KING AND HIS KINGDOM

Scarlet was the color of the clothes traditionally worn by kings and members of royal families. The Roman soldiers placed a robe of this color on Jesus to mock His claim that He was a king. They also placed a reed, representing a royal scepter (see note on Ezekiel 19:11), in His hand and fashioned a crown of thorns for His head (Matthew 27:29).

How ironic it is that the powerful kingdom the soldiers represented—the Roman Empire—has long since disappeared. But the kingdom over which Jesus ruled and about which they were ignorant—the kingdom of God—still exists and includes millions of subjects who acknowledge Him as the everlasting King.

They [the Roman soldiers] stripped him [Jesus], and put on him a scarlet robe.
MATTHEW 27:28

They [the Roman soldiers] crucified him [Jesus], and parted [divided up, NIV] his garments, casting lots.
MATTHEW 27:35

The crucifixion of Jesus.

A BADGE OF HONOR

None of the Gospels (Matthew, Mark, Luke, and John) go into detail about the crucifixion of Jesus. They didn't have to. The people of New Testament times knew all about this cruel form of capital punishment and the pain and suffering it inflicted.

The victim's wrists were nailed to a horizontal cross-beam; then it was raised into position and attached to a stake

fixed firmly in the ground. Sometimes the feet were crossed and nailed to the stake. Without any support for the body except the nails through the feet and wrists, the victim slumped forward on the cross.

This put pressure on the heart and lungs, making breathing difficult. A slow, painful death usually occurred after two or three days from a combination of shock, fatigue, asphyxiation, and loss of blood.

Sometimes the victim's legs were broken with a club as an act of mercy to hasten death. This was not necessary in Jesus' case because He died after only a few hours on the cross (Matthew 27:45–50). The Gospel of John declares that this was a fulfillment of the Old Testament prophecy, "A bone of him shall not be broken" (John 19:36; see Psalm 34:20).

To the Jewish people, crucifixion was a despicable and dishonorable way to die (Galatians 3:13). But Jesus turned the cross into a symbol of hope and a badge of honor and self-sacrifice (Philippians 2:5–8).

A False Charge

They [the Roman soldiers]. . . set up over his [Jesus'] head his accusation written [the written charge against him, NIV], THIS IS JESUS THE KING OF THE JEWS.
MATTHEW 27:36–37

It was customary among the Romans to post a sign at the execution site, declaring the crime for which a criminal was being put to death. This sent a message to the people that the same thing would happen to them if they dared to disobey the law.

The charge against Jesus was that He claimed to be the king of the Jewish people. This was considered an act of sedition against the Roman government. Only the emperor had the authority to appoint rulers over the nations that Rome controlled.

This was actually a false charge, since Jesus never claimed to be a political king. As the Messiah, He was a spiritual leader who came to bring people into a heavenly kingdom— the kingdom of God (see note on Matthew 20:21).

A Door of Stone

Joseph [of Arimathea]. . . laid it [Jesus' body] in his own new tomb, which he had hewn out in the rock: and he rolled a great stone to the door of the sepulchre, and departed.
MATTHEW 27:59–60

The tomb in which Joseph of Arimathea laid the body of Jesus had been hewn out of solid rock (see note on Isaiah 22:16). It was closed by rolling a flat, circular stone across the entrance to keep out animals and grave robbers.

These stone "doors" must have weighed several hundred pounds. When three women went to anoint Jesus' body on Sunday morning after His burial, "they said among themselves, Who shall roll us away the stone from the door of the sepulchre?" (Mark 16:3).

The opening to Jesus' tomb was guarded by a large stone used to seal the tomb entrance.

SEALED AND SURE

These were some of the same religious leaders who had succeeded in having Jesus executed. They started thinking that His disciples might remove the body from the tomb and claim that Jesus had been raised from the dead.

To make sure this didn't happen, they sealed the stone that had been placed across the entrance. They could have stretched a rope across the stone and sealed each end of the rope with clay or wax. If this seal were to be broken, they would know someone had tampered with the stone.

This may have been the way the entrance to the pit was sealed after Daniel was thrown to the lions by King Darius and his aides (Daniel 6:17).

They [the Jewish leaders] went, and made the sepulchre sure, sealing the stone, and setting a watch.
MATTHEW 27:66

MARK

A Wild Man in the Desert

John the Baptist, forerunner of Jesus, lived a plain, simple, solitary lifestyle out in the wilderness, or desert (Mark 1:3). He foraged for his food, eating locusts—flying insects similar to grasshoppers (see note on Joel 1:4)—and honey from the nests of bees. His clothes were made from the hair and skin of animals. Today people would probably consider John a hermit or a fanatical wild man.

Why did John live this type of life? Probably to identify himself with the prophets of Israel's past. It had been more than four hundred years since a prophet had walked among the Jewish people. John wanted to show that the ultimate Prophet—the Messiah who had been promised for centuries—was about to burst upon the scene.

Going through the Roof

This verse shows the determination of the friends of a disabled man to get him to Jesus for healing. They brought their friend in a blanket or pallet to the house where Jesus was teaching. Unable to get into the building because of the crowd, they climbed an exterior stairway to the roof. After ripping a hole in the roof, they lowered him down to Jesus.

The roofs of most houses in Bible times were built in three simple steps. First, beams or logs were laid across the tops of the exterior walls. These beams were then overlaid with thatch, consisting of tree branches and straw. Finally, the thatch was topped with a layer of clay that was hardened in the sun. In a climate in which rainfall was minimal, these roofs would hold up well if the clay was rolled and hardened on a regular basis.

Tearing through a roof like this was a simple matter. It was also easy to repair.

The Term *Children*

Like the word *father* (see note on Genesis 4:21), the term *children* is often used in an idiomatic way in the Bible. It refers to those who have a close identification with certain objects or attitudes. Thus, "children of the bridechamber" refers to friends and relatives who participated in the wedding celebration.

Other similar expressions in the Bible include "children of light" (Luke 16:8), "children of pride" (Job 41:34), "children of wickedness" (2 Samuel 7:10), and "children of the kingdom" (Matthew 13:38).

Jesus said unto them, Can the children of the bridechamber [guests of the bridegroom, NIV] fast, while the bridegroom is with them?

MARK 2:19

A SHINING LIGHT

Jesus was referring to the truths about Him and His work that He was teaching to His disciples. These truths were not to be hidden under a basket or a bed. They should be placed out in the open for everyone to see, just as a lamp was lit and placed on a lampstand to light up a house.

METAPHORICAL LAMPS

1. Job declared that the candle, or lamp, of the wicked would be extinguished (Job 18:5–6).
2. The industrious wife of the book of Proverbs is portrayed as working late into the evening, so that her "candle [lamp] goeth not out by night" (Proverbs 31:18).
3. The prophet Jeremiah described the judgment of God as a force that would put out the lamp of Judah (Jeremiah 25:10).
4. The prophet Zephaniah pictured the Lord as searching Jerusalem with lamps to find and punish sin (Zephaniah 1:12).

The lamps of Jesus' time were small vessels made of clay (see note on Matthew 25:1–3). They could hold about a pint of olive oil, which served as fuel for the lamp (see note on Exodus 27:20). A burning wick inserted into the oil gave off enough light to illuminate a small room.

He [Jesus] said unto them, Is a candle [lamp, NIV] brought to be put under a bushel [bowl, NIV], or under a bed? and not to be set on a candlestick [stand, NIV]?

MARK 4:21

ASLEEP IN THE STORM

Jesus and His disciples were struck by a severe storm while crossing the Sea of Galilee in a fishing boat. Unlike the disciples, who were terrified, Jesus was calmly sleeping in the stern of the vessel.

He [Jesus] was in the hinder part [stern, NIV] of the ship, asleep on a pillow [cushion, NIV].

MARK 4:38

Looking across the bow of a boat in the direction of the rising terrain that marks Gergesa. As Jesus and his disciples traveled east across the Sea of Galilee, the boat was caught in a severe storm.

A "pillow," as rendered by the King James Version, on which Jesus was resting, would have been out of place in a fishing boat. The New International Version renders the word more accurately. He was probably resting on the fleece on which rowers sat when they were pulling at the oars.

LIVING AMONG THE DEAD

There met him [Jesus] out of the tombs a man with an unclean spirit, who had his dwelling among the tombs.

MARK 5:2–3

This man who met Jesus was possessed by demons. He may have been driven out of the villages of "the country of the Gadarenes" (Mark 5:1) and forced to live a life of isolation in a cemetery because of his violent, unpredictable behavior (Mark 5:5).

The "tombs" mentioned in this passage were probably natural caves or burial chambers that had been dug out of solid rock (see note on Isaiah 22:16). Tombs like this were commonly used by the upper-class families of Bible times.

This poor, deranged man may have been living among the bones of the dead in one of these burial caves. The New International Version states specifically that he was living "in the tombs," not "among the tombs."

REJECTING THE REJECTERS

Whosoever shall not receive you. . .when ye depart thence, shake off the dust under your feet for a testimony against them.

MARK 6:11

The Jewish people believed that all Gentiles, or non-Jews, were unclean pagans. When traveling through Gentile territory, they would wipe their feet to remove all traces of unclean soil before reentering Jewish territory.

Jesus picked up on this symbolic action when sending His disciples out on a preaching and healing mission. If anyone rejected their message, the disciples were to treat them as if they were pagan Gentiles who would face the judgment of God for their unbelief.

During their first missionary journey, Paul and Barnabas took this same symbolic action against the unbelieving Jews who drove them out of Antioch of Pisidia (Acts 13:51).

THANKS FOR THE MEAL

When he [Jesus] had taken the five loaves and the two fishes, he looked up to heaven, and blessed [gave thanks, NIV], and brake the loaves.

MARK 6:41

"Saying the blessing" before a meal is how we sometimes describe the practice of offering thanks to God for providing the food we eat. Jesus followed this custom before the meal in which He miraculously multiplied five loaves of bread and two fish into enough food to feed a crowd of more than five thousand people.

Offering thanks to God before meals should remind us every day that God is the Great Provider without whose favor we could not exist. We should never take His blessings for granted.

Jesus and the Scribes

The scribes and Pharisees are often mentioned together as if they were united in their opposition to Jesus (Matthew 15:1; Luke 5:21; John 8:3).

Scribes assumed the responsibility of copying the scriptures.

The office of scribe developed in Old Testament times when scribes were charged with the responsibility of copying the scriptures. Laboriously copying a sacred document by hand was the only way to reproduce and pass on God's commands in written form.

By New Testament times, scribes had assumed the task of interpreting and teaching God's law as well as copying it. This is why they are mentioned often with Pharisees as those who were opposed to Jesus. Both were committed to preserving the traditions that had grown up around the original written law (see note on Matthew 22:15). They considered these additions as binding as the law itself.

Jesus criticized these "sacred traditions," broke many of them Himself during His teaching and healing ministry, and insisted they were not as authoritative as God's law in its original form (Matthew 15:5–6; Mark 7:5–6; Luke 6:1–5).

Then came together unto him [Jesus] the Pharisees, and certain of the scribes [teachers of the law, NIV].
MARK 7:1

HIRED SCRIBES

When the word *scribe* (singular) appears in the Bible, it usually denotes a person who served as a secretary for a king or prophet. His job was to write down dictated messages, decrees, or letters from his employer. Several scribes of this type are mentioned in the Bible.

1. Seraiah was a scribe in the administration of King David of Israel (2 Samuel 8:17).
2. Shebna was a scribe for King Hezekiah of Judah (2 Kings 18:17–18).
3. Shaphan was a scribe for King Josiah of Judah (2 Chronicles 34:15–16).
4. Baruch was a scribe for the prophet Jeremiah (Jeremiah 36:1–4).

Outer or Inner Cleansing?

The washing to which this verse refers is not the normal washing of hands that was done before or after eating meals (see note on 2 Kings 3:11). It refers to the elaborate ceremonial cleaning that Pharisees practiced to purify themselves from anything they had touched that they considered unclean.

The Pharisees, and all the Jews, except they wash their hands oft, eat not, holding the tradition of the elders.
MARK 7:3

195

Ceremonial cleansing involved washing and rewashing the hands up to the elbows several times. This procedure was not prescribed in the law, but it had been added by the Pharisees as a tradition that they considered as authoritative as the original written law (see note on Matthew 22:15).

The Pharisees criticized Jesus and His disciples because they did not perform these ceremonial washings before eating (Mark 7:2, 5). He responded that their traditions had become more important to them than the original law of Moses (Mark 7:8–9). Furthermore, a person could not be made spiritually clean by washing the outside of the body (Matthew 7:15).

GETTING AROUND THE LAW

This charge by Jesus against the Pharisees is a perfect example of how they had replaced the original law with their own traditions (see notes on Matthew 22:15 and Mark 7:3).

The original law specified that people were to honor and take care of their parents (Exodus 20:12). But the Pharisees used their tradition known as Corban—or a gift devoted to God—to get around this commandment.

For example, if the parents of a Pharisee needed financial help, he could say, "My property is Corban," or devoted to God and the temple. He was permitted to continue to use the property as he pleased, but the Pharisaic traditions forbade him from using it to assist his parents, against whom he had invoked the Corban ban.

To Jesus, this was just a clever way of getting around the clear intent of the law. No wonder He condemned them as "hypocrites" (Matthew 23:15), "blind guides" (Matthew 23:16), and "serpents" (Matthew 23:33).

JESUS AND HYPERBOLE

This statement from Jesus is what is known as hyperbole—a deliberate exaggeration in order to make a point. We might compare this to the modern statement, "It's raining cats and dogs." We don't mean that actual cats and dogs are falling from the sky. We are saying that the rain is coming down in a torrential downpour.

The point Jesus was making is that wealthy people tend to put their trust in their riches. It is very difficult for them to release their grasp on the material—things they can see with their physical eyes—in order to commit themselves in faith to spiritual realities that they can't see or feel. Jesus had just seen this difficulty proven by the rich young ruler, who rejected Jesus'

Ye [Pharisees] say, If a man shall say to his father or mother, It is Corban, that is to say, a gift, by whatsoever thou mightest be profited by me; he shall be free.

MARK 7:11

It is easier for a camel to go through the eye of a needle, than for a rich man to enter into the kingdom of God.

MARK 10:25

Bone needles like this were commonly used in Jesus' day. Using hyperbole, He observed that it would be easier for a camel to pass through the eye of such a needle than for a rich person to enter the kingdom of God.

invitation to become His disciple because "he had great possessions" (Mark 10:22).

Other examples of Jesus' use of hyperbole include these: "Ye blind guides [Pharisees], which strain at a gnat, and swallow a camel" (Matthew 23:24), and "If any man come to me, and hate not his father, and mother. . .he cannot be my disciple" (Luke 14:26).

STRAIGHT-UP PRAYER

This teaching of Jesus on prayer and forgiveness shows that standing was one common stance while praying in Bible times. The person would address his prayer to God by lifting his hands toward heaven with his palms up. This is the way King Solomon prayed when he dedicated the newly constructed temple in Jerusalem to the Lord (1 Kings 8:22).

When ye [Jesus' followers] stand praying, forgive, if ye have ought against any [hold anything against anyone, NIV].
MARK 11:25

COUNCILS AND SYNAGOGUES

With these words, Jesus warned His disciples about the persecution they would face from the Jewish religious authorities after His death and resurrection.

The word *councils* (plural) refers to regional courts that were scattered throughout Palestine. The term *council* (singular) describes the highest court of the Jews—the Sanhedrin—that was located in Jerusalem. It consisted of seventy members who ruled on various civil and religious matters that came under its jurisdiction. This was the Jewish body that condemned Jesus for blasphemy (Mark 14:63–64), then took Him to Pilate, the Roman governor, with the recommendation that He be put to death (Matthew 27:1–2).

Synagogues were local Jewish religious centers where people were instructed in the law (see note on Luke 4:16). These organizations apparently had the authority to excommunicate and flog their members as disciplinary measures.

Take heed to yourselves: for they shall deliver you up to councils; and in the synagogues ye shall be beaten.
MARK 13:9

The synagogue was the place of worship for the Jews of Jesus' day. The white stone structure is the synagogue at Capernaum.

Watch ye therefore: for ye
know not when the master
of the house cometh, at
even [in the evening, NIV],
or at midnight, or at the
cockcrowing [when the
rooster crows, NIV], or in
the morning [at dawn,
NIV].

MARK 13:35

There shall meet you a
man bearing a pitcher
[jar, NIV] of water.

MARK 14:13

He [Jesus] answered. . .It
is one of the twelve, that
dippeth with me in the
dish [dips bread into the
bowl with me, NIV].

MARK 14:20

Now at that feast he
[Pilate] released unto them
one prisoner, whomsoever
they desired.

MARK 15:6

NEW TESTAMENT NIGHT WATCHES

During Old Testament times, the Jews divided the night into three "watches" or divisions of time (see note on Exodus 14:24). But after the Romans occupied their territory, they adopted the Roman pattern of the four-watch night.

Jesus referred to these four watches in His instructions to His disciples that they should always be ready for His return: the first ("even") at three hours after sunset, the second three hours later at midnight, the third ("cockcrowing") at three hours before sunset, and the fourth ("morning") at dawn with the rising of the sun.

These were the same times when the Roman soldiers guarding Peter in prison rotated their shifts (see note on Acts 12:4).

A MAN WITH A PITCHER

According to Jesus, this is how the disciples could identify a man who would show them to a room where they could eat the Passover meal together (see note on Matthew 26:19).

Collecting and carrying water from the public water supply was considered women's work (see note on Genesis 24:11). So a man carrying a pitcher of water through the streets of Jerusalem would stand out from the crowd.

This unnamed man was probably a follower of Jesus who had made arrangements in advance for the "large upper room" where they met (Mark 14:15).

BREAD OF BETRAYAL

People of Bible times did not use utensils such as forks and spoons to eat their meals (see note on Genesis 18:7–8). They picked up the food with their hands. But some dishes such as stew or gravy had to be scooped up with a piece of bread. This is the method of eating to which Jesus referred in this verse.

In John's Gospel, this bread used to pick up liquid food is call a "sop." Jesus handed the bread to Judas, clearly identifying him as the betrayer (John 13:26).

BARABBAS, NOT JESUS

At the annual celebration of the Passover in Jerusalem (see note on Matthew 26:19), the Roman governor released one Jewish prisoner who was selected by the people. This was a gesture of goodwill to the Jews, who resented the Roman occupation of their country.

Rather than choosing Jesus for release, the crowd selected

instead a murderer and insurrectionist named Barabbas. The Jewish religious leaders had worked the crowd behind the scenes to influence their choice (Mark 15:11).

THE CRUCIFIXION SITE

The exact location of Jesus' crucifixion is unknown, although there are three suggested sites: (1) the Church of the Holy Sepulcher inside the walls of Jerusalem, (2) an unidentified place outside the city walls, and (3) Gordon's Calvary, a hillside site above a large rock that resembles a skull. This third site is also outside the city walls.

They [soldiers] bring him [Jesus] unto the place Golgotha, which is, being interpreted, The place of a skull.
MARK 15:22

Some interpreters claim that a verse from the book of Hebrews proves the crucifixion occurred outside the walls of Jerusalem: "Jesus also suffered outside the city gate to make the people holy through his own blood" (Hebrews 13:12 NIV). But Jerusalem was destroyed by the Roman army in AD 70, about thirty-five years after Jesus' crucifixion. The city's walls may have been rerouted when they were rebuilt.

The site—wherever it was—was probably the place where all Roman executions in the Jerusalem area were carried out. Both *Golgotha*, Mark and Matthew's Aramaic word (see Matthew 27:33), and *Calvary*, Luke's Latin word (see Luke 23:33), mean "place of a skull."

Gordon's Calvary is one of the sites in Jerusalem identified as the possible location of Jesus' crucifixion.

Equal Access to God

This veil, or curtain, separated the Holy Place from the Most Holy Place in the Jewish temple at Jerusalem. Only the high priest was allowed behind this curtain, and he could go into the Most Holy Place only once a year—on the Day of Atonement—to offer sacrifices to atone for the sins of the people (see note on Leviticus 16:34).

At the very moment when Jesus died, this large curtain was split in two by a miraculous act of God. This signified that Jesus had paid the price for human sin and that all people had access to His love and grace (Hebrews 10:19–22).

Joseph the Bold

The New International Version identifies Joseph of Arimathea as a noted member of the Jewish Sanhedrin. This high Jewish court had condemned Jesus for blasphemy and recommended to Pilate just a few days before that He be executed (see note on Mark 13:9).

Where was Joseph when Jesus was dragged before the Sanhedrin for trial? Why did he not step forward in His defense? We don't know. But we do know that Joseph risked his reputation with that judicial body when he claimed the body of Jesus and laid it in his own new tomb.

Even if Joseph was a "secret disciple" of Jesus, his bold and kind act to give Him a decent burial deserves the admiration and thanks of all believers.

LUKE

ZACHARIAS AND ELISABETH

Zacharias was the father of John the Baptist, forerunner of Jesus. In this verse Luke shows us that Zacharias was a priest of impeccable credentials.

When the priesthood was established in the days of Moses and Aaron, God made it clear that He expected His priests to be physically and morally qualified for the office. They could not have any physical disability or defect (Leviticus 21:16–21). They were to be holy, respecting the Lord and obeying His commands (Leviticus 21:6). Even their wives were to be persons of high moral character (Leviticus 21:7).

Zacharias apparently met all of these qualifications. His wife, Elisabeth, was even a descendant of Aaron, the first high priest of the Israelites (Exodus 28:1, 29–30).

> *There was. . .a certain priest named Zacharias, of the course of Abia: and his wife was of the daughters of Aaron [also a descendant of Aaron, NIV].*
> LUKE 1:5

A BABY NAMED JOHN

The relatives of Zacharias and Elisabeth, parents of John the Baptist, wanted to name the child after his father. But Elisabeth insisted that his name was John, meaning "the favor of Jehovah." Zacharias had been told by an angel several months before that this child of their old age was to be named John (Luke 1:13).

In Bible times a baby was normally named by the mother (1 Samuel 1:20). But sometimes a father exercised this privilege (Exodus 2:22). Other relatives of the child, as in the case of John, sometimes participated in the naming as well. A male infant was named at the time of circumcision, eight days after birth (Genesis 17:12).

> *On the eighth day they [relatives of Zacharias and Elisabeth] came to circumcise the child [John the Baptist]; and they called him Zacharias, after the name of his father.*
> LUKE 1:59

A MESSAGE IN WAX

The tablet on which Zacharias wrote this message was a small block of wood coated with wax on one side. He used a stylus, or metal pen, to write his message in the wax. This is the only way he could communicate, since an angel had taken away his speech for expressing doubt that he and Elisabeth could conceive a child in their old age (Luke 1:20).

> *He [Zacharias] asked for a writing table [tablet, NIV], and wrote, saying, His name is John.*
> LUKE 1:63

Wax tablets were used for writing brief documents such as letters and lists (Isaiah 30:8; Habakkuk 2:2). Messages could be erased easily from the soft wax, and the tablet could be used over and over again. Longer documents that needed to be preserved were written on scrolls of parchment or animal skin (see note on Jeremiah 36:18).

A King in a Stable

She [Mary] brought forth her firstborn son, and wrapped him in swaddling clothes, and laid him in a manger; because there was no room for them in the inn.

Luke 2:7

After His birth in a stable in Bethlehem, the baby Jesus was placed in a manger, a feeding trough for livestock. This manger may have been hewed out of rock. Stone mangers about three feet long, eighteen inches wide, and two feet deep have been discovered in the ruins of King Ahab's stables at the ancient city of Megiddo.

The "swaddling clothes" in which Jesus was wrapped after His birth were strips of cloth that were wound tightly around a newborn's body to restrict movement. This custom is also mentioned in Ezekiel 16:4.

The inns or public lodging places of Bible times were nothing like our modern motels. They were little more than primitive shelters or camping sites near a well where people and their animals could bed down for the night. Travelers were expected to provide their own bedding, food, and cooking utensils.

The inn at Bethlehem had no lodging spaces left when Mary and Joseph arrived in town. But they were allowed to sleep in the adjoining stables where the animals of travelers were kept.

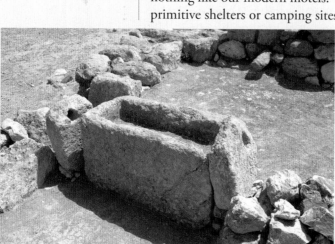

A stone feeding trough from the ancient city of Megiddo.

They [Mary and Joseph] found him [Jesus] in the temple [temple courts, NIV], sitting in the midst of the doctors [teachers, NIV], both hearing [listening to, NIV] them, and asking them questions.

Luke 2:46

Jesus among the Teachers

This account from Luke is the only information about the childhood of Jesus recorded in any of the Gospels. His parents found Him among the learned Jewish teachers after they accidentally left Him behind after a Passover celebration in Jerusalem.

The doctors or teachers among whom Jesus was sitting were experts in the Old Testament law. After expounding on the law in a temple service, they invited any interested persons to meet with them for further learning and discussion. Jesus was eager to learn, and He impressed them with His probing questions (Luke 2:47).

Luke tells us through this event that Jesus grew up like any Jewish boy. Although He was aware of His mission as the Messiah from an early age, He did not launch His public ministry until He was about thirty years old (Luke 3:23). Throughout His early years, He was subject to His parents, and He "increased in wisdom and stature, and in favour with God and man" (Luke 2:52).

CHAFF AS A METAPHOR

1. Job declared that the Lord would scatter the wicked, like the "chaff that the storm carrieth away" (Job 21:18).
2. God promised through the prophet Isaiah that He would restore his people Israel to greatness and turn their enemies into mounds of useless chaff (Isaiah 41:14-16).
3. The prophet Hosea portrayed the nation of Israel as chaff "driven with the whirlwind" because of the coming judgment of the Lord (Hosea 13:3).

The Separating Messiah

A fan or winnowing fork was used by farmers of Bible times to separate grains of wheat from useless stalks and hulls in a process known as winnowing (see note on Ruth 3:2). People scooped up the wheat and the chaff together with a wooden fork similar to a pitchfork and tossed them into the air. A brisk wind separated the useless chaff from the wheat.

To John the Baptist, the winnowing process symbolized God's judgment through the Messiah, who would separate the righteous from the sinful.

Reading in a Synagogue

This synagogue in which Jesus read the Old Testament scriptures was in Nazareth, his hometown in the province of Galilee. Synagogues were built in towns and cities throughout Palestine. Their purpose was not to replace the temple in Jerusalem that served as the central place of worship and sacrifice for all Israel. Synagogues existed to teach the law to local people.

A community synagogue was presided over by a leader who had been elected by its members. Priests had no official role in synagogues, although they often attended and were honored by being asked to read the scriptures during the service.

Jesus was not a priest or a member of the religious

Whose fan [winnowing fork, NIV] is in his [the Messiah's] hand, and he will thoroughly purge his floor [clear his threshing floor, NIV].
Luke 3:17

A winnowing fork was used by farmers to toss the mixture of grain and chaff into the air.

He [Jesus] went into the synagogue on the sabbath day, and stood up for to read.
Luke 4:16

establishment. His reading in the Nazareth synagogue shows that common, everyday "laypeople" who were known in the community were often asked to participate in the service. In addition, His ministry as a teacher and healer had begun to attract attention throughout Galilee (Luke 4:14–15).

Jesus read from the book of Isaiah and identified Himself as the servant of the Lord whom the prophet had written about (Luke 4:17–21).

A DISAPPOINTING NIGHT ON THE LAKE

We [Peter and his fishing partners] have toiled all the night, and have taken [caught, NIV] nothing.
LUKE 5:5

Every fisherman knows how disappointing it is to fish all day and not catch a thing. But Peter and his partners had been fishing all night without catching a single fish. And they were commercial fishermen, so their poor catch was a more serious matter.

Commercial fishing on Lake Galilee—the livelihood of Peter and his partners—must have been done at night, perhaps to escape the heat of the day or because conditions were more favorable then. Nighttime fishing also freed up the daylight hours for cleaning and mending their nets.

The practice of fishing at night is also referred to in John 21:3.

Commercial fishing on the Sea of Galilee continues today as it did in the days of Jesus.

He [Jesus]. . .saw a publican [tax collector, NIV], named Levi, sitting at the receipt of custom [his tax booth, NIV]: and he said unto him, Follow me.
LUKE 5:27

UP FROM THE TAX BOOTH

Matthew was busy at his job of collecting taxes when Jesus called him to become one of His disciples (see note on Matthew 9:10).

The citizens of Palestine were heavily taxed by the occupying Roman government in New Testament times. They had to pay a poll (head) tax, a property tax on the land they owned, a tax on the crops and herds they produced, a tax on all goods imported into and exported out of the country, and a tax on everything bought and sold within Jewish towns.

This heavy taxation naturally resulted in a hatred of Rome among the Jewish people. Anyone—whether Roman or Jewish—who participated with the government of Rome in collecting taxes was hated, as well. They were grouped with "sinners" as people who were degenerate and corrupt (Matthew 9:10–11; Mark 2:15).

Yet Jesus selected Matthew the tax collector as one of the Twelve. This shows that God's covenant of grace extends to all people and that no one is beyond the reach of His mercy and love.

A Funeral Procession

This verse gives us insight into a burial custom from New Testament times. A widow's son had died, and a coffin with his body inside was being carried outside the city for burial. The woman's friends and neighbors were walking along with her.

This is similar to our modern custom of forming a funeral procession to follow the casket of a deceased person to the cemetery for burial. It is a gesture of respect that assures the survivors of our love and support.

What Jesus did for this widow who had lost her only son was more than a gesture of respect. In an act of compassion, He raised him from the dead and then "delivered him to his mother" (Luke 7:15).

He [Jesus] came nigh to the gate of the city, behold, there was a dead man carried out, the only son of his mother, and she was a widow: and much people of the city [a large crowd from the town, NIV] was with her.

Luke 7:12

Eyes Straight Ahead

The primitive plows of Bible times were hard to handle, particularly when trying to prod the ox that was pulling the plow into action at the same time (see notes on Judges 3:31 and 1 Kings 19:19). Plowing a straight furrow required eyes-ahead concentration at all times.

No man, having put his hand to the plough, and looking back, is fit for the kingdom of God.

Luke 9:62

Plows were difficult to handle, requiring the farmer to focus intently on the process in order to keep the furrows straight.

205

Just like a plowing farmer, the believer must commit himself to the Lord and keep looking ahead to the work to which he has been called. It is impossible to serve the Lord if we refuse to let go of the old habits and patterns of life from the past.

DON'T WASTE TIME

Salute [greet, NIV] no man by the way [on the road, NIV].
LUKE 10:4

Jesus gave these instructions to seventy of His followers when He sent them out on a teaching and witnessing mission. It seems strange that He would forbid them from greeting the very people whom they were sent to reach.

But Jesus did not restrict them from greeting strangers with a friendly "hello." He was referring to the elaborate and drawn-out salutations with which the Jewish people sometimes greeted one another. They would bow again and again, ask about the health and welfare of all the members of their respective families, and repeat their wishes for the peace and prosperity of the other several times.

This type of greeting took a lot of time. "Greet people quickly, and be on your way," is what Jesus was saying. "Let's use every precious minute we have to bring people into God's kingdom."

TWO HEALING AGENTS

A certain Samaritan. . . went to him [a wounded traveler], and bound up [bandaged, NIV] his wounds, pouring in oil and wine.
LUKE 10:33–34

This verse from Jesus' parable of the good Samaritan describes how he treated the wounds of the traveler who had been beaten by thieves on the road from Jerusalem to Jericho.

Because of its alcohol content, wine was often used as a medicine (see note on 1 Timothy 5:23). Olive oil also soothed the traveler's wounds and aided the healing process.

A segment of the Roman road connecting Jerusalem with Jericho. This road was the setting for Jesus' parable of the good Samaritan.

A Crowded Bedroom

This verse comes from a parable of Jesus that emphasizes the need for persistence in prayer. The man in the parable first refused his neighbor's request to borrow some bread to feed a late-night guest. But he finally got up and gave him what he wanted because the neighbor kept on asking.

Most of the houses of Bible times had one bedroom where the entire family slept. Separate mats on the floor served as their mattresses. They were not all sleeping together in the same bed as the King James Version implies. A better translation is, "My children and I are in bed" (CEV).

He from within shall answer. . .Trouble me not: the door is now shut, and my children are with me in bed.
LUKE 11:7

Bread, Not Rocks

This verse continues Jesus' teaching on prayer. It emphasizes the truth that our loving heavenly Father is eager to give us what we need if we will ask in prayerful trust and faith.

The small round cakes into which bread was baked in New Testament times had some resemblance to flat circular rocks. This is why Jesus used the imagery of a loving father not giving stones to a son who asked him for bread. This is also the imagery behind Satan's challenge to Jesus during His temptation in the wilderness: "If thou be the Son of God, command that these stones be made bread" (Matthew 4:3).

If a son shall ask bread of any of you that is a father, will he give him a stone?
LUKE 11:11

True Riches

With these words, Jesus encouraged His followers to build up heavenly treasure, or the favor of God—not to stockpile earthly riches that will not stand the test of time.

The bags or purses that He mentioned were leather pouches in which royal treasures were stored. Treasures like this can be lost or stolen (Luke 12:33). But God's love and favor toward believers will last forever.

Provide yourselves bags [purses, NIV] which wax not old [will not wear out, NIV], a treasure in the heavens that faileth not [will not be exhausted, NIV].
LUKE 12:33

The Power of Leaven

In the process of baking bread, leaven or yeast was added to the dough to cause it to rise. Thus, Jesus was saying that the kingdom of God had a power out of proportion to its size that caused it to permeate and influence all of society.

Jews ate unleavened bread during the celebration of the Passover to remember the circumstances under which the Israelites were delivered by the Lord from Egyptian slavery. They left so quickly that they didn't have time to add leaven to the bread they were baking at the time (Exodus 12:34, 39).

The kingdom of God. . . is like leaven [yeast, NIV], which a woman took and hid [mixed, NIV] in three measures of meal [a large amount of flour, NIV], till the whole was leavened [until it worked all through the dough, NIV].
LUKE 13:20–21

DINING WITH A PHARISEE

Jesus' clash with the Pharisees throughout the Gospels may lead us to believe that all Pharisees were bad or that Jesus condemned them all. But this verse shows us otherwise.

A leader among the Pharisees apparently invited Jesus to dine in his home on the Sabbath, and He accepted the invitation. Jesus used the occasion to teach this man and several other Pharisees about His healing mission and His superiority over the Sabbath (Luke 14:3–6).

Two other Pharisees in the Gospels are also worthy of commendation. Nicodemus was a Pharisee who was known for his inquiring mind and seach for truth (John 3:1–12). Joseph of Arimathea was probably a Pharisee since he was a member of the Sanhedrin. He claimed the body of Jesus and buried it in his own new tomb (see note on Mark 15:43).

A SQUANDERED INHERITANCE

This verse is part of Jesus' parable of the prodigal son (Luke 15:11–32). An estate was normally divided by a father among his sons at his death. But the father in this parable did so while he was still alive.

Under Jewish law, the firstborn son received a double portion of his father's estate (Deuteronomy 21:17) because he assumed responsibilities as head of the clan. Since there were two brothers in this parable, the younger son received one-third of the inheritance and the older son received two-thirds.

The younger son turned his inheritance of property and goods into cash ("got together all he had," Luke 15:13 NIV), left the country, and wasted it all on a spending spree. The father's love when he welcomed his destitute son back home represents God's love and forgiveness of repentant sinners.

A RESOURCEFUL STEWARD

In this parable (Luke 16:1–8) Jesus told about a person who had been employed by a rich man to look after his property. As a steward or manager, he was like a financial agent who made investments to increase his employer's wealth and look after his business affairs.

Through carelessness and mismanagement, this steward lost a lot of his employer's money. Facing the loss of his job, he made secret deals with his employer's creditors to make sure they would come to his aid after he was fired. His resourcefulness and foresight were commended by his employer.

The message of Jesus' parable is that all believers are stewards of the blessings of God. We should be wise and creative in taking care of the resources—both physical and spiritual—that God has committed to our care.

Twice-a-Week Fasting

These are the words of the self-righteous Pharisee in Jesus' parable about the Pharisee and the tax collector. Fasting twice a week, as the Pharisee claimed to do, was not commanded in the law of Moses. This was probably a custom instituted by the Pharisees as an addition to the law that they practiced scrupulously.

The message of this verse is that we can't buy our way into heaven by observing certain rituals. We are justified in God's sight only through faith in Jesus Christ and His atoning death on our behalf.

I [a self-righteous Pharisee] fast twice in the week, I give tithes of all that I possess.
Luke 18:12

Grief over Sin

This verse is also part of Jesus' parable of the Pharisee and the tax collector. He contrasted the self-righteous attitude of a proud Pharisee with the humble and penitent attitude of a tax collector.

Jesus declared that the tax collector, rather than the Pharisee, was favored by God. This must have been a surprise to many in the audience, because the Jews considered tax collectors to be traitors and degenerate sinners (see notes on Matthew 9:10 and Luke 5:27).

But the tax collector's attitude was what mattered to Jesus. He expressed his extreme remorse over his sin by beating his breast, a gesture of grief and mourning (Nahum 2:7 NIV). He recognized his sin, repented of it, and pleaded for God's mercy and grace.

The publican [tax collector, NIV], standing afar off, would not lift up so much as his eyes unto heaven, but smote [beat, NIV] upon his breast, saying, God be merciful to me a sinner.
Luke 18:13

Herod's Temple in Jerusalem

When Jesus entered Jerusalem for the Passover celebration, His disciples were impressed with the Jewish temple that was being remodeled in a project launched by Herod the Great, Roman ruler over Palestine. According to the Jewish historian Josephus, its white marble and gold trim was dazzling to the eyes.

Herod began this building project about 15 BC in order to curry the favor of the Jews. It was still

Some spake of the temple, how it was adorned with goodly [beautiful, NIV] stones and gifts [gifts dedicated to God, NIV].
Luke 21:5

The Temple in Jerusalem was remodeled by Herod the Great.

under construction about forty-five years later when Jesus and His disciples came to the holy city to observe the Passover. Finally completed in AD 64, the temple was destroyed—as Jesus predicted (Luke 21:6)—when the Roman army put down a rebellion by the Jewish people in AD 70.

The temple in Jerusalem has never been rebuilt. Today a Muslim mosque known as the Dome of the Rock occupies the site.

THE JEWISH SCRIPTURES

All things must be fulfilled, which were written in the law of Moses, and in the prophets, and in the psalms, concerning me [Jesus].

LUKE 24:44

Jesus spoke these words to His disciples when He appeared among them in Jerusalem after His resurrection. He declared that He had fulfilled all of the things foretold about the Messiah in the Jewish scriptures.

The scriptures used by the Jews in Jesus' time included the books in our present Old Testament, but they were arranged differently than in our modern Bibles. Jesus mentioned the three major divisions of the Jewish scriptures.

1. *The Law of Moses*. This is what we refer to today as the Pentateuch—Genesis, Exodus, Leviticus, Numbers, and Deuteronomy.

2. *The Prophets*. This section included Joshua, Judges, 1 and 2 Samuel, 1 and 2 Kings, and all of the prophets except Daniel.

3. *The Psalms*. Included in this section were the Psalms, the book for which the entire section was named, as well as Proverbs, Job, Song of Solomon, Ruth, Lamentations, Ecclesiastes, Esther, Daniel, Ezra, Nehemiah, and 1 and 2 Chronicles.

JOHN

HUMILITY OF JOHN THE BAPTIST

He [Jesus] it is. . .whose shoe's latchet [thongs, NIV] I [John the Baptist] am not worthy to unloose.

JOHN 1:27

Although John the Baptist was divinely selected to serve as the forerunner of Jesus (Luke 1:76), he was aware of his unworthiness of such an honor. He declared in this verse that he was not even worthy to bend down and untie the leather thongs that held Jesus' sandals on His feet.

But Jesus recognized John's greatness and commended

him for his faithfulness: "Among them that are born of women there hath not risen a greater than John the Baptist" (Matthew 11:11).

WATER INTO WINE

This is the only place where the word *firkin* appears in the Bible. It was the main liquid measure of the Roman world in New Testament times. A firkin was equal to about nine gallons.

Jesus directed that these huge jars should be filled with water, then He turned the water into wine (John 2:7–9). According to the Gospel of John, this was the first of Jesus' many miracles (John 2:11).

JOHN, THE BRIDEGROOM'S FRIEND

These words of John the Baptist show his joy at being chosen as the forerunner of Christ. He compared himself to the friend of the bridegroom, a close friend or relative of the groom who helped plan and arrange the wedding.

According to John, the duties of the friend of the groom would end when the groom—or Jesus the Messiah—appeared to wed His bride. The modern custom of the groom's best man is based loosely on this "friend of the bridegroom" tradition.

DRAWING FROM JACOB'S WELL

The well at which Jesus talked with this Samaritan woman was known as Jacob's Well (John 4:6). Although it is not mentioned in the Old Testament, it was named for the

There were set there six waterpots of stone. . . containing two or three firkins apiece [each holding from twenty to thirty gallons, NIV].
JOHN 2:6

Stone water jars like these played a role in Jesus' first miracle at Cana in Galilee.

The friend of the bridegroom, which standeth and heareth him, rejoiceth greatly because of the bridegroom's voice.
JOHN 3:29

The woman saith unto him [Jesus], Sir, thou hast nothing to draw with, and the well is deep.
JOHN 4:11

The traditional site of Jacob's Well, where Jesus spoke with the Samaritan woman (John 4).

211

patriarch Jacob, who lived many centuries before Jesus' time. It was a community well (see note on Genesis 24:11) that provided water for citizens of the village of Sychar (John 4:5). This well, still visible today, is a popular stopping spot on Holy Land tours.

WELCOME TO WOMEN

Upon this [Just then, NIV] came his [Jesus'] disciples, and marvelled [were surprised, NIV] that he talked with the woman.
JOHN 4:27

The attitude of Jesus' disciples toward this Samaritan woman was typical of the views of Jewish males toward all women during New Testament times. Women were considered inferior to men. They were not to be greeted in the streets or instructed in the law as males were. Certainly, no respectable Jewish teacher would talk with a woman in a public place.

But Jesus rejected this stereotype, just as He rejected prejudice toward any group of people (see notes on Matthew 9:10; Matthew 20:2; and John 8:48). He included women in His teaching and healing ministry (Mark 1:29–31; Luke 8:43–48; 10:38–42), treated them with kindness and respect (John 8:1–11), and welcomed them as His followers (Mark 15:40–41).

SUDDEN STORMS ON THE SEA OF GALILEE

The sea arose by reason of a great wind that blew.
JOHN 6:18

Jesus' disciples were crossing the Sea of Galilee in a small fishing boat when they were caught in a sudden storm.

This freshwater lake, about thirteen miles long by eight miles wide, is fed by the Jordan River. It sits about seven hundred feet below sea level in an area surrounded by high mountains. Cool winds frequently rush down from these mountains and mix with the warm air on the surface of the lake. The result is a sudden, violent storm such as that which overwhelmed the disciples.

The Sea of Galilee.

THE GREAT THIRST-QUENCHER

This verse refers to the Feast of Tabernacles. An eight-day festival, it commemorated the years of wandering of the Jewish people in the wilderness after their release from slavery in Egypt. Jesus was in Jerusalem for this celebration because it was one of the three great festivals that adult Jewish males were required to attend in the holy city (see notes on Exodus 23:14; Exodus 23:15–16; and Exodus 23:17).

On the last day of the festival, a priest poured water on the altar in the temple. This represented God's provision of water for the Israelites in the wilderness (Numbers 20:1–11). This was the moment when Jesus declared that He had been sent as living water to quench the spiritual thirst of all people (John 7:38).

In the last day, that great day of the feast [the last and greatest day of the Feast, NIV], Jesus stood and cried, saying, If any man thirst, let him come unto me, and drink.
JOHN 7:37

JEWS AND SAMARITANS

The Jewish religious leaders attempted to discredit Jesus and His work by resorting to name-calling and insults. They told Him that He was possessed by a demon—or deranged and out of His mind. What's worse, they called Him "a Samaritan." This was the ultimate insult among Jews of Jesus' time.

Samaritans were former Jews who had corrupted their bloodline by intermarrying with pagans and foreigners several centuries before New Testament times. They lived in their own separate territory in the central section of Palestine. Most Jews refused to even travel through this region. They would take a wide detour around the Samaritan's homeland when traveling across Palestine.

Jesus had no such prejudice toward the Samaritans. He talked with a Samaritan woman at a well outside her village and offered her "living water" during one of His trips through Samaria (see note on John 4:27). He told a parable about a kind Samaritan traveler who came to the aid of a wounded man, even when this man's fellow Jewish citizens refused to get involved (Luke 10:25–37).

Say we [Jewish religious leaders] not well that thou [Jesus] art a Samaritan, and hast a devil [are. . . demon-possessed, NIV]?
JOHN 8:48

THE LONG ARM OF THE SYNAGOGUE

The Pharisees were angry because Jesus had healed a blind man on the Sabbath (John 9:1–7). They first questioned the man himself about his healer and then interviewed the man's parents. They refused to get involved, because they knew they could be excommunicated from their local synagogue if they did not give testimony that pleased the Jewish religious leaders.

These words spake his [blind man healed by Jesus] parents, because. . . the Jews had agreed already, that if any man did confess that he was Christ, he should be put out of the synagogue.
JOHN 9:22

213

Excommunication from the synagogue was a serious matter to the Jews. A person was banned from attending synagogue services and hearing instruction from the law. The most serious form of excommunication cut a person off from all connection with his fellow Jews.

This most severe penalty may have been pronounced by the Pharisees against this healed man because he claimed that Jesus was a divine teacher sent from God (John 9:30–34).

THE RIGHT CREDENTIALS

A sheepfold was a fenced area in which sheep were bedded down for the night to keep them safe from wild animals and thieves. This pen had only one door, and the shepherd slept near the door as an additional security measure.

With this imagery, Jesus declared Himself to be the true shepherd of Israel. The Pharisees claimed to be the leaders, or shepherds, of God's people, but they were actually false prophets who were leading the people astray.

Jesus was the Good Shepherd who had entered the sheepfold with the right credentials. He was God's Son who had been sent by the Lord Himself as the Savior and Redeemer of His people.

Shepherds made enclosures from fieldstones in which to bed down their flocks for the night.

FOLLOWING THE SHEPHERD

Shepherds of Bible times did not use dogs to keep their sheep in line. They relied on a system of verbal commands, using the voice to move them around, to call straying sheep back to the flock, and to lead them to grass and water.

Jesus used this imagery to show how He as the Good Shepherd takes care of His flock. He is a leader—not a driver—of His sheep. Believers recognize His call and follow Him willingly because they know He wants only the best for His flock.

THE JEWISH CLOCK

To the Jews of New Testament times, sundown marked the end of an old day and the beginning of a new day. The twenty-four-hour period between each sundown was divided into twelve hours of night—beginning about 6:00 p.m.—and twelve hours of daylight—beginning with dawn at about 6:00 a.m.

Thus, the "third hour of the night" (Acts 23:23) was about 9:00 p.m., and the "third hour" of the day (Matthew 20:3) was about 9:00 a.m.

The Romans used a different system for measuring the hours of the day and night. It is not always possible to tell whether the Jewish or the Roman system is being cited in the New Testament. Thus, one modern translation of the Bible renders the "tenth hour" in John 1:39 as "10 in the morning" (HCSB), three stick with the King James Version by rendering it "tenth hour" (ESV, NASB, NKJV), and three translate it as "four o'clock in the afternoon" (CEV, NCV, NRSV).

Are there not twelve hours in the day [twelve hours of daylight, NIV]?
JOHN 11:9

THOMAS THE TWIN

Thomas was one of the twelve disciples of Jesus. This is one of four places where he is mentioned in the Gospel of John (14:5–6; 20:24–29; 21:2). Except for the listing of his name (Matthew 10:2–4; Mark 3:14–19; Luke 6:12–16), he is not mentioned in the other three Gospels.

Thomas was the Aramaic form of his name, and Didymus was the Greek version. Both names mean "twin," so Thomas must have had a twin brother or sister.

Then said Thomas, which is called Didymus. . .
JOHN 11:16

RECLINING WHILE EATING

This verse describes the scene when Jesus was eating the Last Supper with His disciples on the night before He was crucified. They were not seated at a high table, as some popular paintings show, but were reclining around a low table, in accordance with the custom of that time.

Each person thrust his legs out to the side and leaned on his elbow while taking food from the table. This is how it was possible for John, the "disciple whom Jesus loved," to be leaning back against the bosom of Jesus, who was immediately behind him.

There was leaning [reclining, NIV] on Jesus' bosom one of his disciples, whom Jesus loved.
JOHN 13:23

It was the custom in Jesus' day to eat while reclining around a low table.

CARRYING THE CROSS

A cross strong enough to hold the weight of a man and long enough to be placed in the ground and have the victim elevated at the same time would probably be too heavy for a person to carry.

Thus, Jesus probably carried only the horizontal beam to the crucifixion site. Here he was stripped naked, laid on the ground, and nailed to the beam, which was then raised and attached to the upright post.

This form of execution (see note on Matthew 27:35) was so cruel and degrading that it was never imposed by the Roman government against its own citizens.

A JEWISH BURIAL

Before placing Jesus' body in his own new tomb (see note on Mark 15:43), Joseph of Arimathea, along with Nicodemus, wound it in strips of cloth. These men also placed aromatic spices among the folds of the cloth, probably to mask the odor when the body began to decay.

This was the customary method of burial among the Jews. They buried a body quickly after death, making no attempt to preserve it, as the Egyptians did with their embalming process (see note on Genesis 50:2–3).

SUPERNATURAL PEACE

According to John's Gospel, this was Jesus' first appearance to His disciples after His resurrection. His first word to them was the common greeting used by the Jewish people of that day—a wish for their peace, wholeness, and well-being.

When Jesus greeted them with these words, perhaps the disciples remembered a promise of His supernatural peace and presence that He had made to them while training them for the task of carrying on His work: "Peace I leave with you, my peace I give unto you: not as the world giveth, give I unto you. Let not your heart be troubled, neither let it be afraid" (John 14:27).

WISHES FOR PEACE

1. A kind old man in the city of Gibeah greeted a stranger in town with the words, "Peace be with thee" (Judges 19:20).
2. David instructed his men to introduce themselves to the wealthy herdsman Nabal with this elegant greeting: "Peace be both to thee, and peace be to thine house, and peace be unto all that thou hast" (1 Samuel 25:6). David hoped that Nabal would provide food for his hungry warriors.

ACTS

A SHORT WALK

Jesus ascended to heaven from the Mount of Olives after delivering a farewell message to these believers (Acts 1:6–9). This hill east of Jerusalem is just a few minutes' walk from the city. This tells us that a "sabbath day's journey" was probably less than a mile.

The prohibition against working on the Sabbath (Exodus 20:8–11) led to this regulation about a Sabbath day's journey. Walking farther than this short distance permitted on the day of worship was considered work, and thus a violation of the Sabbath law.

Jesus may have had this regulation in mind when He told His followers they might have to flee to escape persecution in the end times: "Pray ye that your flight be not. . .on the sabbath day" (Matthew 24:20).

The Bible also speaks of a "day's journey" (see note on 1 Kings 19:4).

Then returned they [early believers] unto Jerusalem from the mount called Olivet, which is from Jerusalem a sabbath day's journey [walk, NIV].
ACTS 1:12

The Tower of Ascension, located on the Mount of Olives, marks the traditional location for Jesus' ascension into heaven.

DEATH BY STONING

Executing a person by bludgeoning him to death with stones was the form of execution preferred by the Jewish people during Bible times.

Stephen, the first martyr of the Christian movement, was stoned to death by the Jewish Sanhedrin on the charge

[The members of the Jewish Sanhedrin] cast him [Stephen] out of the city, and stoned him.
ACTS 7:58

that he spoke blasphemously against the temple (Acts 7:47–49) and claimed that Jesus was the Messiah, whom they had crucified (Acts 7:52).

Normally only the Romans could administer the death penalty in Palestine. But they may have turned a deaf ear in this case because they considered the Jewish charge of blasphemy against Stephen an internal religious matter that did not merit Roman attention.

In addition to blasphemy, the Old Testament law listed several offenses for which stoning was specified: child sacrifice (Leviticus 20:2), consultation with witches and mediums (Leviticus 20:27), violation of the restriction against working on the Sabbath (Numbers 15:32–36), worship of false gods (Deuteronomy 13:10), and rebellion against one's parents (Deuteronomy 21:18–21). The account of Jesus' encounter with a woman accused (John 8:3–11) shows that adultery was also considered a capital offense for which stoning was mandated.

Praying on the Roof

Peter went up upon the housetop [roof, NIV] to pray about the sixth hour [about noon, NIV].
Acts 10:9

This may seem to us like a strange place to pray, but it made perfect sense to Peter.

The roofs of houses in Bible times might be compared to our modern patios. They were flat and easily accessible by an exterior stairway. People often went to the roof for rest and relaxation, particularly at night to catch a cooling breeze (see note on Deuteronomy 22:8).

Peter probably went to the roof so he could be alone in prayer, since he was a visitor in the house of Simon the tanner (Acts 10:5–6).

Peter's Jail Break

When he [Herod] had apprehended him [Peter], he put him in prison, and delivered him to four quaternions of soldiers [four squads of four soldiers each, NIV] to keep him.
Acts 12:4

Peter must have been considered a dangerous criminal if sixteen Roman soldiers were assigned to guard him! Actually, he was guarded by four soldiers at a time. These four sentinels were rotated every three hours, at the beginning of every "watch" into which the night was divided (see note on Mark 13:35).

The apostle was chained between two of these soldiers in his cell, and the other two stood guard at the door (Acts 12:6). But God released his shackles and had him walk out of the prison in a trance, and none of the soldiers even realized he was gone (Acts 12:7–11).

THE SYNAGOGUE LEADER

During Paul's first missionary journey, he and his associate, Barnabas, attended worship services at the local synagogue (see note on Luke 4:16) in Antioch of Pisidia. They were invited to speak to the other worshipers by the rulers or presiding officers of the synagogue.

A synagogue ruler was elected to his position by other members of the congregation. His responsibility was to plan the services, enlist readers and speakers, and preside at the worship proceedings.

Most mentions of this synagogue officer in the New Testament refer to only one ruler (Mark 5:36–38; Luke 13:14). But this passage in Acts mentions more than one ruler. Perhaps a division of responsibilities was required in larger synagogues.

> *The rulers of the synagogue sent unto them [Paul and Barnabas], saying. . .*
> *If ye have any word of exhortation [message of encouragement, NIV] for the people, say on.*
> ACTS 13:15

The synagogue located somewhere amidst the ruins of Pisidian Antioch hosted Paul and Barnabas on Paul's first missionary journey.

GODS IN HUMAN FORM

During Paul's first missionary journey, he and Barnabas visited the city of Lystra in the province of Lycaonia. After Paul preached the gospel to the people of the city, he healed a crippled man. They were so impressed that they hailed the missionaries as pagan gods who had come down to them "in

> *They [the citizens of Lystra] called Barnabas, Jupiter; and Paul, Mercurius, because he was the chief speaker.*
> ACTS 14:12

219

the likeness of men" (Acts 14:11).

Jupiter was the supreme god of all the pagan deities. Mercurius was the god of speech and eloquence. Since Paul was the chief speaker, the people identified him as Mercurius.

BULLS AND GARLANDS FOR JUPITER

One of the priests at the temple of Jupiter just outside the city of Lystra heard about the visit of Paul and Barnabas (see note on Acts 14:12). He wanted to get in on the action, so he brought bulls, along with garlands of flowers or leaves, to present as offerings to Jupiter.

This account of Paul and Barnabas in Lystra demonstrates the spiritual bankruptcy of the first-century world. The old Greek and Roman gods were losing their appeal. The people's eagerness to worship pagan gods in human form shows that ignorance and superstition were widespread. Into this religious vacuum, Paul and Barnabas introduced a revolutionary new spiritual reality: "For God so loved the world, that he gave his only begotten Son, that whosoever believeth in him should not perish, but have everlasting life" (John 3:16).

RIVERSIDE WITNESSING

When Paul and Silas arrived in Philippi, they did not find a Jewish synagogue, probably because there were few Jews in this region of the Gentile world. Ten Jewish men were the minimum required before a synagogue could be established.

But the two missionaries did find a synagogue substitute—an outdoor spot by the river outside the city where the few Jews in the region met for prayer on the Sabbath.

Here Paul and Silas met a Jewish woman named Lydia,

Then the priest of Jupiter [Zeus, NIV], which was before [outside, NIV] their city, brought oxen [bulls, NIV] and garlands [wreaths, NIV] unto the gates [city gates, NIV], and would have done sacrifice with the people.

ACTS 14:13

On the sabbath we [Paul and Silas] went out of the city [Philippi] by a river side, where prayer was wont to be made.

ACTS 16:13

Beside this river located just outside Philippi, Paul and Silas witnessed to Lydia.

who became a believer after she heard about Jesus and His sacrificial death. Lydia and her household were baptized, and she provided lodging for the two missionaries while they witnessed to others in Philippi (Acts 16:14–15).

Lydia's conversion shows that any place—even a spot by the river—is an appropriate setting for sharing the gospel with others.

HAPPENINGS BY RIVERS

1. The baby Moses was hidden by his mother in a basket on the Nile River (Exodus 2:3).
2. Naaman, a Syrian military officer, was healed of his leprosy when he bathed in the Jordan River at the prophet Elisha's command (2 Kings 5:9–14).
3. The Jewish exiles wept by "the rivers of Babylon" when they remembered the city of Jerusalem and their native land (Psalm 137:1).
4. The prophet Daniel had a vision of the future while standing by the river Ulai in Babylon (Daniel 8:2).

A DESPERATE JAILER

God sent an earthquake to release Paul and Silas from their prison cell in the city of Philippi. Along with these missionaries, all of the other prisoners were also set free.

Under Roman law, prison keepers were held strictly accountable for the prisoners under their guard. If one escaped, the keeper assumed his punishment. It is likely that some of these prisoners were being tortured or would face such treatment in the future or were being held for capital crimes. Since all of the prisoners in this situation were set free, the jailer considered committing suicide a better fate than undergoing these punishments.

He [the jailer at Philippi] drew out his sword, and would have killed himself, supposing that the prisoners had been fled.
Acts 16:27

CIVIL RIGHTS VIOLATIONS

With these words, Paul condemned the officials of the city of Philippi for breaking the Roman law by throwing him and Silas—both Roman citizens—into prison.

Roman citizens had certain rights in New Testament times (see note on Acts 25:12). If charged with a crime, they could not be beaten or imprisoned without a trial. The high-handed treatment of Paul and Silas by the officials of Philippi was a violation of both of these rights.

They [the magistrates of Philippi] have beaten us [Paul and Silas] openly uncondemned, being Romans, and have cast us into prison.
Acts 16:37

PAUL IN THE MARKETPLACE

When Paul arrived in the city of Athens, the cultural center of ancient Greece, he presented the gospel first to the Jewish citizens in their synagogue. Then he moved into the open-air marketplace for discussions with other citizens of the city.

The agora, or marketplace, in cities of New Testament times was a public place where merchants sold their wares

Therefore disputed he [Paul]. . .in the market daily with them [citizens of Athens] that met with him.
Acts 17:17

The marketplace provided a welcome location for Paul to discuss the gospel message with the residents of Athens.

(see note on James 4:13) and day laborers went to be hired (see note on Matthew 20:3).

Here people also gathered to catch up on the latest news and strike up conversations with their friends and strangers to the city. This was an ideal spot where Paul could mingle with the crowd and witness for Jesus Christ.

PAUL THE TENTMAKER

Because he [Paul] was of the same craft, he abode with them [Priscilla and Aquila], and wrought [worked, NIV]: for by their occupation they were tentmakers.
ACTS 18:3

Paul spent eighteen months in the city of Corinth (Acts 18:11), working with Priscilla and Aquila at their mutual trade of tentmaking to support himself. During this time they established a church in this thriving, paganistic city.

The craft of tentmaking involved sewing together pieces of cloth or animal skins, adding ropes and loops for staking the tent, and cutting and sewing flaps for the tent door (see note on Genesis 18:1). Paul may have learned this trade from his father. Jewish men considered it their responsibility to pass on their trades to their sons.

A PUBLIC BOOK BURNING

Many of them [citizens of Ephesus] also which used curious arts [sorcery, NIV] brought their books [scrolls, NIV] together, and burned them before all men.
ACTS 19:19

Paul spent at least two years in Ephesus (Acts 19:10)—longer than he did in any other city where he established a church. This verse shows the cumulative impact the gospel had on the city's practitioners of black magic.

Many of them who became Christians gathered up their occultic books and burned them in a public gesture of their contempt for their old way of life. Luke, author of the book of Acts, adds this note on what was happening in this pagan city: "In this way the word of the Lord spread widely and grew in power" (Acts 19:20 NIV).

DIANA AND HER TEMPLE

A city of about 300,000 people, Ephesus was a strategic center for the planting of the gospel in the Gentile world (see note on Acts 19:19). The pride of the city was a large, ornate temple devoted to worship of Diana, or Artemis, a pagan fertility goddess. This building was one of the seven wonders of the ancient world.

Bigger than a football field, it was flanked by several ornate columns more than fifty feet tall. People from all over the province of Macedonia came to worship the multibreasted Diana at this sacred site.

Demetrius and other craftsmen of the city made their living by making and selling miniature replicas of Diana. These were probably worn as charms on necklaces or bracelets by her worshipers.

When the citizens of Ephesus began turning to the Lord and quit buying these pagan charms, Demetrius incited a riot against Paul (Acts 19:24–29). Religious tolerance was out of the question when pagan profits were at stake.

A certain man [of Ephesus] named Demetrius, a silversmith, which made silver shrines for Diana [Artemis, NIV], brought no small gain unto the craftsmen.
ACTS 19:24

DISTURBANCE AT THE THEATER

The riot inspired by Demetrius spilled over into the entire city. The people gathered at the amphitheater to join in the demonstration.

The Roman theater at Ephesus has been unearthed by archaeologists. Built similar to a modern stadium, it had row upon row of tiered seats built of stone. It could seat about twenty-five thousand people.

Huge amphitheaters like this were built by the Greeks

The whole city [of Ephesus] was filled with confusion [in an uproar, NIV]: and. . .rushed with one accord into the theatre.
ACTS 19:29

The Roman theater in ancient Ephesus. The citizens of this city rioted when Paul confronted them with God's Word.

223

and Romans throughout the ancient world. Others have been discovered at Athens, Corinth, Miletus, Pergamos, and Philippi.

PAUL'S RIGHT OF APPEAL

Festus. . .answered, Hast thou [Paul] appealed unto Caesar? unto Caesar shalt thou go.
ACTS 25:12

Festus was the Roman governor of Judea who agreed to hear the charges against Paul brought by the Jewish leaders. When Festus suggested that the apostle be sent back to the Jewish court, Paul invoked his rights as a Roman citizen (see note on Acts 16:37). He appealed his case to Rome, the capital city, where he would be assured of a fair trial (Acts 25:10–11).

In Paul's time, a person could become a Roman citizen by birth or by buying this special status. Roman officials often granted these rights to non-Romans who had rendered special service to the empire. Although Paul was a Jew, he had been born a Roman citizen (Acts 22:28). How his parents had obtained their citizenship rights is unknown.

PERILS ON THE SEA

Fearing lest we [Paul and his shipmates] should have fallen upon rocks, they [the sailors] cast four anchors out of the stern, and wished for the day [prayed for daylight, NIV].
ACTS 27:29

Acts 27 reports on the voyage of Paul to Rome and the wreck of his ship in a ferocious storm. Ancient sailing ships were at the mercy of the winds. The crew tossed out four anchors from the rear of the ship to keep it from being broken to pieces on the rocky shore.

This chapter of Acts also tells us that the captain of this ship was pushing his luck by sailing to Rome so late in the year. Most ships that sailed the Mediterranean Sea apparently docked in a protected bay or inlet until the storms of winter were over (Acts 27:7–12).

Several actions were taken to save the ship when the storm struck with its full fury. The crew pulled ropes or cables tightly around the hull to keep it from breaking apart (Acts 27:17). They also lightened the ship by throwing the cargo and even its pulleys and ropes for hoisting the sails into the sea (Acts 27:19, 38).

ROMANS

GREEKS AND BARBARIANS

Paul meant by these words that he was under obligation—by virtue of his call from God—to share the gospel with all types of people. This included the Greeks, a highly civilized and cultured people, as well as the barbarians—a general term for the unlearned and unsophisticated.

The Greeks referred to any person who was not a citizen of Greece as a "barbarian," just as the Jews thought of all non-Jewish people—no matter what their ethnic background—as "Gentiles."

> I [Paul] am debtor [obligated to, NIV] both to the Greeks, and to the Barbarians [non-Greeks, NIV]; both to the wise, and to the unwise [foolish, NIV].
> ROMANS 1:14

ADOPTION AND SALVATION

Paul compared the process by which believers are justified to the process of adoption in Roman culture. If a Roman man had no son by biological birth, he could adopt one. One of his slaves might even be adopted as a son. The adopted son took the name of the father and had all of the rights that would have been extended to a biological child.

Paul also made this comparison between adoption and salvation in his letter to the Galatians. After being delivered from bondage to sin and adopted into God's family, a believer is "no more a servant, but a son; and if a son, then an heir of God through Christ" (Galatians 4:7).

> Ye [believers in Christ] have received the Spirit of adoption [sonship, NIV], whereby we cry, Abba, Father.
> ROMANS 8:15

TREATMENT OF ENEMIES

This advice from the apostle Paul is based on Jesus' teaching from His Sermon on the Mount: "Love your enemies, bless them that curse you, do good to them that hate you" (Matthew 5:44).

But Paul adds an observation about the response that our kindness will kindle in our enemies. "Heaping coals of fire" on the heads of one's enemies refers to the sense of remorse they will feel about their hateful behavior. The refusal to retaliate with like behavior toward hate and unkindness is one of the hallmarks of a believer (see note on Matthew 5:38).

> If thine enemy hunger, feed him; if he thirst, give him drink: for in so doing thou shalt heap coals of fire on his head.
> ROMANS 12:20

225

Paul's "Holy" Kiss

Salute [Greet, NIV] one another with an holy kiss.

Romans 16:16

In three other of his epistles, Paul instructed believers to greet one another in this way (1 Corinthians 16:20; 2 Corinthians 13:12; 1 Thessalonians 5:26). Thus, we can assume that the holy kiss ("kiss of charity," 1 Peter 5:14) was practiced widely among the early New Testament churches.

This is one of those biblical customs that we find surprising and puzzling because of the romantic and sexual overtones attached to kissing in our culture. The New Living Translation takes the easy way out and renders this verse, "Greet each other in Christian love." But greeting others with a kiss had no erotic meaning in Bible times. We might compare it to a handshake in the modern world. It was simply the customary way to greet others (see note on Genesis 29:13).

It is interesting that Paul added the word *holy* to this standard kiss of greeting. Early believers could greet one another with a "holy" kiss because they were members of God's family who had been cleansed and justified by the blood of Christ.

1 CORINTHIANS

Gladiator Apostles

I [Paul] think that God hath set forth us the apostles last, as it were appointed to death: for we are made a spectacle unto the world, and to angels, and to men.

1 Corinthians 4:9

Paul compared himself and the other apostles of the New Testament to the gladiators who were "set forth. . .last" in the Roman arena. These were slaves or criminals who were forced to fight experienced gladiators or wild animals without weapons and who were quickly "appointed to death."

Paul was saying that he and the other apostles of New Testament times had made sacrifices to advance the gospel—and the Corinthian believers had been blessed by their witnessing efforts.

Paul's words were prophetic. Most of the apostles of the early church, including this great missionary to the Gentiles, were eventually martyred for their faith.

This arena at Miletus witnessed the life and death struggle of gladiators. Paul compared his ministry to life as a gladiator in 1 Corinthians 4:9.

DISCIPLINE AND TRAINING

This is one of many references in Paul's writings to the Greek games that were similar to our modern Olympics. An athlete who expected to win at these games had to be "temperate in all things," or undergo a strict regimen of discipline and training.

Paul was comparing the Christian life to the discipline required of these Greek athletes. Believers are saved to a life of service in the cause of Christ. Every day should bring us closer to the goal of total commitment to Christ and His work.

The winners of the various contests in these games were recognized by having a crown made from leaves placed on their heads. Paul compared this makeshift earthly crown that would soon wither away with the crown of eternal life awarded to followers of Christ. This crown would last forever.

Every man that striveth for the mastery [competes in the games, NIV] is temperate in all things [goes into strict training, NIV]. Now they do it to obtain a corruptible crown; but we an incorruptible [a crown that will last forever, NIV].
1 CORINTHIANS 9:25

NO SHADOW BOXING

This is another reference by Paul to the Greek athletic games. In this verse he referred to the boxers in training who practiced shadow boxing, throwing punches at an imaginary opponent.

Unlike these athletes who engaged in make-believe boxing, Paul labored in the cause of Christ with a definite aim and purpose in mind. He made every blow count in a real battle as he worked to establish churches and present the claims of the gospel to the Gentile world.

So fight I [Paul], not as one that beateth the air.
1 CORINTHIANS 9:26

During Bible times, metal mirrors provided the user with a poor reflection of reality.

SPEECH BASED ON LOVE

The Greek word translated as "charity" or "love" in this verse is *agape*—self-giving love that asks for nothing in return. No matter how eloquent in speech a person may be—even if he speaks several languages—his eloquence amounts to nothing if his words are not spoken in love.

Pagan worship in Paul's time was often accompanied by strange noises, the clang of gongs and cymbals, and loud blasts on trumpets. Paul declared that the words of the Corinthian believers were no better than these meaningless rituals unless spoken in love.

A BETTER REFLECTION

The New International Version renders the phrase "now we see through a glass, darkly" as "now we see but a poor reflection as in a mirror." Paul referred to mirrors of Bible times that were made of highly polished metal (see note on Exodus 38:8).

Unlike our modern glass mirrors, these metal mirrors gave a poor reflection. Paul was saying that our spiritual vision as believers is blurred by earthly distractions as long as we remain in this world. It's just like looking at ourselves in an inferior looking glass. But we will be able to see and understand more distinctly when we are face-to-face with the Lord in heaven.

RAISED THE THIRD DAY

Jesus was in the tomb only about thirty-six hours (from late Friday afternoon until early Sunday morning)—not three full days as some people might conclude from Paul's statement that He was raised on the third day.

The day for the Jewish people during New Testament times began after sundown and ended at the following sundown (see note on John 11:9). They referred to a partial day as if it were a full day.

Thus, Jesus was laid in the tomb on late Friday afternoon, just before the day ended. He was in the tomb one full day—from sundown on Friday until sundown on Saturday, the Jewish Sabbath. He was resurrected early on Sunday morning, or on the "third day" by Paul's Jewish method of reckoning time.

2 CORINTHIANS

TRIUMPHANT IN CHRIST

Paul compared the victory of Christ over death to a Roman military procession. A victorious general and his army would return from a battle with captives and spoils of war in tow. The entire city of Rome would turn out to welcome the warriors with loud shouts and joyful music.

To Paul, Christ's victory over the grave was more impressive than Roman military triumphs that led to such lavish displays. And more significant, all believers share in this victory procession of Christ.

The Arch of Titus depicting a Roman military procession. Although this portrays the victory of Rome over Jerusalem, Paul uses such an image to describe the triumph of Christ over his enemies (2 Corinthians 2:14).

PRECIOUS TREASURE IN A CHEAP POT

The "treasure" to which Paul referred is God's gift of salvation through His grace. He compared himself—and others who preach this gospel—to "earthen vessels," the common and inexpensive clay pots that held waste matter and garbage.

By using frail and weak human messengers to preach the glorious gospel, God declares that salvation is the result of His power and not of any power that resides in them. His might and glory are separate from and superior to those who declare His power to others.

JUDGMENT OF BELIEVERS

The Corinthian believers would have understood exactly what Paul was saying in this verse. In the city square of Corinth stood the *bema*, an elevated seat where Roman officials sat to render judgments in judicial proceedings. This is the Greek word Paul used that is rendered as "judgment seat" in reference to the judgments of Christ.

Paul was referring to the judgment of believers. The service we have rendered in His name and for His cause will be

> *Thanks be unto God, which always causeth us to triumph [leads us in triumphal procession, NIV] in Christ.*
>
> 2 CORINTHIANS 2:14

> *We have this treasure in earthen vessels [jars of clay, NIV], that the excellency of the power may be of God, and not of us.*
>
> 2 CORINTHIANS 4:7

> *We must all appear before the judgment seat of Christ.*
>
> 2 CORINTHIANS 5:10

laid open to review. Or as one translation renders the verse, "We must all have our lives laid open before the tribunal of Christ" (NEB).

GIVE UP THE PAST

Be ye [Corinthian believers] not unequally yoked together with unbelievers.

2 CORINTHIANS 6:14

Paul was probably alluding in this verse to a familiar prohibition in the Mosaic law: "Thou shalt not plow with an ox and an ass [donkey, NIV] together" (Deuteronomy 22:10).

The reason for this law may have been that a donkey was considered an unclean animal, while the ox was among the clean animals that Jews were permitted to eat (see note on Leviticus 11:29–30, 33). What's more, they would have been out of step with each other in their pull against the plow.

Paul's point is that the believers of Corinth should leave the patterns and habits of their old life of unbelief behind. They should live in accordance with their new status as members of God's family.

PAUL'S ESCAPE IN A BASKET

Through a window in a basket was I [Paul] let down by the wall.

2 CORINTHIANS 11:33

The event to which Paul referred in this verse is reported in the book of Acts (9:22–25). Paul traveled to the city of Damascus to persecute Christians. But after his dramatic conversion, he witnessed for Christ among the Jews of the city. Other believers had to help him escape over the city wall when the Jews determined to kill him.

The window out of which Paul escaped may have been in a house that was built into or on top of the defensive wall of Damascus. Such "wall houses" were common in some cities. This was the type of house in which Rahab the prostitute lived. She helped several Israelite spies escape over the city wall from the window in her house in Jericho (see note on Joshua 2:15).

GALATIANS

"UP" TO JERSUALEM

Paul indicated in the previous verse that he had been in Damascus, Syria (Galatians 1:17), until he traveled to Jerusalem to see Peter.

Damascus was north of Jerusalem. Why didn't Paul say that he went "down" to the city to see Peter? To most people today, "up" refers to northern locations and "down" to southern sites.

Jerusalem was built on high hills in a mountainous territory about 2,500 feet above sea level. To the Jews, whatever the direction from which they approached Jerusalem, it was always "up" (Luke 2:42).

After three years I [Paul] went up to Jerusalem to see [get acquainted with, NIV] Peter.
GALATIANS 1:18

Jerusalem is a city built on hills that rise above sharply-cut valleys.

NO SAVING POWER

The Greek word behind "schoolmaster" in this verse refers to a slave or servant in wealthy Roman families who performed duties similar to those of a modern nanny. He took care of the children, taught them manners and customs, disciplined

The law was our schoolmaster to bring us unto Christ.
GALATIANS 3:24

231

them when necessary, and escorted them to and from school.

Paul used this word in his letter to the Galatian Christians to show them the shortcomings of the law in comparison to the grace of Christ. Like a schoolmaster, the Jewish law could teach the people morals and right behavior. But it did not have the power to save them from their sin. This was possible only through the atoning blood of Jesus Christ.

The New Revised Standard Version has the best translation of this verse: "The law was our disciplinarian until Christ came."

MARKS OF PERSECUTION

I [Paul] bear in [on, NIV] my body the marks of the Lord Jesus.
GALATIANS 6:17

In Paul's time, slaves were branded with distinctive marks to show that they belonged to their masters, much as cattle are branded in modern times (see note on Psalm 40:6). Paul declared that his body bore marks from the persecution he had endured in Christ's service. These showed that he belonged to the Lord Jesus.

The apostle named some of these marks of persecution in 2 Corinthians 11:24–25: "Five times received I forty stripes save one. Thrice was I beaten with rods, once was I stoned."

EPHESIANS

SEALED BY THE SPIRIT

After that ye [Ephesian believers] believed, ye were sealed with that holy Spirit of promise.
EPHESIANS 1:13

Paul referred in this verse to the distinct mark of identification that was placed on a letter, contract, or other legal document in Bible times. This seal proved the document's authenticity (see note on 1 Kings 21:8).

Likewise, believers are sealed or authenticated by the Holy Spirit after their conversion. His mark in our lives results in holy and righteous living. God also gives us His spirit as His pledge of our future inheritance of eternal life (2 Corinthians 1:22).

Spiritual Battle Gear

Paul told the Ephesian believers they needed to equip themselves for spiritual battle, just as the Roman soldiers of his day put on their battle gear to get ready for war.

The apostle compared the breastplate of righteousness to the armor that protected a soldier's upper body (Ephesians 6:14). The hobnail shoes that soldiers wore symbolized the believer's sure footing in the gospel. Believers also should carry with them into battle the "shield of faith," the "helmet of salvation," and the "sword of the Spirit, which is the word of God" (Ephesians 6:16–17).

These items will assure victory in the spiritual battles that believers face in the world.

Take unto you [Ephesian believers] the whole [full, NIV] armour of God, that ye may be able to withstand [stand your ground, NIV] in the evil day.
EPHESIANS 6:13

PHILIPPIANS

The Real Deal

The word *sincere* in this context translates a Greek word meaning "genuine" or "authentic." Paul wanted the Philippian believers to have a faith that was real—not fake or counterfeit. Only a genuine faith would carry them through the tough times and point others toward the all-sufficient Lord whom they served.

"Without offence" means "blameless." The Philippians were to set a positive example for others through their godly behavior.

That ye [Philippian believers] may be sincere and without offence till the day of Christ.
PHILIPPIANS 1:10

Poured Out for the Lord

The New International Version translates this verse, "Even if I am being poured out like a drink offering on the sacrifice and service coming from your faith." Paul was comparing himself and his life to a sacrifice known as the drink offering.

In this ceremony, the worshiper poured wine on the altar on which animals were sacrificed as burnt offerings (see note on Leviticus 23:18). Wine was a valuable commodity in Bible times (see note on Matthew 21:33), so this offering represented the worshiper's commitment to the Lord.

Paul viewed his life as a drink offering. He rejoiced that

If I [Paul] be offered upon the sacrifice and service of your [Philippian believers'] faith, I joy, and rejoice with you all.
PHILIPPIANS 2:17

it was being poured out in sacrifical service on behalf of the Philippians and other early believers.

A Heavenly Book

My [Paul's] fellowlabour-ers, whose names are in the book of life.
PHILIPPIANS 4:3

Many people worked with the apostle Paul in founding and leading churches that brought honor and glory to Christ. In his letter to the Philippians, he declared that all of these believers had their names written in the heavenly book of life because they were believers who belonged to Christ.

The concept of a book of life may have originated with Moses. He prayed that God would erase his name from His book instead of wiping out the Israelites because of their worship of the golden calf in the wilderness (see Exodus 32:32 and note on Exodus 32:3–4).

At the final judgment those whose names are written in the Lamb's book of life will dwell with God in the New Jerusalem (Revelation 21:27).

COLOSSIANS

Salvation and Circumcision

In whom [Jesus] also ye [Colossian believers] are circumcised with the circumcision made without hands.
COLOSSIANS 2:11

Circumcision—the removal of the foreskin from the male sex organ—was a mark of the covenant between God and His people, the Israelites (Romans 4:11; see note on Genesis 17:11).

In this verse Paul compared the death of Christ on the cross to this ritual. This "circumcision" of Jesus was the event that provided for the salvation of believers. We are also "circumcised" when we die to our sins by committing ourselves to Him as our Lord and Savior.

Christ at God's Right Hand

Seek those things which are above, where Christ sitteth on the right hand of God.
COLOSSIANS 3:1

In Bible times an aide who sat at a king's right hand was his most trusted and influential adviser. With this image of Jesus at God's right hand, Paul portrayed Him as God's second in command (see note on Matthew 20:21).

Several other passages in the New Testament refer to this exalted position of Christ. At God's right hand He intercedes for us (Romans 8:34), serves as our High Priest (Hebrews 8:1), and rules over angels and other authorities and powers (1 Peter 3:22).

GRACEFUL AND SALTY TALK

You can tell a lot about a person by the way he talks. In this verse Paul gave some sound advice on the speech of believers. Speech characterized by grace is Christlike, kind, gracious, and humble. But what did Paul mean by speech that is "seasoned with salt"?

Perhaps he meant talk that is honest and free of hypocrisy. Or since salt was used as a preservative and seasoning agent in Bible times (see note on Matthew 5:13), maybe he was saying that our speech should be worthwhile and profitable—not dull, flat, or aimless.

Talking gently but with conviction at the same time is a challenge. Most of us go to one extreme or the other. Maybe we need to pray this prayer more often: "Let the words of my mouth. . .be acceptable in thy sight, O LORD, my strength, and my redeemer" (Psalm 19:14).

> *Let your speech be always with grace, seasoned with salt.*
> COLOSSIANS 4:6

1 THESSALONIANS

PROTECTED BY FAITH AND LOVE

In his letter to the Ephesian Christians, Paul instructed them to put on the "breastplate of righteousness" (see Ephesians 6:14). Here he exhorted the Thessalonian believers to put on the "breastplate of faith and love."

The breastplate, or body armor, of a Roman soldier protected the vital organs of the upper body. Likewise, believers are protected from giving in to temptation when we focus on His love for us and exercise faith in His promises.

> *Let us [believers]. . .be sober [self-controlled, NIV], putting on the breastplate of faith and love.*
> 1 THESSALONIANS 5:8

2 THESSALONIANS

PAUL'S OWN HANDWRITING

The salutation [greeting, NIV] of Paul with mine own hand, which is the token [distinguishing mark, NIV] in every epistle: so I write.

2 THESSALONIANS 3:17

In Bible times many people wrote letters by dictating them to a secretary—a professional amanuensis, or scribe. This apparently was done occasionally by Paul, the most prolific letter writer of the New Testament.

To prove to the recipients of 2 Thessalonians that this letter was from him—even though it had been written by someone else—Paul wrote the final words in his own handwriting. He also closed 1 Corinthians (16:21) and Colossians (4:18) in the same way.

In Paul's letter to the Romans, his secretary identified himself and included his own greeting to the Roman Christians: "I Tertius, who wrote this epistle, salute you in the Lord" (Romans 16:22).

1 TIMOTHY

DRESSED FOR WORSHIP

That women adorn themselves in modest apparel. . .not with broided [braided, NIV] hair, or gold, or pearls, or costly array [expensive clothes, NIV].

1 TIMOTHY 2:9

There is nothing wrong with women wanting to look their best. Paul's point in this passage is that flamboyance and immodesty in dress are out of place in public worship. Our appearance should not be a distraction to others as they seek to commune with the Lord. And this applies to men as well as women!

John Chrysostom's comments on this verse are still appropriate, even though they were written more than fifteen centuries ago: "Are you come to a ball? a marriage-feast? a carnival? There such costly things might have been seasonable: here not one of them is wanted. You have come to pray."

Above-and-Beyond Hospitality

In this verse Paul gave Timothy some criteria by which he could determine if a widow in the church was a sacrificial servant of the Lord who should receive financial assistance from her fellow believers.

One mark of her character was that she had shown hospitality to strangers. Throughout the New Testament, the grace of welcoming strangers into one's home is commended (Romans 12:13; 1 Peter 4:9).

Another thing that Timothy was to look for was whether a widow had gone beyond what was expected in the hosting of strangers. Washing a guest's feet, for example, was considered the job of a lowly slave.

If she [a widow] have lodged strangers, if she have washed the saints' feet...
1 Timothy 5:10

Medicinal Use of Wine

Contaminated water was a problem in Bible times, just as it still is in many parts of the world. Paul's practical advice to Timothy was to drink a little wine along with the water that he had been drinking, which had caused a stomach ailment.

In addition to serving as the common beverage of Bible times, wine was used for medicinal purposes. People drank it to ease physical pain and suffering (Mark 15:23), as well as mental distress (Proverbs 31:6). Sometimes it was poured on wounds (Luke 10:34).

Drink no longer water [Stop drinking only water, NIV], but use a little wine for thy stomach's sake and thine often infirmities.
1 Timothy 5:23

Thou [Timothy] therefore endure hardness [hardship, NIV], as a good soldier of Jesus Christ. No man that warreth entangleth himself with the affairs of this life; that he may please him who hath chosen him to be a soldier [his commanding officer, NIV].

2 TIMOTHY 2:3–4

Roman soldier in bronze. Paul encouraged Timothy to give obedience to God, as a Roman solider obeyed his commander (2 Timothy 2:3–4).

There is laid up for me [Paul] a crown of righteousness, which the Lord, the righteous judge, shall give me at that day.

2 TIMOTHY 4:8

HARDSHIP AND SACRIFICE

Paul continued his imagery from the Roman military (see notes on Ephesians 6:13 and 1 Thessalonians 5:8) by referring to the discipline and singleness of purpose required of a Roman soldier.

The ordinary foot soldier in the Roman military was loaded down with his armor and weapons, tools, and rations that would last him for several days. He was sworn through strict discipline and training to obey the orders of his commanding officer without question.

Paul was telling Timothy that the Christian life—while it has its rewards—is not an easy path. It requires discipline and sacrifice.

A CROWN OF RIGHTEOUSNESS

This crown spoken of by Paul represents the righteousness that belongs to every believer. This righteousness has three dimensions.

First, we are made righteous or justified by Christ when we accept Him as Lord and Savior (Romans 4:6). Second, we grow in Christ's righteousness through a lifetime of commitment to Him (1 Peter 2:24). Finally, Christ perfects His righteousness in us when we enter heaven. This final dimension of righteousness is what Paul was referring to in this verse.

OTHER CROWNS

1. Paul described the believer's hope in Christ as a "crown of rejoicing" (1 Thessalonians 2:19).
2. Paul declared that Jesus' promise of eternal life for believers is an "incorruptible" crown—one that will never fade away (1 Corinthians 9:25).
3. The apostle Peter promised that all people who claim Christ as their personal Savior will receive "a crown of glory" (1 Peter 5:4).

PAUL'S SIMPLE NEEDS

Paul wrote his second letter to Timothy while imprisoned in Rome. Timothy planned to visit him soon, so Paul asked him to bring these three items when he came.

The apostle's needs were simple—a cloak, or his long outer robe, to keep him warm, and several scrolls and parchments. These were writing materials similar to our modern paper (see notes on Job 19:23–24 and Isaiah 34:4).

Were these scrolls and parchments blank? If so, did Paul plan to use them to write letters to other churches and church leaders, just as he had written this letter to Timothy? Or had these materials already been written on? Did they contain copies of the Old Testament scriptures, perhaps, or other sacred writings that Paul planned to read and meditate on to help pass the time in prison?

We don't know. What we do know is that Paul had learned the secret of abundant living in the midst of sparse circumstances. On another occasion he expressed it like this: "I have learned, in whatsoever state I am, therewith to be content" (Philippians 4:11).

The cloke that I [Paul] left at Troas with Carpus, when thou [Timothy] comest, bring with thee, and the books [scrolls, NIV], but especially the parchments.

2 TIMOTHY 4:13

The Mamertinum Prison at Rome. Paul wrote his second letter to Timothy while imprisoned in Rome.

TITUS

FAITH, NOT FABLES

Not giving heed to Jewish fables [myths, NIV], and commandments of men, that turn from the truth.

TITUS 1:14

Paul wrote this letter to his missionary helper Titus, whom he had placed in charge of the church on the island of Crete.

One purpose of this letter was to instruct Titus in how to deal with the false teachers who had infiltrated the church. They were members of a group known as the Judaizers, who taught that Gentiles could not become Christians unless they submitted to certain Jewish rituals, including being circumcised, refusing to eat unclean foods, and observing Jewish feasts and holy days.

To Paul, these were Jewish fables or myths that had no part in a person's salvation. God accepted both Jews and Gentiles on the basis of their faith in Jesus Christ and their commitment to Him as Lord and Savior (Ephesians 2:8–9).

PHILEMON

PHILEMON'S HOUSE CHURCH

To the church in thy [Philemon's] house: Grace to you, and peace.

PHILEMON 1:2–3

Paul sent greetings in this verse to the believers who met in Philemon's house. Groups of believers in New Testament times did not have church buildings, so they usually met in private homes.

Priscilla and Aquila apparently made their home available as meeting places in both Rome (Romans 16:3–5) and Ephesus (1 Corinthians 16:19). Early believers also met in the home of Nymphas (Colossians 4:15–16).

HEBREWS

BOLD ACCESS TO THE KING

As a person becomes famous or rises to a high position, he limits his accessibility to others for his own protection. Many kings of Bible times, for example, could not be approached by anyone but their most trusted advisers. The Persians had a law that anyone who came into their king's presence without his permission could pay with their lives (see note on Esther 4:11).

This verse from Hebrews, when seen against the background of these "unapproachable" kings, makes us realize what a revolutionary Savior Jesus is. Although He is exalted to the highest position as God's Son, He is still as approachable to us as a member of the family or a close friend. We can bring our needs boldly to Jesus and expect to be received joyfully into His presence.

> *Let us [believers] therefore come boldly unto the throne of grace, that we may obtain mercy, and find grace to help in time of need.*
> HEBREWS 4:16

EXECUTION BY SAWING

This verse appears in the famous "roll call of the faithful" chapter in Hebrews. The writer pays tribute to the people of past generations who remained faithful to God, in spite of great persecution.

Execution by being sawed in two is cruel and inhumane by modern standards, but this form of capital punishment was apparently practiced in the ancient world. It was not out of character for the cruel Assyrians, who were known to cut off the ears and hands of their victims just for sport (see note on Judges 1:6).

But even King David of Judah may have practiced this form of torture and execution against the Ammonites. After capturing their capital city, Rabbah, he "brought out the people that were in it, and cut them with saws, and with harrows of iron, and with axes" (1 Chronicles 20:3).

> *They were stoned, they were sawn asunder [sawed in two, NIV], were tempted, were slain with the sword.*
> HEBREWS 11:37

A Lifetime Race

Let us [believers] lay aside every weight, and the sin which doth so easily beset us, and let us run with patience [perseverance, NIV] the race that is set before us.

HEBREWS 12:1

This verse compares the Christian life to the footrace in which athletes competed in the Greek games (see note on 1 Corinthians 9:25). The foot race was one of the most popular events of the Greek games that were held every year in Athens.

To prepare themselves for these races, runners underwent rigorous training, trimming down their bodies to eliminate every ounce of excess fat. On race day they wore light clothing—perhaps no clothes at all—to give themselves every possible advantage in the competition against other runners. These races covered various distances—from short sprints where speed was called for, to longer runs where stamina and endurance were more important.

In Paul's thinking, the Christian life is like a marathon. It is important for us to remain faithful to Christ during a lifetime of service so we can say with the apostle at the end of the race, "I have finished my course, I have kept the faith" (2 Timothy 4:7).

This stadium at Perge hosted foot races common during the New Testament time. Paul compared the Christian life to such a race. (Hebrews 12:1)

JAMES

AN ETERNAL CROWN

Crowns were worn by kings as symbols of authority and power (2 Samuel 1:10). James compared the believer's inheritance of eternal life through the atoning death of Jesus Christ to a crown.

This crown, unlike earthly and physical status symbols, will never grow tarnished or lose its luster because of changing cultural standards. It has an "eternal lifetime" warranty from the King of kings and Lord of lords (Revelation 21:5–7).

Blessed is the man that endureth temptation [perseveres under trial, NIV]: for. . .he shall receive the crown of life, which the Lord hath promised to them that love him.
JAMES 1:12

FIRST OF THE BEST

In the Old Testament, firstfruits were the first and best of the crops that were to be presented to God as an offering (Exodus 23:19). In giving the firstfruits to the Lord, the people expressed their faith that He would fulfill His promise of an abundant harvest to come.

In this passage, James compared believers to these firstfruits. We are the first evidence of God's future new creation (2 Peter 3:1–10). Our new life in Christ is only a glimpse of our future glory with Him.

We [believers] should be a kind of firstfruits of his [God's] creatures.
JAMES 1:18

MERCHANTS ON THE GO

Many people of Bible times made their living as itinerant merchants. They would carry their wares to a distant city, sell or trade them there for a while, then move on to another city and repeat the operation.

These merchants became experts at catching the local markets at times when people were open to buying what they had to sell. They often traveled in caravans (see note on Genesis 37:25).

James did not condemn this practice in this passage. He used it as an illustration to show that people's best-laid plans can be thwarted by God: "Ye know not what shall be on the morrow. . . . Ye ought to say, If the Lord will, we shall live, and do this, or that" (James 4:14–15).

Go to now [Now listen, NIV], ye that say, To day or to morrow we will go into such a city, and continue there a year, and buy and sell [carry on business, NIV], and get gain [make money, NIV].
JAMES 4:13

LORD OF SABAOTH

The word *Sabaoth* means "hosts." Thus, James is speaking of the Lord of hosts. While this title for God appears frequently in the Old Testament (see 1 Samuel 15:2; Isaiah 3:1), this is the only place in the New Testament where it is used.

This verse describes God as hearing the cries of the poor who are being oppressed by the rich. The Lord of all the hosts of heaven and earth is on the side of the poor, and He will render justice on their behalf (James 5:7–8; see note on Deuteronomy 24:10–11).

PATIENT WAITING

The land of Palestine, known for its dry climate, had limited rainfall. Moisture for crop production was supplemented by heavy dews (Deuteronomy 33:13).

But every farmer knew that at least two major rainfalls during the year were essential for crops to grow. The early rain in October and November softened the soil for planting. The latter rain of March and April brought a needed boost for the crops before they ripened fully for the harvest.

James declared that just as farmers waited patiently from the early rain to the latter rain for their crops to mature, so believers must wait patiently for the second coming of Jesus (2 Timothy 4:8).

1 PETER

CLEAR THINKING

Both men and women of Bible times wore full-body outer robes that extended almost to the feet. If a person needed to run or do strenuous work, he would tuck the bottom part of his robe into the belt or sash around his waist (see note on 1 Kings 18:46). This gave him greater freedom of movement.

This practice is described by the King James Version as "girding up the loins." In this verse, Peter described thinking constructively as girding up "the loins of your mind." The

New International Version translates it, "Prepare your minds for action." Peter meant that believers should think clearly and reject the hindrances and temptations of the world by focusing on God and His grace.

Tucking the robe into the belt is sometimes referred to in the Bible in a figurative sense to denote strength and determination (Job 40:7; Psalms 65:6; 93:1).

JESUS THE CHIEF SHEPHERD

In Bible times, wealth was often measured by the size of one's flocks and herds of livestock (see note on Job 1:3). Some wealthy people had hundreds of sheep, and caring for these animals required the services of several shepherds. These shepherds would be supervised by a chief shepherd or master shepherd (1 Samuel 21:7).

Peter compared Jesus Christ to a chief shepherd. This title is similar to His designation as "that great shepherd of the sheep" in Hebrews 13:20.

All ministers who lead God's people should remember that they are undershepherds who work under the supervision of the Great Shepherd or Chief Shepherd—Jesus Christ. He enables them to take care of God's people with wisdom and kindness.

> When the chief Shepherd [Jesus] shall appear, ye shall receive a crown of glory that fadeth not away.
> 1 PETER 5:4

2 PETER

JESUS THE LIGHT

The apostle Peter declared in this verse that Jesus the Messiah had been foretold in the Old Testament. These prophecies were like "a light that shineth in a dark place." But when He arrived on earth, the full light of His glory burst forth, like the dawning of a new day.

Jesus as the light is a central theme of the New Testament. He Himself declared, "I am the light of the world" (John 8:12). Believers are known as "children of light" (Ephesians 5:8).

> We [believers] have also a more sure word of prophecy; whereunto ye do well that ye take heed, as unto a light that shineth in a dark place, until the day dawn, and the day star [morning star, NIV] arise in your hearts.
> 2 PETER 1:19

1 JOHN

BOWELS OF COMPASSION

Whoso. . .seeth his brother have need, and shutteth up his bowels of compassion from him [but has no pity on him, NIV], how dwelleth the love of God in him?

1 JOHN 3:17

In Bible times, the bowels were considered the seat of emotions and feelings. According to the apostle John in this passage, a person who shuts his "bowels of compassion" has no pity or empathy toward those in need. In our modern figure of speech, we would probably say that a person like this does not have a compassionate heart.

The apostle John made it clear throughout this epistle that love and compassion toward others are two of the marks of an authentic believer: "This commandment have we from him, That he who loveth God love his brother also" (1 John 4:21).

2 JOHN

THE ELDER AND THE LADY

The elder unto the elect [chosen, NIV] lady and her children.

2 JOHN 1:1

The apostle John identified himself as "the elder," a term that means "pastor" or "bishop." He was an important leader in the early church. Many believe he was associated with the church at Ephesus.

The phrase "elect (or chosen) lady," referring to the letter's recipient, is puzzling. Some interpreters think it was a code name for a specific congregation, while others believe John addressed an unnamed female believer. If John did have a specific person in mind, 2 John is the only New Testament letter addressed to a woman.

3 JOHN

A SHORT LETTER

John addressed this brief letter to a church leader named Gaius. He purposely kept the letter short because he planned to talk personally with Gaius very soon.

The ink mentioned by John was probably the same as that used by Jeremiah's scribe, Baruch (see note on Jeremiah 36:18). Writing pens of Bible times consisted of hollow reeds cut diagonally on one end to give them flexible writing points.

These hollow reeds held only a small amount of ink, so they had to be dipped repeatedly in ink to replenish the supply. The points of these pens would wear down with use, and they were sharpened with a scribe's knife or penknife (Jeremiah 36:23).

I [the apostle John] had many things to write, but I will not with ink and pen write unto thee [Gaius]: but I trust I shall shortly see thee, and we shall speak face to face.

3 JOHN 1:13–14

JUDE

THE LOVE FEAST

The phrase "feasts of charity" that Jude used in this verse probably referred to the love feast, a meal that early Christians ate together as part of their observance of the Lord's Supper. The purpose of this meal was to remember the sacrifice of Christ, since he was eating the Passover meal with His disciples when He turned it into a memorial of His sacrificial death (Luke 22:14–20).

In its early years, the love feast was also known as the agape meal. It became a charity meal for the poor in some Christian traditions. Most Christian groups today have dropped this communal meal from their observance of the Lord's Supper.

These are spots [blemishes, NIV] in your feasts of charity [love feasts, NIV], when they feast with you, feeding themselves without fear [eating with you without the slightest qualm, NIV].

JUDE 1:12

REVELATION

A Stone for the Winner

To him that overcometh will I [Jesus] give. . . a white stone.

Revelation 2:17

This imagery of a white stone has been explained in various ways by interpreters: as a badge of acquittal in a legal case, as an expression of welcome by a host to his guests, or as a voting token used by a voter to indicate his choice of a candidate.

Perhaps the most believable explanation is that the apostle John, the author of Revelation, was referring to a white stone given to the winner of an athletic contest. This stone was an admission ticket to the winner's celebration at a later time. This may refer to the time when faithful, persevering believers will receive eternal life and experience the Lord's great victory celebration in heaven.

Symbols of Victory and Joy

A great multitude. . .stood before the throne, and before the Lamb, clothed with white robes, and palms [palm branches, NIV] in their hands.

Revelation 7:9

The "palms" held by this great multitude of believers were palm branches. These were considered symbols of victory and joy (Leviticus 23:40; Nehemiah 8:15).

Jesus was welcomed on His triumphant entry into Jerusalem by crowds waving palm branches (John 12:13). In the New Jerusalem, or heaven, believers will acclaim Jesus as the triumphant Lamb or Savior by waving these same symbols of victory and gladness.

Palm tree on a Judea Captive coin. Among the Jews, the palm branch was a symbol of victory and freedom.

THE NUMBER SEVEN

The Jewish people thought of seven as a sacred number. It is used often in the Bible to show fullness, completion, and perfection (Genesis 2:2–3; Daniel 9:25).

The apostle John used the number seven throughout the book of Revelation: seven churches (1:4), seven stars (2:1), seven lamps (4:5), seven seals (5:1), seven angels with seven trumpets (8:2), seven thunders (10:4), a beast with seven heads (13:1), seven vials or bowls (17:1), and seven kings (17:10).

By using this number, John declared that God will bring about His perfect judgment in the end time. All believers will participate in the full and complete victory of Christ over the forces of evil.

And I [the apostle John] saw another sign in heaven. . .seven angels having the seven last plagues.
REVELATION 15:1

A KING WITH MANY CROWNS

John borrowed this imagery from the custom of kings who ruled over more than one country. They would wear several crowns to represent all of the nations under their control. For example, the kings of Egypt wore a two-in-one crown to represent the unification of Upper and Lower Egypt under their rule.

To the apostle John in this verse, the many crowns worn by Jesus show His universal reign as Savior and Lord throughout the world. The hymn writer expressed it like this:

His [the reigning Christ's] eyes were as a flame of fire, and on his head were many crowns.
REVELATION 19:12

> Crown Him with many crowns,
> The Lamb upon His throne;
> Hark! how the heav'nly anthem drowns
> All music but its own!
>
> Awake, my soul, and sing
> Of Him who died for thee,
> And hail Him as thy matchless King
> Thro' all eternity.
>
> —MATTHEW BRIDGES,
> "CROWN HIM WITH MANY CROWNS"

INDEX

PAGE NUMBERS IN BOLD TYPE REFER TO AN IMAGE THAT ILLUSTRATES A MAIN ENTRY.

Aaron, 30, 42, 47, 52, 57–58, 201
Abed-nego, 107, 154
Abib, 44
Abigail, 76
Abner, 13, 80, 85
Abraham, 7–21, 23, 27, 60, 107, 144
Absalom, 40, 76, 87–89
Accidental death, 63
Achan, 69
Adam, 87
Adoni-bezek, 70
Adonijah, 91
Adoption, 225
Agag, 153
Agape meal, 247
Agora, 221
Ahab, 8, 28, 40, 59, 62, 96, 98–99, 101–102, 158, 181, 202
Ahaz, 53
Ahaziah, 100
Ahijah, 94
Ahimaaz, 88
Ahimelech, 83
Aholah, 151
Aholibah, 151
Alms, 172
Aloes, 121
Altar, 27, 50, 110, 120, 213, 233; horns of, **91**
Amanuensis, 236
Amasa, 90
Amaziah, 106
Ammonites, 53, 59, 86, 151, 241
Amnon, 141
Amon, 145
Amon-Ra, 145, 149. See also *Ra; Sun worship.*
Amorites, 60
Amos, 94, 106, 158–159
Anathoth, **144**
Anger, expression of, 88
Animals: Clean and unclean, 51, 149, 230; cut into two pieces to seal a covenant, 144; horn of, symbol of strength, 122; humane treatment of, **43;**

offered as sacrifices, 48–49, 51, 58, 61, 95, 139, 180, 233; skins of, made into containers or writing material, 117, 123, 137, 174, 202
Ankle bracelet, 133
Anointing, 102, 119, 190
Anthropomorphism, 140
Antioch of Pisidia, 194, **219**
Anvil, 133
Apis, **46**
Aquila, 222, 240
Arabian Desert, 130
Araunah, 92
Arch of Titus, **229**
Ark of the covenant, 13, 42, 45, **47**, 72, 79
Arm, baring the, 139
Armor, 79, 80, 233, 235
Arrows, 115, 136, 151
Artaxerxes, 109, **111**
Artemis. See *Diana.*
Asa, 106
Asahel, 80
Ashdod, 79
Asher (tribe), 67
Asherah, **71**
Assassination, 102, 112
Assyria/Assyrians, 28, **106, 119**, 138, 176; condemned by Nahum, 163; cruelty of, 102, 164, 165, 241; defeated the Northern Kingdom, 103, 104, 146, 151; fond of costly clothing, 73
Astrology, 139, 170
Athens, 221, **222**, 224
Atonement, 49, 52. See also *Day of Atonement.*
Axe, 63, 146
Azariah, 188
Baal, **59**, 62, 70, 95–96, 155, 172
Baalam, 59
Babel. See *Tower of Babel.*
Babylon/Babylonians, 30, 44, 55, 93, 107, 110, 136, 154; cruelty of, 104; defeated the

Southern Kingdom, 108, 144–145, 147–149, 151–152, 154–155, 160, 165; known for astrology, 139, 170; pagan gods of, 138, 164
Bagpipe, 124, 153
Balak, 59
Balm, 142. See also *Medical treatment.*
Banner, 57. See also *Standard.*
Banquet, 111, 113, 182, 185
Barabbas, 199
Barbarian, 225
Barefoot, 87
Barley, 42, 66, 77, 137, 176. See also *Wheat.*
Barnabas, 194, 219, 220
Baruch, 145, 195, 247
Bashan, 60
Bath (liquid measure), 42, 152
Bathsheba, 65, 86–87, 121
Battle axe, 146
Beard, 30, 54, 86, 90, 134. See also *Hair.*
Beersheba, 91, **97**
Bel, 138
Bellows, 142
Belt, 96, 245. See also *Clothing.*
Benammi, 7
Ben-hadad, 98, 101
Benjamin (son of Jacob), 32–34
Benjamin (tribe), 82
Bereavement. See *Grief; Mourning for the dead.*
Beth Horon, 105
Bethel, 100
Bethlehem, 17, 26, 76, 78, 202
Beth-shan, 122, 147
Betrothal, 169. See also *Marriage.*
Bildad, 116
Birthright, 20–21, 33. See also *Inheritance practices.*

Biscuit, 94
Bitumen, 7, 36, 135
Black magic. See *Occult.*
Blacksmith, 133, 142
Blasphemy, 218
Blessing, declaration of, 21
Blood, eating of, forbidden, 61
Boaz, 11, 13, 42, 75–77
Book of Life, 234
Booth. See *Hut.*
Boundary stone, **64**
Bow (weapon), 165
Bowels, 246
Bowing to others, 11
Boxing, 227
Bracelet, **18**, 84
Bread, 12, 20, 39, 77, 80, 94, 194; baking of, 12, 39, 51, 94, 207; manna as substitute for, 41; staple food, 32; unleavened, 39, 49, 207
Bread of the Presence, 45
Breastplate of righteousness, 233, 235
Bricks, 7, 118, 154, 164; Babylonian, 7; without straw, **37**
Bridal payment, 17–19, 24, 26, 169
Bridle, 99
Brother (as a word), 9, 23
Buckler. See *Shield.*
Bul, 93
Burial and funeral practices, 16, 35, 103, 122, 143, 175, **186,** 194, 205, 216; of Egypt, 35; of Judah, for selected kings, 91
Burning bush, 10, 97
Burnt offering, 48–50, 54, 110, 233
Butter, 12, **128,** 134
Buying and selling, 15, 67, 152, 180, 221, 243; honesty in, **67**
Camel ornaments, 73
Caravan, 28, 142, 243
Catapult, **107**
Cave, 16, 136, 194

Ceremonial washing, 185, 195–196

Chaff, 77, 203

Chamberlain, 112

Chariots: Assyrian, 164; Egyptian, **40;** running in front of, 96; those of Syria captured by David, 105

Cheese, 80

Chemosh, 59

Chief priest, 188

Child sacrifice, 53, 59, 101, 218

Childlessness, 9, 79

Children (as a word), 7, 192–193

Church of the Holy Sepulcher, 199

Circumcision, 10, 16, 68, 234

Cistern, 27, 88, **141.** See also *Pit.*

Cities of refuge, 63, 91

City Gate. See *Gate of the city.*

Clay pots, 229

Clay tablets, 117–118, **148.** See also *Writing.*

Cloak. See *Outer garment.*

Clothing: As gifts, 34, 82; considered suitable for a royal wedding, 182; dressed in white, 129; freshened with oil and spices, 120; tearing of, 87, 112

Communion with the dead, 62–63

Concubine, 112

Contempt, expression of, 88, 110

Corban, 196

Corinth, 222, 224, 229, **230**

Cornet. See *Sistrum.*

Coronation ceremony, 102

Courier. See *Messenger on foot.*

Covenant, 9–10, 17, 21, 27, 49, 144, 170, 234

Cracknel. See *Biscuit.*

Cremation, 106, 122. See also *Burial and funeral practices.*

Crescent necklace, 133

Crete, 240

Cross (crucifixion instrument), 190, 216

Cross-dressing, 65

Crown, 84, 113, 140,

227, 238, 243, 249

Crucifixion, 188, **189,** 190, 199, 215

Cubit, 45. See also *Span.*

Cupbearer, 109

Curds. See *Butter.*

Cush. See *Ethiopia.*

Cymbal, 105

Cyrene, 188

Cyrus, 108, **155**

Cyrus Cylinder, **155**

Dagon, 75

Damascus, 71, 230–231

Dancing, 26, 41, 47, 82, 133

Daniel, 72, 107, 129, 153–154, 191, 221

Darius, 153–154, 167, 191

Darkness, 116

Darnel, 176

David, 11, 13–14, 35, 40–41, 47, 72, 76, 80–92, 100, 102, 104, 119, 155, 170, 195, 216, 241; committed adultery with Bathsheba, 65, 121; organized temple musicians, 105

Day. See *Time.*

Day of Atonement, 52, 55, 200. See also *Atonement; Scapegoat.*

Day's journey, 97

Dead Sea, 8, 14, 106, 170

Dead Sea Scrolls, **14,** 145

Death penalty, 64

Deborah, 72–73

Debt, 55. See also *Lending laws.*

Deed for property, 144

Delilah, 74

Demetrius, 223

Denarius, 175, **178,** 179

Dew, 244

Diana, 223

Didymus. See *Thomas.*

Divination, 62; with a cup, 33, 62; with a liver, 151. See also *Occult.*

Dog, 85

Dome of the Rock, **92,** 210

Donkey, **43,** 230

Doorkeeper. See *Porter.*

Dowry. See *Bridal payment.*

Drachma, 178

Dreams, 30, 153

Drink offering, 27, 54, 233

Drinking customs, 111, **163**

Dulcimer, 153

Ear: Metaphor for God's power, 140; piercing of, 120

Earring, 18

Eating customs, 12, 100, 196, 198, **215**

Ebenezer, 22

Edom/Edomites, 7, 106, **160**

Eglon, 71

Egyptians, 8, 11, 27, 30, 38–39, 43, 61, 107, 118, 121, 135, 142, 145, 149–150, 152, 157, 207, 249; burial practices of, **35;** pagan gods of, 8, 10, 33, 38, **39, 46,** 57; social distinctions among, 32. See also *Pharaoh of Egypt.*

Elam, 136

Elder, 246

Eleazar, 58

Eli, 13, 78, 125

Eliakim, 107, 136

Eliezer, 16

Elijah, 8, 11, 28, 59, 94, **95,** 96–97, 99–100, 172, 181

Elimelech, 78

Eliphaz, 116

Elisabeth, 201

Elisha, 11, 18, 26, 98, 100–103, 221

Emasculation, 112

Ephah, 42, 152

Ephesus, 222, **223,** 240

Ephron, 15

Esau, 7, 11, 20–21, 82

Esther, 112–114, 150, 154

Ethanim, 93

Ethiopia, 135

Eunuch. See *Chamberlain.*

Euphrates River, 109

Eutychus, 72

Evening sacrifice, 96

Excommunication from the synagogue, 197, 213

Execution: By burning, 154; by crucifixion, 189, 216; by decapitation, 102; by hacking to pieces, 153; by sawing in two, 241; by stoning, 217; by tossing from a cliff, 106

Eyes: Beautification of, by Jezebel, 101; beautiful, desired by women, 23; closing of, at death, 34

Ezekiel, 73, 148–152, 162

Ezra, 86, 93, 134, 137, 188

Face: Between the knees, 96; covering of the, 162

False gods. See *Idolatry.*

False prophets, 214

False teachers, 240

Famine, **8,** 30–31

Fan. See *Winnowing fork.*

Farthing, 175

Fasting, 52, 209

Father (as a word), 7

Feast of Harvest, 43–44

Feast of Ingathering. See *Feast of Tabernacles.*

Feast of Passover, 39, 43–45, 180, 187, 198, 202, 207, 209–210, 247

Feast of Purim, 114

Feast of Tabernacles, 43, 44, 86, 93, 213

Feast of Trumpets, 54

Feast of Unleavened Bread, 39, 43

Feast of Weeks. See *Feast of Harvest.*

Fenced city. See *Walled city.*

Fertility enhancement, 25. See also *Childlessness.*

Festus, 224

Fig, 162

Firkin, 211

Firstborn: Death of Egyptian, 39; rights of, 20–21, 24, 208. See also *Birthright; Inheritance practices.*

Firstfruits, 243

Fish, 177, 194

Fishing, 135, **177,** 193, **204,** 212

Fist, shaking the, 165

Flesh pot, 41

Flogging, 188, 197

Flute, 90, 124, 143, 153

Foot on enemies' necks, 70

Foot washing. See *Washing of feet.*

Footrace, **242**

Footstool, 123

Fortune telling, 62

Fowler, 123

Fox, 148

Friend of the bridegroom,

Fuel for ovens and lamps, 122, 193

Funeral. See *Burial and funeral practices.*

Gaius, 247

Galilee, 203

Games of children, 175

Garden of Gethsemane, 188

Gate of the city, 13, 85, 119, 140, 179; business transacted at, 15; opened and closed by porters, 89; reinforced with heavy timbers, 105; some massive in size, 85, **119;** two gates at Mahanaim, 88; where elders rendered judgments, 64

Gentiles, 139, 176, 182, 194, 220, 225–226, 240

Gerah, 56

Gershon, 57

Giants, 60

Gibeah, 216

Gibeonites, **69**

Gideon, 73

Gifts, 26, 34, 101, 196

Gilead, 28, 142

Girding up the loins, 96, 244

Girdle. See *Belt.*

Gladiator, 226, **227**

Gleaning, 42, 66, 75, **76.** See also *Poor, treatment of.*

Goat, 187

Goat worship, 53

Goliath, 79–83, 102

Golden calf, 234

Gomorrah, 8, 14, 170. See also *Sodom.*

Good Shepherd, Jesus as, 214

Gordon's Calvary, **199**

Goshen, 32

Grain: Threshing of, 77, 115, 137, 159; winnowing of, **77,** 203; grinding of, 75, 128, 147, 159; roasting of, 77, 80; storage of, **31,** 145

Grain offering, 50

Grape, 150, 155, 166, 181

Greaves. See *Armor.*

Greek games, 227, 242

Greeks, 225

Greetings, 76, 206, 216, 226

Grief, expression of, 28, 87–89. See also *Mourning for the dead.*

Habakkuk, 164

Hadarezer, 105

Hagar, 9–10, 14

Haggai, 166

Hair: Arranged by Jezebel, 101; immodesty in style of, condemned by Paul, 236; mark of Jewish pride, 133; pulling out of, 110; trimming of, by men forbidden, **54**

Haman, 28, 30, 112–114

Hand mill, 75, 178

Hands: Clasped over the head, 141; enemies hung up by, 147; lifted in prayer, 93; metaphor for God's power, 140; shaking of, in agreement, 126; striking the, together, 151; washing of, 100

Hand-to-hand combat, 82, 116, 136, 164

Hannah, 74, 78–79

Hanun, 86

Haran, 9, 17, 82

Harem, 112

Harmonica, 124

Harp, **25,** 26, 105, 120, 153. See also *Lyre.*

Harvesting, **76,** 115

Hathor, **39**

Hazael, 101

Head: Ashes on, 112, 140–141; covering of, 87; dust on, 87; objects carried on, **29;** wearing ropes on, 99

Headband, 133

Heave offering, 51. See also *Wave offering.*

Hebron, 13, 85

Helmet, 79, 233

Heman, 105

Herod the Great, 16, 209

Herodians, 183

Hezekiah, 28, 115, 136, 195

High place, 56, 59. See also *Idolatry; Pagan gods.*

High priest, 46, 52, 58, 127

Hiram, 92

Hissing, 165

Holy kiss. See *Kiss of greeting.*

Holy of Holies/Most Holy Place, 47, 57, 200

Homicide, 63

Honey, 49, **134,** 145, 192

Horn, 105

Horse, 105, 138, 159, 167

Hosea, 155–156, 203

Hospitality, 11, 119, 237

House, 136, 192; bedroom of, 100, 207; built of flimsy materials, 116, 118; door and locks of, 71, 128; flat roofs of, 65, 68, 86, 116, 124, 127, 192, 218; gateway and courtyard of, **126;** pegs in walls of, 136, 150; some built into city walls, 68, 89, 230; windows of, 72, 230

Household engravings, 127

Household idols, 25, **55,** 155

Hushai, 87

Hut, 86, 98, 127, 132

Hyperbole, 196–197

Hyssop, 121

Idolatry, 45–46, 55, 60, 65, 132, 135, 142, 149, 155, 159. See also *High place; Pagan gods.*

Incense, 48

Inheritance practices, 20, 208. See also *Birthright; Firstborn.*

Ink, 145, **149,** 247

Inn, 202

Inner garment, 139. See also *Outer garment.*

Irrigation, 38, 61, 118

Isaac, 14, 16–17, 19–21

Isaiah, 52, 83, 89, 118, 132–139, 152, 181, 204

Ishmael, 9, 145

Ivory, 94, **158**

Jackal, 148

Jacob, 9, 11, 14, 17, 20–28, 32, 34–36, 57, 82, 89, 97, 107

Jacob's Well, **211**

Jael, 72

Jairus, 143

Jar, 94

Javelin, 80. See also *Spear.*

Jehoahaz, 107, 143, 150

Jehoram, 40, 117

Jehu, 40, 72, 101–102

Jeremiah, 13, 27, 59, 106, 118, 141–148, 156, 165, 193, 195

Jericho, 68, 206, 230

Jeroboam, 94, 125

Jerusalem, 45, 47, 87, 89, 91, 97, 107, 109–110, 124, 132, 136, 138–139, 142, 144, 146–149, 154, 160, 165–166, 197–200, 202, 206, 209, 217, 231, **248**

Jesse, 76, 80

Jethro, 36

Jewelry, 18, 37, 133

Jezebel, 59, 62, 72, 97, 99, 101, 125, 181

Jezreel, 96, 102

Joab, 13, 85, 90

Joash, 102

Job, 14, 21, 28, 84, 114–117, 193, 203

Joel, 133, 157

John (apostle), 215, 246, 248–249

John the Baptist, 29, 74, 138, 192, 201, 203, 210–211

Jonah, 28, 97, 154, 161, 176

Jonathan (son of Saul), 82–83, 85

Jonathan (spy for David), 88

Jordan River, 22, 47, 88, 90, 212, 221

Joseph (husband of Mary), 97, 169, 202

Joseph of Arimathea, 136, 190, 200, 208, 216

Joseph (son of Jacob), 7–8, 11, 27–35, 107, 142, 166

Joshua, 13, 22, 37, 58, 69

Josiah, 25, 195

Jot, 171

Jubal, 7

Jubilee. See *Year of Jubilee.*

Judah (son of Jacob), 35

Judaizers, 240

Judas Iscariot, 127, 187, 198

Judgment seat, 78, 229, **230**

Jupiter, 220

Kedar, 130
Key, 71, **136,** 177. See also *Lock.*
Kidron Valley, 170
Kiln, 154
Kir, 136
Kiss of greeting, 23, 34, 90, 119, 226
Kneading trough, 39. See also *Bread.*
Knife, 69
Kohath, 57
Laban, 21–26, 82, 97
Lamb, 187
Lamp, 166, **186,** 193
Lampstand, 193
Last Supper, 215
Launderer, 168
Laziness, 128
Leah, 23–25
Leaven, 49, 207. See also *Bread.*
Lending laws, 65, 158. See also *Debt.*
Leprosy, 121, 162, 173
Letter (correspondence), 110. See also *Writing.*
Levi, 57
Levirate marriage, 66. See also *Marriage.*
Levites, 57, 105, 108, 110, 127, 188
Life for life principle, 63, 172
Light, 116, 245
Lion, 150
Lock, 71, **136.** See also *Key.*
Locust, 157, 192
Lord's Supper, 247. See also *Love feast.*
Lot (nephew of Abraham), 7, 9, 13, 170
Lots, casting of, 110, 114, 127, 151, 161
Love feast, 247. See also *Lord's Supper.*
Lycaonia, 219
Lydia, 220–221
Lyre, 26, 105, 120. See also *Harp.*
Lystra, 219–220
Mace, 146
Macedonia, 223
Machpelah, **16**
Magi, 170
Magic. See *Occult.*
Mahanaim, 88
Mamertinum Prison, **239**
Manasseh (king), 53
Manasseh (tribe), 60
Mandrake plant, **25**

Manger, **202**
Manna, 41–42, 48, 76
Mantle. See *Outer garment.*
Marathon race, 242. See also *Greek games.*
Marduk, 138
Marketplace, 221, **222**
Marriage, 17, 23–24, 64; arranged by parents, 17, 169; betrothal prior to, 169; celebrated with a feast, 24, 182, 186, 193; intermarriage with pagans condemned, 110; of a deceased brother's wife, 66. See also *Levirate marriage; Wedding.*
Mary (mother of Jesus), 79, 97, 169, 202
Mattaniah, 107
Matthew, 204–205
Matthias, 127
Maul, 146
Meat offering, 49
Meat pot, 41
Medes, 154
Medical treatment, 132, 206. See also *Balm.*
Meditation, 96
Mediterranean Sea, 92, 135, 224
Megiddo, **31, 88,** 202
Memorial stones. See *Stone memorials and monuments.*
Mephibosheth, 85
Merari, 57
Merchants, 28, 125
Mercurius, 220
Merodach, 138
Mesha, **117**
Meshach, 107
Mesopotamia, 16–17, 23, 26
Messenger on foot, 115
Metalworking, 127, 168
Micah, 162
Michal, 72
Midian/Midianites, 36, 73
Miletus, 224, **227**
Military duty, 64
Military procession, **229**
Milk, 12, 80, 128, 134
Millstone, 178
Miriam, 41, 83
Mirror, 47, **228**
Moabite Stone, **117**
Moab/Moabites, 7–8, 59,

101, **117,** 134–135, 146
Molech, 53, 59
Money, 15, 56
Money changers, 180
Moon worship, 60, 73. See also *Star worship; Sun worship.*
Mordecai, 28, 30, 112–114, 168
Mortar (cement), 51, 164
Mortar (used for grinding grain), 128
Moses, 8, 10, 30, 36–39, 42–43, 47, 54, 58, 67, 92–93, 97, 135, 201, 221, 234
Most Holy Place. See *Holy of Holies/Most Holy Place.*
Mount Carmel, **95,** 172
Mount Gilead, 97
Mount Moriah, 92
Mount of Olives, **217**
Mount Sinai, 14
Mourning for the dead, 15, 21, 110, 134. See also *Grief.*
Music, 25–26, 41, 90, 105
Mutilation of captives, 70
Myrrh, 121. See also *Spices.*
Naaman, 18, 26, 221
Nabal, 76, 216
Naboth, 99, 125
Nahor, 17
Nahum, 163–164
Nain, 13
Naming of children, 201
Naomi, 8, 77–78
Nathan, 87
Nathanael, 162
Nazareth, 203
Nazarite vow, 74
Nebo, 138
Nebuchadnezzar, 55, 107, 138–139, 152–153
Necklace, 133
Nehemiah, 89, 109–110, 188
Net, 117, 123, 135, **177.** See also *Trap.*
Nethinims. See *Temple servants.*
New Moon celebration, 108
Nicodemus, 208, 216
Night watches. See *Watches of the night.*
Nile River, 8, 29, 32, 36,

38, 61, 118, 135, 145, 221
Nineveh, 97, 102, 163–165, 176
Nisan, 44
No. See *Thebes.*
Noah, 7–8, 181
Nose ring, 18
Nymphas, 240
Oaths, swearing of, 9, 16–17
Obadiah, 160
Occult, 62, 222. See also *Divination.*
Og, 60
Olive press, **166**
Olive tree, 66; leaf of, 7; oil from its fruit, 27, 46, 67, 102, 119, 193, 206
Omer, 42
Ossuary, **186**
Outer garment, 22, 27, 65, 83, **86,** 87, 96–97, 109, 139, 158, 239, 244–245
Oven, **12,** 51, 156
Ox goad, 71, 146
Oxen, **98,** 138, 156, 205, 230
Pagan gods, 8, 62, 75, 133, 138, 141, 151, 158, 161, 228; Ammonite, 53, 59; Assyrian, 165; Babylonian, 138; Egyptian, 8, **39, 46,** 149; Greek and Roman, 220; Moabite, 59; Philistine, 75. See also *High place; Idolatry.*
Palanquin, 131
Palm tree, **248**
Papyrus plant, 36, 117, 135, 137
Parched corn, 77. See also *Grain.*
Passover. See *Feast of Passover.*
Paul (apostle), 68, 71–72, 156, 161, 194, 219–240
Peace offering, 49
Peg, 136, 150
Penknife, 247
Pentecost, 44
Pergamos, 224
Persia/Persians, 28, 30, 104, 108–113, 150, 153–154, 163, 167–168, 241
Pestle, 128. See also

Mortar.
Peter, 86, 173, 198, 204, 218, 231, 245
Pharaoh of Egypt, 7, 28–30, 34, 36, 40, 97, 107, 157, 166
Pharisees, 172–173, 175, 179, 182–186, 195–196, 208–209, 213–214
Philemon, 240
Philip, 162
Philippi, **220**, 221, 224
Philistines, 17, 20–22, 47, 71, 74–75, 79, 81, 84, 102, 104, 122, 146–147
Phylactery, **184**
Pilate, 188, 200
Pit, 27. See also *Cistern.*
Pitcher, 94
Plow, 98, 132, **205**
Poor, treatment of, 65, 157–158, 172, 244. See also *Gleaning.*
Porter, 89
Portions at meals, 33. See also *Eating customs.*
Potiphar, 28
Pottage, 20
Pottery, 143, 164
Praetorium, 189
Prayer, 14, 93, 154, 172–173, 185, 194, 197, 207, 218
Priestly clothes, 48
Priscilla, 222, 240
Prison, 27–29, 198, 221. See also *Cistern; Pit.*
Prisoners, treatment of, 70, 104
Psaltery. See *Harp; Lyre.*
Purim. See *Feast of Purim.*
Purse, 207
Queen of Sheba, 26, 74
Ra, 8, 38, 60, 145, 149. See also *Amon-Ra; Sun worship.*
Rabbah, 241
Rachel, 9, 23–25, 32, 36
Raft, 92
Rahab, 68, 86, 230
Rainfall, 27, 244
Raisin cake, 155
Ramah, 84
Rebekah, 17–19, 23
Red heifer, 58
Red Sea, 82
Redemption of property, 78
Rehoboam, 156
Restitution, 42, 51

Reuben, 24, 33
Riddle games, 74
Ridicule, expressing, 165
Right hand as place of honor, 180, 234
Road, 138
Roasted grain, 77, 80. See also *Grain.*
Robbers, 116
Roman citizenship, 221, 224
Roman Empire, 189–190, 204, 224
Roman soldier, 233, 235, **238**
Rome (city), 224, 229, 239–240
Ropes on the head, 99
Royal birthday feast, 29
Ruth, 11, 13, 42, 75–77
Sabbath, 213, 217–218
Sabbath day's journey, 97, 217
Sabbatical year, 55
Sackbut, 153
Sackcloth, 28, 112, 133. See also *Grief; Mourning for the dead.*
Saddle, 14
Sadducees, 183
Salt, 49, 170, 235
Samaria, 94, 98, 110, 146, 158
Samaritans, prejudice toward, 213
Samson, 74, 104
Samuel, 22, 40, 74, 84, 100, 102, 153
Sanballat, 110
Sandals, 11, 158
Sanhedrin, 171, 197, 200, 208, 217
Sarah, 9, 12, 16, 19, 107
Sash, 96
Saul (king), 11, 76, 80, 82–84, 88, 102, 104, 106, 122, 147
Scapegoat, **52,** 127. See also *Day of Atonement.*
Scepter, 113, **150,** 189
Schoolmaster, 231
Scourging. See *Flogging.*
Scribes, 172, 175, **195,** 236
Scroll, 117, **137,** 145, 202, 239
Sea of Galilee, 193, **204, 212**
Sealing wax, 110, 191
Search and seizure, 65
Seat of judgment. See *Judgment seat.*

Sebat, 167
Secretary. See *Amanuensis.*
Self-mutilation, 95
Sennacherib, 138
Seraiah, 195
Sermon on the Mount, 225
Servants, 120, 124, 231; Abraham's chief servant, 16; Gibeonites made, by Joshua, 69; in a king's court, 112; in the temple, 108; Rebekah's nurse, 19
Seven (as a sacred number), 249
Seventh-month Festival. See *Feast of Trumpets.*
Shadrach, 107
Shallum. See *Jehoahaz.*
Shamgar, 71, 146
Shaphan, 195
Shebna, 136, 195
Shechem, 116
Sheep, **131,** 187, 214
Sheepfold, **214**
Shekel, 15, 18, 56, 187
Shepherd, 22, **23,** 34, 36, 56, 82, 187, 214; an occupation detested by the Egyptians, 33; Jesus as the Chief, 245
Shewbread. See *Bread of the Presence.*
Shield, 116, 135, 163, 165, 233; large, used by Goliath, 80; ornamental, owned by Solomon, 93
Shiloh, 13
Shimei, 87
Ship, 224
Shofar, **73**
Shulamite, 130–131
Sieve, 159
Signet ring, 30, **99,** 166
Silas, 220–221
Silver coin, 187
Simon of Cyrene, 188
Simon the Tanner, 86, 218
Sin offering, 49–50, 54
Singing, 82–83, 142
Sisera, 72–73
Sistrum, 85
Sitting on the ground, 134
Slavery, 158, 187, 225, 232
Slime, 7
Sling, **81**
Snake charming, 121

Sodom, 8–9, 13, 170. See also *Gomorrah.*
Solomon, 26, 31, 74, 122, 125, 128–129, 131, 154, 156, 197; administration of his government, 91; his ornate throne, 94; temple built by, 108
Sons of the prophets, 100
Sop, 198
Sorcery, 62
Span, 46. See also *Cubit.*
Sparrow, 175
Spear, 80, 117, 132. See also *Javelin.*
Spices, 120–121, 137, 142
Spoils of war, 73
Spring (water source), 141
Staff, 81
Standard (sign), 57. See also *Banner.*
Star worship, 60. See also *Moon worship; Sun worship.*
Stealing, 42, 64, 78
Stephen, 217
Steward, 208
Stomacher, 133
Stone memorials and monuments, 14, 22, 26, 69, 117, 163
Stylus, 117, 148, 201
Succoth, 18
Sun worship, 8, 38, 60, 145, 149. See also *Moon worship; Star worship.*
Superstition, 25, 155–156, 161, 220
Swaddling clothes, 202
Swearing. See *Oaths.*
Sword, 81, 83, 117, **132,** 233
Sycamore figs, **159**
Sychar, 17, 212
Synagogue, 185, **197,** 203, 219
Syria/Syrians, 26, 40, 98–99, 101–102, 105, 231
Tabernacle, 37, 45, 47–48, **50,** 57, 91–92, 105. See also *Temple in Jerusalem.*
Tabret, 25–26, 133
Tamar, 141
Tambourine, 41, 85, 133, 143
Tar, 7, 36, 135

Tares, 176–177
Tassel, 184
Tattooing, 54
Tax collector, 173–174, 205, 209
Taxes, 91, 178, 204
Tears in a bottle, **121**
Tekoa, 159
Temple in Jerusalem, 45, 127, 149, 154, 166, 170, 178, 188, 200, 203, 213, 218; built originally by Solomon, 92; rebuilt after the exile, 30, 108, 166; remodeled by Herod the Great, **209.** See also *Tabernacle.*
Temple servants, 108, 110
Ten Commandments, 14, 55
Tent, **10,** 13, 222
Teraphim. See *Household idols.*
Tertius, 236
Thebes, 145, **146**
Thief. See *Robbers.*
Thomas, 215
Thorn, 122, 181
Threshing. See *Grain.*
Timbrel, 25, 41
Time, Jewish reckoning of, 96, 215, 228
Timothy, 237–239
Tithing rod, 56
Tittle, 171
Titus, 240
Tomb, 103, 186, 190, **191,** 194, 208, 216
Tower of Ascension, **217**
Tower of Babel, 7
Town crier, 175
Transfer of property, 15
Transvestitism. See *Cross-dressing.*
Trap, 117, 123. See also *Net.*
Trespass offering, 49, 51, 54
Trumpet, 172
Tunic. See *Outer garment.*
Tyre, 92
Ur, 99, 101
Uzziah, 106–107, 188
Vashti, 111
Veil, **19**
Vineyard, 99, 106, 135, 150, 179, 181
Wages, 179
Walled city, 68, **88,** 89, 105, 119, 230; guarded

by watchmen, 89, 131; offered protection from intruders, 105; subjected to siege warfare, 105, **106;** topped by defense towers, 107. See also *Gate of the city.*
Wallet, 109
War club, 146
Warfare, 98–99, 102, 115, 146, 152, 164, 167
Washing of feet, 11, 237
Watches of the night, 40, 198, 218
Watchmen, 89, 131
Watchtower, 106, **181**
Water carriers, 69. See also *Servants.*
Water of separation, 58
Wave offering, 51. See also *Heave offering.*
Wax tablets, 202. See also *Writing.*
Weaning of children, 14
Wedding, 142, 175, 182, 186, 193
Well (water source), 17, 20, 22, 27, 198, 212
Wheat, 42, 66, 77, 176–177. See also *Barley; Grain.*
White donkey, 72
White stone, 248
Whitewashed tombs, 186
Wick, 193
Widow, 237
Window, **72,** 143, 156, 230
Wine, 54, 74, 76, 111, 125, 137, 147, 166, 181, 185, 206, 233, 237
Winepress, 147, 166, 181
Wineskin, 121, 174
Winnowing fork, **203.** See also *Grain.*
Wise men. See *Magi.*
Witchcraft, 62
Woodcutter, 69. See also *Servants.*
Writing, 117, 149, 152, 195, 201, 236, 239, 247. See also *Letter.*
Year of Jubilee, 55
Yeast, 39, 49, 207. See also *Bread.*
Yoke, 156, 175–176
Zacharias, 201
Zalmunna, 73
Zarephath, 94
Zeba, 73

Zechariah, 167
Zedekiah, 104, 107, 146
Zephaniah, 165, 193
Zerubbabel, 30, 108, 166
Zif, 93
Zion. See *Jerusalem.*
Zobah, 105

ART CREDITS

Dr. Jack Beck: 54

Direct Design: 8, 23, 29, 43, 76, 86, 114, 131, 204

The Israel Museum, Jerusalem: 169

Dr. James C. Martin: 10, 12 (top), 16, 25 (top), 32, 39, 47, 58, 61, 64, 69, 73, 79, 84, 88, 91, 92, 95, 107, 121, 128, 130, 134, 141, 144, 150, 159, 160, 181, 184, 186 (both), 191, 193, 196, 199, 202, 205, 206, 211 (bottom), 214, 217, 219, 220, 222, 223, 227, 230, 242

Dr. James C. Martin, The Amman Archaeological Museum, Amman, Jordan: 14, 149 (Photographed by permission.)

Dr. James C. Martin, The British Museum: 12 (bottom), 25 (bottom), 55, 67, 71, 72, 106, 119, 132, 148, 155, 238 (Photographed by permission.)

Dr. James C. Martin, The Burnt House Museum, Jerusalem: 182 (Photographed by permission.)

Dr. James C. Martin, The Cairo Museum: 40, 46, 228 (Photographed by permission.)

Dr. James C. Martin, The Egyptian Ministry of Antiquities: 35, 37 (Photographed by permission.)

Dr. James C. Martin, The Eretz Israel Museum, Tel Aviv: 166 (Photographed by permission.)

Dr. James C. Martin, Illustration by Timothy Ladwig: 173, 177, 189, 195, 215

Dr. James C. Martin, The Isma-iliya Museum, Isma-iliya, Egypt: 18 (Photographed by permission.)

Dr. James C. Martin, The Istanbul Archaeological Museum: 99 (Photographed by permission.)

Dr. James C. Martin, On licence Ministero per I Beni e le Attivita Culturali— Soprintendenza Archaeologica di Roma, Rome, Italy: 229

Dr. James C. Martin, "Reproduction of the City of Jerusalem at the time of the Second Temple—located on the grounds of the Holyland Hotel, Jerusalem": 180, 209 (Photographed by permission.)

Dr. James C. Martin, Sola Scriptura: The Van Kampen Collection on display at the Holy Land Experience in Orlando, Florida: 137 (Photographed by permission.)

Dr. James C. Martin, St. Catherine's Monastery: 174 (Photographed by permission.)

Garo Nalbandian: 77

Preserving Bible Times: 19, 98

Preserving Bible Times and Dr. James C. Martin: 31, 50, 52, 97, 146, 197, 212, 231

Preserving Bible Times and Dr. James C. Martin, The British Museum: 81, 101, 103, 111, 158, 163, 248 (Photographed by permission.)

Preserving Bible Times and Dr. James C. Martin, The Eretz Israel Museum, Tel Aviv: 126, 203 (Photographed by permission.)

Preserving Bible Times and Dr. James C. Martin, The Israel Museum, Jerusalem: 59, 211 (top) (Photographed by permission.)

Preserving Bible Times and Dr. James C. Martin, The Israel Museum: Shrine of the Book, Jerusalem: 136 (Photographed by permission.)

Preserving Bible Times and Dr. James C. Martin, On licence Ministero per I Beni e le Attivita Culturali—Soprintendenza Archaeologica di Roma, Rome, Italy: 239

Preserving Bible Times and Dr. James C. Martin, Mus'ee du Louvre: 117 (Autorisation de photographer et de filmer—LOUVRE, Paris, France. Photographed by permission.)

Preserving Bible Times and Dr. James C. Martin, The Rockefeller Museum, Jerusalem: 178 (Photographed by permission.)